The Magnificent Experiment

The Magnificent Experiment

*Building the Salt River
Reclamation Project
1890-1917*

KAREN L. SMITH

The University of Arizona Press
TUCSON

About the Author

KAREN L. SMITH, senior planning analyst in the Department of Strategic Planning of the Salt River Project, earned a Ph.D. in history from the University of California at Santa Barbara in 1982. She has served on the boards of directors for the National Council of Public History and the Coordinating Council for History in Arizona. In the early 1980s, as director of a research consulting firm, she was a consultant on water rights and related issues.

All photographs in this book are courtesy of the Salt River Project.

THE UNIVERSITY OF ARIZONA PRESS

Copyright © 1986
The Arizona Board of Regents
All Rights Reserved

This book was set in 10/12 Linotron 202 Baskerville.
Manufactured in the U.S.A.

Library of Congress Cataloging-in-Publication Data

Smith, Karen L.
   The magnificent experiment.

   Bibliography: p.
   Includes index.
   1. Salt River Project—History.   2. Water resources
development—Arizona—Phoenix Metropolitan Area—
History. 3. Irrigation—Arizona—Phoenix Metropolitan
Area—History. I. Title.
TC424.A6S65   1986   627'.12'0979173   85-24628

ISBN 0-8165-0921-2 (alk. paper)

To my parents,
Edward and Mary Smith

Contents

ILLUSTRATIONS

MAPS

Preface

As a child living in Phoenix in the early 1960s, I knew little about the problems of water in the desert and nothing at all about the Salt River Project. I simply assumed that water would come out of the tap when I turned the faucet and out of the control valve in the middle of the yard when it was our turn in the neighborhood to irrigate. I left the valley for more humid regions of the country and soon forgot about irrigating altogether. It was only when I returned to Phoenix as a graduate student that the connection between Phoenix and water became more important.

On the face of it, the growth of metropolitan Phoenix from a dusty village located near the Salt River to the ninth-largest city in the United States has been something of an anomaly. There was no major railroad connection to Phoenix until the 1920s, no harbor or navigable river to spawn commerce, and no major trail or crossroads to lure tired travelers to stop. Farmland was rich and would grow any number of crops year-round if there was an artificial way to put water on the soil. But the water supply was uncertain; desert rivers are flashy and unpredictable, one year sending torrents of water to flood and the next hardly providing sufficient amounts to grow crops. The key to sustained growth had to be insuring the water supply.

The history of metropolitan Phoenix and much of the growth of Arizona is, thus, linked inseparably to an assured, developed water supply; this association is true for much of the West. When Paul G. Weimann asked me to return to Phoenix from the University of California at Santa Barbara to help him with a historical research project he had undertaken at the Salt River Project, I jumped at the chance to explore further the history of the federal reclamation project and water institution which has meant so much to Arizona.

As I began to examine the early history of the Project, I found that it was interwoven with the history of social reform in the United States during the period of time generally known as the Progressive Era (roughly dating from the 1890s to the 1920s). The relationships between the Salt River Valley water users and the government's Reclamation Service seemed to me to tell an important story about the false starts and early successes of implementing a national reform policy—federal reclamation—at a local level. Instead of simply writing a history about the early years involved with building the Salt River Project, the significant story, I thought, lay in the shifts in policy and institutions which resulted from the local water users' hammering out a means to live with the federal reclamation requirements. The resulting compromise provided the framework for city-building in the Salt River Valley and served as a model for reclamation projects throughout the arid West.

There is a poignant human story involved with the building of the Salt River Project as well. Men who believed firmly in the social goals of the reclamation reform movement became bitter when others throughout the West did not share their crusading spirit. Strong friendships were made and broken as engineers and farmers attempted to build their dreams into a realistic reclamation project. The engineers of the United States Reclamation Service, the agency charged with implementing national reclamation, were eager to have a successful project to demonstrate the virtues of conservation. The excellent physical conditions and the organized landowners in the valley made the Salt River Project a likely candidate. Moreover, the valley's population of cautious, small-acreage-holding farmers seemed ideal. For Salt River Valley landowners, however, government subsidy through the reclamation program also meant federal control. The reconciliation of federal reclamation principles with local irrigation practices shaped the direction the reclamation program would follow, both within the Salt River Valley and across the arid West. Conflict between the engineers and the farmers over project control, accountability for construction costs, repayment policy, and conservation philosophy highlighted both the strengths and weaknesses of national reclamation as it was implemented at Salt River. The resulting compromise suggested that reclamation as progressive reform would become less a crusade than a business, driven more by politicians than technical experts.

While the engineers were perhaps less expert with the politics of reclamation, they proved to be marvels at constructing the necessary facilities to bring water to the desert. By 1911 the water-storage dam that Salt River Valley landowners had longed for majestically filled the Tonto site, forming behind it a lake both to hold the water for dry years and to regulate the river. Phoenix grew, prospered, and conquered the desert; pioneer Darrel Duppa's 1870 prophecy of a great city rising within the Salt River Valley became a twentieth-century reality. The government engineers and Salt River Valley farmers made it possible; together they built the Salt River reclamation project.

The history of the Salt River Project from 1890 to 1917 is the story of the implementation of federal reclamation policy. It shows the process by which reclamation as progressive reform became reclamation as bureaucracy and it suggests how local leaders adapted, rebelled, and adapted again to the marriage of their traditional irrigation practices and government reclamation policy. It also traces the origin of the special relationship that the Salt River Project and the Department of Interior have maintained since the turn of the century. This case study of one reclamation project cannot suffice as evidence of the program's success or failure, but those interested in the reclamation movement and the development of western water resources will find Salt River's story revealing.

In the 1980s the Salt River Project has been a controversial institution, supplying electrical energy and managing the water resources for most of metropolitan Phoenix. This history of its early years points out the deep roots that the project has in central Arizona and, indeed, in the national reclamation scene. As city and farm continue to compete for greater shares of an already scarce resource, it will become increasingly important to understand why the Salt River Project was built.

ACKNOWLEDGMENTS

This history of the Salt River Project from 1890 to 1917 would not be possible but for some extraordinary support from friends, family and colleagues. Paul Weimann served as both inspiration and sounding board as I shifted the setting and focus of the book. I am certain that this story would not have been written without him. My doctoral committee at the University of California at Santa Barbara reviewed its arguments and logic at an early stage: G. Wesley Johnson, Jr., Carroll Pursell, Jr., Patricia Cline Cohen, and Dean Mann. Carroll

Pursell was especially helpful in his constructive advice concerning the role of the Reclamation Service in light of the early twentieth-century attitude toward science and technology. Pat Cohen provided some thoughtful direction as I turned the dissertation into a book.

Rochelle Bookspan cheerfully read every draft of every chapter and gave me both valuable ideas and friendship along the way. Rebecca Conard also shared some of the joys and agonies of writing this book, giving reams of moral support. Karen Engberg shared her Washington, D.C., apartment with me as I finished research in that city, and never complained when the Salt River Project intruded upon her medical studies. My sister, Kathleen, and my brothers, Steven and Scott, also lent encouragement to this effort.

Renee M. Jaussaud at the National Archives provided invaluable assistance as I pored over the early reclamation records. I cannot thank her enough for keeping me away from avoidable detours. Ken Rossman at the Federal Records Center at Laguna Niguel, California, also allowed me every courtesy as I worked in that fine facility.

Many people at the Salt River Project were helpful throughout the process of researching and writing this book, and I regret that space will not allow me to recognize them individually. I must thank two people, however, for their encouragement: Jack Pfister and Dick Silverman.

Lavina Paulsell has spent almost as much time with this project as I have. Her critical eye for the right word saved many a sentence from mediocrity. Lyn Oldenkamp typed this book through at least one draft.

Part of the first chapter of this book first appeared in somewhat altered form in the Summer 1981 issue of *Arizona and the West*. I thank the Arizona Board of Regents for permission to reprint some of it. I also thank Gene Gressley and the American Heritage Center at the University of Wyoming, Laramie, for permission to use the Frederick H. Newell *Autobiography*. Christine Marín at the Arizona State University Arizona Collection and Susie Sato at the Arizona Historical Foundation also rendered me special assistance.

Finally, my husband, Gary Robinson, and Erin Robinson, lived with both me and this project cheerfully and without complaint. Their support and encouragement kept me and the book on track, and for that and more I am grateful.

KAREN SMITH

The Magnificent Experiment

The Campaign for Water Storage

The need for a secure water supply is a timeless one in the arid lands
of the world. Arizona's Salt River Valley, which extends along the Salt
River from the Verde River to the Gila River, is typical of the arid
American Southwest; no crop will grow without the artificial application of water to the soil. Desert rivers, which seem at first the antidote
to the region's limited rainfall, complicate southwestern agriculture
because they are not reliable sources of water; their sometimes violent
flood and drought cycles make water supply chaotic.

The campaign for a stable water supply in the Salt River Valley
dominated economic and political affairs in the area since the time of
the first American settlements in the 1860s. It was clear to farmers
and landowners as early as the 1880s that a water-storage system was
the essential ingredient in maintaining the valley's growth.

NATIONAL IRRIGATION POLICY AT THE
TURN OF THE CENTURY

In 1889 the United States Senate created the Committee on Irrigation and Arid Lands; its stated purpose was "to consider the subject
of irrigation and the best means of reclaiming the arid lands of the
United States."[1] The members of the newly formed committee traveled throughout the West, gathering information and prompting
local communities to explore various reclamation proposals. In the
Salt River Valley of south-central Arizona, farmers and landowners
had recognized the importance of obtaining a water-storage dam to

[1]

regulate the Salt River and provide a stable water supply for agricultural growth. Learning that the Senate Committee on Irrigation
and Arid Lands planned to visit the valley, the Maricopa County
Board of Supervisors authorized a survey team to find a site for such a
dam. Led by County Surveyor W. M. Breakinridge, the team found a
potential site near the confluence of the Salt River and Tonto Creek.
When the senators arrived in Phoenix, the county seat and capital of
territorial Arizona, the Board of Supervisors and local citizens enthusiastically presented their Tonto-site data.

Neither the senators nor the Salt River Valley proponents of a
reclamation program realized in 1889 that the Tonto damsite and the
Salt River Valley would become one of the most successful federal
reclamation projects ever constructed. There was no mandate, in
1889, for a federal reclamation program. Discussion was enthusiastic
for some sort of national irrigation policy, but most in the West,
indeed across the nation, believed such a program would entail land
grants to the states.[2] There was a general consensus in the Salt River
Valley that the traditional irrigation values of individual effort and
responsibility were inadequate to satisfy the needs of a growing
region. Many believed some larger program was necessary to make
the valley prosper. Landowners and farmers were sensitive, however,
to the issue of control of the water supply. While they understood the
ramifications of the building of a water-storage dam by private enterprise, they had little appreciation for what a government reclamation
program could do for them.

At the same time that Salt River Valley landowners and farmers
debated how they should construct their water-storage dam at the
Tonto site, the nation as a whole entered an active period of reform,
which historians characterize as the Progressive Era. Among the
reformers of this era were conservationists, whose principles stressed
the efficient development of America's natural resources without the
waste so often seen with private exploitation. Conservation emphasized foresight, prudence, thrift, and intelligence in dealing with public matters, and "the application of common sense to the common
problems for the common good."[3] In this way, the people, as chief
forester Gifford Pinchot declared, "shall get their fair share of the
benefit which comes from the development of the country which
belongs to us all."[4] Conservation was more than common sense; it was
also technical. Trained experts developed new ways to minimize waste
while getting projects done quickly.[5]

National irrigation became an integral part of the conservation
reform program. Instead of leaving implementation of a reclamation
policy to the states and private enterprise, which would be inefficient

and potentially scandalous, proponents of national irrigation advocated a national reclamation program, whereby government engineers would construct the projects and the proceeds from the sale of public lands would finance them. The object of the government in sponsoring a national reclamation program was to open the arid lands west of the 100th meridian to settlers who would build homes and family farms upon them. National reclamation would make the desert bloom as a rose, and open the arid West for settlement.

Those who supported a national irrigation policy convinced the Congress that reclamation and settlement of the country's arid lands would enrich every region within the United States; increased demand for manufactured articles would stimulate industrial production in the East and the Asian trade would consume what would otherwise be an increase in food supplies. The nation as a whole would profit, not only through enlarged markets, but because, as President Theodore Roosevelt told the Congress, "successful home-making is but another name for the upbuilding of the nation."[6]

On June 17, 1902, Roosevelt signed into law the National Reclamation Act, a bill designed to make useful the streams and rivers of the arid region. Under this act the federal government would build engineering works for water storage. This legislation, combined with the Roosevelt Administration's great emphasis on conservation reform, provided a unique opportunity for Salt River Valley landowners to build their water-storage project at the Tonto site.

EARLY IRRIGATION IN THE
SALT RIVER VALLEY

Although the need was plain for construction of a storage dam on Salt River to retain floodwaters for use in dry years, such large projects were expensive and beyond the individual capabilities of the valley's inhabitants. Residents in the Salt River Valley explored water-storage financing alternatives rather than relying on either the vagaries of the river or the efforts of small groups of landowners organized in irrigation canal companies. Chief among the options considered by the citizens were (1) soliciting private investment capital to build the water-storage facilities and (2) government subsidy.

The West had traditionally been a place for eastern capital to turn a profit, and many thought reclamation of the arid lands an investment comparable to the transcontinental railroads. Salt River Valley landowners were skeptical, however, of private control over something as critical to their life as the water supply. They, therefore, broached the possibilities of entrepreneurial development of the water-storage project carefully. While the subject of government aid to irrigation in the West had grown in popularity since 1878, when John Wesley Powell published his seminal work on lands of the arid region of the United States, residents of the valley had no clear vision of what sort of government aid they favored. They well understood the precedents of government subsidy in river and harbor appropriations and in canal and railroad construction, but they did not yet have an appreciation as to how their own project fit within that framework. Debate over whether government aid or private investment should be solicited to construct the water-storage dam for the Salt River Valley was lively, filled with controversy and personalities. Most landowners realized that the decision they would make was important not only for their own future, but for the valley's as well.

When the valley was first settled in the late 1860s, growing hay to sell to the United States Army's Camp McDowell and grain crops of wheat and barley to trade with the mining districts to the north were its settlers' principal agricultural pursuits. Jack Swilling, an ex-Confederate wagonmaster, was the first to act upon the potential the abandoned irrigation ditches of the prehistoric Hohokam Indians held for successful farming, and with twelve men and $10,000 in capital he had dredged the "community ditch" from one of the prehistoric canals by 1868. Continued work on the irrigation ditch in 1871 resulted in expanded capacity, so that 200 cubic feet per second (c.f.s.) could supply about 4,000 acres.7

Swilling's canal venture was a cooperative association. The community ditch (later the Swilling Ditch) represented a community of interest, of rights and obligations among those contributing to its construction and maintenance. The basis of one's share in the irrigation community was generally the proportionate part of his land served by the ditch. The more land served by water from the ditch, the more work or capital the owner of that land put into the canal's maintenance. To meet expenses, assessments in the form of cash or labor performed on the canal or headgates were levied against the shares each farmer held in the venture.

While cooperative in its construction, the Swilling Ditch Association was unlike many other cooperative irrigation ventures, in that it was not communal. Decisions about the amount of water to be used to irrigate crops, defined as the duty of water, were made individually, determined by a settler's claim to the river. By the 1860s the doctrine of prior appropriation, or first in time is first in right, had been accepted as water law in most parts of the West. Based upon mining custom, the only condition for a claim was that the water be put to a beneficial use; a water right could be forfeited if it was not used within a five-year period. Communal associations usually determined beneficial uses and made provisions for sharing a water shortage, but the Swilling group did not, relying instead on individual exploitation of the environment. Similarly, communal associations usually developed a wide variety of administrative, economic, and social organizations centered upon irrigation; the Mormons of Utah provide a useful example. Early settlers in the Salt River Valley, however, seemed more concerned with personal rights and economic success than with group obligations or community benefits.[8]

The Swilling Ditch served as a model for several new canals dredged during the 1870s, and these were also primarily cooperative ventures. As more land was brought into cultivation during the 1880s, most of the canal companies in the valley became corporate associations issuing capital stock. The casual operation and maintenance procedures and the informal management of water shortage and distribution of the early ditch days were no longer enough for the increasing number of people using the canals. More business propositions than agricultural tools, these corporate canal companies leased and assigned water rights within the service limits of an irrigation ditch with little regard for the primacy of prior appropriation. Water certificates gradually became common currency, as more and more of them found their way into the hands of persons who were not owners of the land, but were instead money lenders collecting defaulted loans. The significance of the shift from cooperative to corporate irrigation can be seen largely in the changing purposes of the canal companies; making a profit from land sales, not controlling the water supply or farming, became the motive force.[9]

The population of the Salt River Valley was about 11,000 in 1890, a considerable rise from the 235 people noted in the 1870 census. The heavy reliance on grain crops for economic profit had caused a brief recession in the late 1870s, as the prices of wheat and barley fell after a small boom earlier in that decade. Farmers began to diversify their crops in the 1880s, discovering that some fruit trees did well in the valley's mild climate; they planted peach, apricot, fig, and citrus trees next to alfalfa, clover, and grain fields. On the north side of the river alone 50,000 acres, irrigated by the Arizona, Maricopa, Grand, and Salt River Valley canals, were planted with alfalfa, orchards, and grain. As community and corporation boosters publicized nationally the quality of Salt River Valley citrus and other crops, and with the completion of the railroad spur from Maricopa to Phoenix in 1887, which finally enabled the Salt River Valley to market its products via the mainline Southern Pacific railroad, more settlers came to build homes and farm the rich, alluvial soil.[10]

By 1900 Maricopa County (of which the Salt River Valley is the population center) had 20,457 residents farming about 113,000 acres with water from ten major canals. The dredging of the ancient canals had given way by the late 1880s to a technology focusing on crib dams and cross-cut laterals to connect the larger, north-side canals in order to provide more efficient water delivery, but canal and land promoters lusted for even more water so that more farms could be sold; the canal companies were interested more in land speculation than in water distribution.[11]

Despite the decision by Judge Joseph Kibbey in *Wormser v. Salt River Valley Canal Company* (1892), which re-emphasized the public ownership of the water of Salt River and set forth the legal principle that water was appurtenant, or tied to the land, canal companies continued to barter water certificates in their efforts to realize sizeable profits from the undeveloped arid lands of the valley. Additional legal challenges to the canal companies by prior appropriators dominated court agendas throughout the 1890s, and the result was greater insecurity over water rights. More water was claimed from the river than flowed normally, and it was quite clear that the inadequate supply running in Salt River hampered the canal companies' plans. Estimates of acreage which could be potentially cultivated ranged as high as 500,000, and, although these estimates were usually exaggerated, speculators, boosters of the valley's major town, Phoenix, and businessmen were "too ambitious to be satisfied with conditions that [fell] short of the best possibilities."[12]

While all were in agreement that some project to increase the water supply of the Salt River was necessary, there was little consonance among the various canal companies, citizen groups, and landowners as to how this should be achieved. The major problem in the valley, in addition to esteem for individual action, was a lack of investment capital.

Just as in the early part of the nineteenth century, when there were no large pools of venture capital in the eastern United States, so there were none in the West in the latter part of the nineteenth century. As a result, Arizona and the Salt River Valley, like much of the West, "found itself under the sentence of economic colonialism," dependent on the East to finance its large and significant improvements.[13] Construction of the Arizona Canal provides a useful example. Unable to find sufficient capital in Phoenix and Arizona to build the $650,000 Arizona Canal system, W. J. Murphy, one of its early promoters, traveled to San Francisco, Detroit, and Chicago, as well as New York and other major cities in the East, to secure the needed funds to begin construction. Investors in these cities, like many at home in Arizona, were primarily interested in land speculation, not water distribution. As costs on the Arizona Canal quickly increased, due to flood damage and extensions of the approximately forty-mile system, eastern capital and credit became more difficult to obtain. The national depression of the 1890s further dissuaded prospective investors, and the Arizona Canal went into receivership in the 1890s.[14]

IRRIGATION AND THE FEDERAL GOVERNMENT

The indifferent success of constructing irrigation works by private means kept the subject of government enterprise alive.[15] Major John Wesley Powell of the United States Geological Survey created great excitement when he published his report on the arid lands in 1878, which stated that a great number of farms could be carved out of the public lands west of the 100th meridian if water were made available. When he was appointed to head the Survey in 1881, Powell urged Congress to deal directly with the irrigation question. Congress authorized, in 1888, an investigation of the practicability of constructing water-storage reservoirs in the arid region and sent into the field a Senate Subcommittee on Irrigation. Chaired by Senator William Stewart of Nevada, the subcommittee stopped at least once in every state and territory, holding fifty-three sessions to hear testimony. Notified in early 1889 that Phoenix was scheduled as one of the subcommittee's stops, the Phoenix Chamber of Commerce passed a resolution in the summer of that year asking the Maricopa County Board of Supervisors to finance exploratory efforts to find suitable water-storage sites within the watersheds of the Salt and Verde rivers.[16]

The "scent of government appropriations" spurred the county to send three men into the field: county surveyor W. M. Breakinridge, John Norton, and James McClintock.[17] The most promising of the many damsites the trio discovered was near the confluence of Salt River and Tonto Creek:

> There was a narrow canyon for the dam, in hard rock of advantageous stratification, furnishing the best of building material. Above was a wing-shaped double valley, within which was storage capacity for all the floods of an average season.[18]

When the Stewart subcommittee arrived in Phoenix in the fall of 1889, city officials handed the Senate representatives the notes of the Breakinridge survey. Spirited testimony throughout the West by men almost exclusively from groups that would benefit directly from any steps the government might take to render the arid lands more valuable helped to target the Stewart subcommittee's criticism chiefly on Powell for having spent most of his 1888–1889 appropriation of

$350,000 on topographical maps and for withholding surveyed lands from settlement.[19]

Charges that the federal government was disrupting private efforts to build profitable irrigation works made Congress focus its irrigation legislation on assisting the states to develop projects in conjunction with private enterprise. An 1890 statute revoked that part of the 1888 law which called for the reservation of public irrigable lands, limiting reservation simply to reservoir sites. The next year Congress provided for right-of-way over public lands for private- or state-sponsored irrigation companies.

More lay behind the reluctance of the federal government to involve itself in a national reclamation program during the 1890s than a laissez-faire attitude or the constitutional argument that this was a job for the states. Tension between the underdeveloped West and the developed East often caused the West to resist what it perceived as controls from the East. Westerners argued against federal involvement because the government was too far away and the arid regions too unlike each other, while easterners argued that it was not fair to take taxes from one set of citizens to use in developing the property of another.[20]

The philosophy of state control over potential government irrigation projects and the resistance on the part of easterners to use tax money to pay for western development both found a legislative home in the Carey Act of 1894, which provided that the President could authorize allocation of a maximum of one million acres within each state's public lands for irrigation, reclamation, settlement, and cultivation; surplus funds were to be used for reclaiming other lands within the state. The Carey Act was ineffective, however, largely due to the lack of private financing, and little of the public domain was reclaimed under this legislation.[21]

Arizona, as a territory, was not eligible for Carey Act funds until 1909, when Congress extended its provisions to the territories of both Arizona and New Mexico. When Wells Hendershott, a lawyer and promoter from the East, filed claim in 1893 to the reservoir site upon which the Breakinridge survey recommended constructing a storage dam, valley land speculators and Phoenix businessmen were delighted. The Tonto Basin was to be turned into a lake by Hendershott's newly formed Hudson Reservoir and Canal Company, with the primary goal of storing flood waters for the irrigation of a large expanse of dry land east of the town of Mesa. The Hudson Company, financed almost entirely by the New York interests of Man and Man, a firm of lawyers and engineers, opened offices in Phoenix in 1894 and composed engineering plans for a masonry dam 225 feet high to create a thirty-square-mile reservoir. Included within the construction plans was a proposal to build a diversion dam at the Granite Reef site which would divert water into the north-side and south-side canal systems. Throughout the 1890s, the Hudson Company performed stream measurements, calculated depth to bedrock for its storage dam, and surveyed several potential lines for a canal route to carry the water to those lands to the southeast which Hendershott had initially favored. The Company, in 1897, even applied for a federal right-of-way through the Gila River Indian Reservation in exchange for supplying water to those Indians living along the right-of-way.[22]

Despite solid plans and sound engineering measurements, the Hudson Reservoir and Canal Company was unable to convince outside investors of the three-million-dollar project's feasibility as a profit-making venture. The company's management even tried to secure from the Arizona Improvement Company (successor to the Arizona Canal Company) north-side water rights and land claims as collateral for the Tonto project to borrow upon, but the shaky financial status of the Arizona Improvement Company prevented this arrangement. All the acreage in the valley would have to be taken up and the rate for water rental doubled before Henry Man believed the Tonto project would be remunerative to a reservoir company.[23]

Consolidation of all the lands in the valley under a privately owned reservoir company was unrealistic, given the vested water rights of early settlers under the doctrine of prior appropriation. Formation of the Old Settlers' Protective Association in 1898 to protect the rights of prior appropriators indicated the resistance the Hudson Company, or any other private corporation, would face in trying to unite all the valley lands. Those with old water rights were entitled to the present supply of water, and although water storage would insure that amount, these farmers were reluctant to be treated on the same terms as new settlers to the valley, who would benefit the most from an increased water supply.[24]

Believing that Arizona had reached the limits of its agricultural development without an increased water supply (the Salt River Valley being the dominant agricultural region in the territory), many valley farmers called for government reclamation. In anticipation of the Fifth National Irrigation Congress to be held in Phoenix in December 1896, William "Bucky" O'Neill, a territorial legislator and Arizona delegate to the Irrigation Congress, submitted in July a national irrigation bill to the Congress's participants. Modeled in some respects after California's Wright Act, which allowed the formation of tax-levying irrigation districts, O'Neill's plan, in simple form, called for the national government to advance the money to state-recognized

irrigation districts to reclaim desert lands. The loans were not to
exceed one million dollars in any given year, and the cost per acre was
not to exceed twenty-five dollars. The charge of the loan was to be a
lien on both the lands and the irrigation works. Every dollar lent by
the government was to be repaid in full, and the charges to the settlers
were to be graduated.[25]

To those whose laissez-faire philosophy prohibited the entrance
of the government into the reclamation business, O'Neill prepared
this reply:

> After the expenditure of millions in improving Eastern harbors
> and rivers, building post office and other edifices, after guaran-
> teeing the bonds of railroad companies to the extent of millions,
> with the Republican and Democratic parties advocating the
> expenditure of one hundred million dollars to build the Nic-
> aragua canal, after the payment of over twelve million dollars in
> bounties to the sugar growers of the South, after the establish-
> ment of protective tariffs for over fifty years for the benefit of the
> manufacturers of the East, there is no reason why such a bill as
> herein proposed [the national irrigation bill] should not be
> passed.[26]

The government had always granted aid to special interests, from
financing eastern turnpikes and canals in the early nineteenth century (either through direct investment in private corporate stock or
through the sale of state bonds) to the granting of vast tracts of the
public domain both to canal projects and to the transcontinental railroads. The concept of social overhead—that some improvements are
worthwhile to society despite their failure to earn a fair return on the
capital invested in them—underlay much of the government's efforts
in financing internal improvement projects; a canal was usually more
useful to the public than to the owners. With this understanding of
the role of the government in improvement projects, Governor Benjamin Franklin of the Arizona Territory echoed O'Neill's sentiment in
his welcoming words to the Irrigation Congress.[27]

Despite O'Neill's preparations for a discussion of specifics regarding national irrigation, delegates to the Irrigation Congress evaded
particulars and talked only in generalities. When, in frustration,
O'Neill took the floor during an afternoon session to criticize the
delegates for talk without action, many members chastised the Arizonan for his behavior. Before the congress had begun, Frederick
Newell, representing the U.S. Geological Survey, answered a
reporter's question about the probable influence the congress would
have in securing government reclamation. While no effect would be

seen for a couple of years, if the congress persisted, Newell asserted that the government would eventually become convinced that the matter was of more than ordinary importance and would legislate accordingly. After the congress, Newell must have been considerably less optimistic.[28]

Perhaps in accord with O'Neill's frustration, Salt River Valley farmers called a mass meeting to discuss their water problems immediately after the conclusion of the Fifth National Irrigation Congress. A citizens' water-storage committee was appointed to investigate three possibilities for water storage in the valley: private ownership, corporate ownership, and government construction. Their report proposed several financing schemes with both public and private elements, including: creation of irrigation districts modeled after California's Wright Act, tax levies on the land, exemption from taxation of water-storage works, and new canals to encourage development.[29]

Yet the owners of the old lands remained reluctant to participate in a privately held water-storage proposition without special provisions. They wanted to insure that the farmers' interests were protected in any canal and reservoir company proposal, especially those interests related to water distribution. In 1898 farmers specifically wanted assurances that they would receive all their water after they had helped construct the reservoir and not have to submit to a four-day-out-of-eight rule of distribution.[30]

Despite the lack of sustained support for federal reclamation, men like Newell and other John Wesley Powell protégés within the U.S. Geological Survey's hydrography branch persisted in their efforts to convince the Congress that some national irrigation bill should be passed. The Chittenden Report (1897), the result of a Congressional directive to examine reservoir sites and report upon the practicability of constructing hydraulic works for water storage, recommended government construction, ownership, and operation of storage works in the West.[31] While the Chittenden Report marked the beginning (or at least the official beginning) of the movement for national irrigation by declaring the problem one with which only the federal government could cope, it also suggested that federal reclamation for water storage might be included with river and harbor concerns. The fact that Captain Hiram Chittenden was with the Army Corps of Engineers and that the report's chief sponsor, Senator Francis Warren of Montana, placed reclamation legislation within river and harbor bills and thus with the Corps, could not have pleased Newell and the Geological Survey; the federal bureaucracy concerned itself with "turf" at the turn of the century, much as it does today. The

Frederick Newell was an important contributor to the development of federal water policy from
the beginning of his government
career. He joined the U. S. Geological Survey in 1887 and became
director of the U. S. Reclamation
Service in 1902. For Newell, reclamation of the arid lands of the
West was a great social experiment in home-building, to which
he dedicated his considerable
political energy and engineering
skill.

drive to persuade Congress to enact national irrigation legislation
took on an added dimension as the Survey worked to regain control.
Frederick Newell was very much at the center of the efforts to pass
national irrigation legislation and to insure that the Geological Survey
was responsible for its implementation.[32]

Frederick Newell, chief hydrographer for the United States Geological Survey in 1897, was an ambitious man. He was born of Puritan
stock in the small mining and lumber town of Bradford, Pennsylvania, in March 1862. While still a baby, he moved from aunt to aunt
and from Pennsylvania to Brookline, Massachusetts, after his mother
died. His early life and primary education were scattered. Because his
father owned a large number of oil fields in western Canada and
Pennsylvania, Newell had the opportunity to learn surveying,
mechanics, bookkeeping, and printing, and by the time he was ready
for high school, was "better equipped than most of the youngsters."[33]
Although his father was anxious for him to finish high school and
enter the oil business, Frederick Newell believed that a degree in
mining engineering from the Massachusetts Institute of Technology
would help him in the business. Despite the fact that he had had to
leave high school after three years to manage the company when his
father contracted malaria, Newell was accepted at M.I.T. in 1880.[34]

Alone much of his early years, except for cousins to play with,

Newell channeled a tremendous amount of energy toward succeeding, whether it was building up his thin physique so that he would be healthier or setting formidable goals for himself. His father was an important stimulus in this process. "There was nothing I would not undertake," Newell wrote, "if he [his father] assumed that it could not be done, whether laying gas lines, plumbing, designing houses or straightening out the books of some company and discovering blunders or worse on the part of the people with whom he was doing business."35 After Newell had completed only one term at M.I.T., however, his father moved to Florida and the son left school to manage the family interests. Before he reentered M.I.T. in 1883, Newell visited Colorado and organized the Columbia Gold Mining Company (of which he was secretary-treasurer) and helped to start a brick, tile and ceramic works and a glass factory in Bradford.36

Yet Frederick Newell was not the type of man who would become a "robber baron," interested only in personal aggrandizement. Geology had captivated his interest by 1883, as had the liberal Henry George's single-tax theory, which would exempt from taxation every article of wealth owing its existence to human effort. In need of material for a doctoral dissertation in geology at M.I.T., Newell joined the U.S. Geological Survey in 1887. Major John Wesley Powell succeeded in diverting Newell's interests from geology and mining to developing water resources in the West. In 1888 the new Survey employee became an assistant hydraulic engineer responsible for carrying out Congress's newly mandated irrigation survey of the arid West. He traveled widely through the West for this purpose, and saw first-hand the difficulties settlers in the arid region faced when they tried to farm the dry land. From the very start of his official career with the government, Newell was an important contributor to the development of federal water policy. He would apply his personal drive to accomplish what others could not to the problem of national irrigation.37

Congress allocated $50,000 to the Survey in 1896 for gauging streams, in order to determine the water supply of the United States, and for preparing reports on the best methods of using the water resources of the country's arid and semi-arid sections. The second water-supply and irrigation paper issued by the Survey was on irrigation near Phoenix, Arizona. While the report focused on the Gila and Verde rivers as well as Salt River, and while it provided little new information on the Tonto site beyond that researched by the Hudson Company, Newell and Arthur P. Davis (a hydraulic engineer and John Wesley Powell's nephew) emphasized in its pages the role that the federal government could take in reclamation. Newell believed that private investors would rarely find irrigation projects lucrative ventures, yet he was also aware that the concept of social overhead would require too much federal largesse. Costs could be repaid in full if they were distributed uniformly to all who benefited, and Newell seemed to advocate this approach as early as 1897. The chief purpose of his investigation, and probably of others similarly undertaken, was twofold: to gather scientific and technical data useful to planning reclamation projects, and to publicize the potential reservoir sites to Congress. Davis wrote of the Tonto site: "There can be no doubt that in this reservoir site lies one of the most important possibilities for the future of agriculture in southern Arizona."[38] Statements like this one indicated government interest in water storage in the Salt River Valley, and encouraged local citizens to include government support on their reclamation agenda.

There was, however, no clear vision of what sort of government aid Salt River Valley landowners favored. On one side of the argument were those who favored trusting the U.S. Geological Survey to administer national irrigation through continuous appropriations from Congress. The other side, favored by Governor Nathan Oakes Murphy, advocated the cession of public lands to the states and territories in which they were located—a variation of the Carey Act theme. Congress's failure to enact any legislation for national reclamation by 1900 disappointed many farmers and landowners.

ORGANIZATION OF VALLEY WATER USERS

Combined with a serious drought, which began in 1897, federal inaction and the failure of the Hudson Company to construct the Tonto Dam prompted the formation of a new citizens' committee on water storage. Created by the Phoenix and Maricopa County Board of Trade, the Water Storage Committee was composed of five successful community leaders: Sam McCowan, John W. Evans, B. Heyman, Benjamin Fowler, and Vernon Clark. Their charge was to investigate the possibilities of water storage for the valley and to recommend to the Board of Trade how to increase the water supply. Their report, published in April 1900, advocated what the citizens' water-storage committee had briefly considered in 1896: constructing a storage dam through the issuance of county bonds.[39]

Brashly proposing to purchase the Tonto Basin reservoir site, construct a dam, and buy all the canal systems in the valley, the Water Storage Committee favored bonding Maricopa County, which was assessed at about ten million dollars, at $4\frac{1}{2}$ percent annually, to retire an estimated project indebtedness of over six million dollars. To make this possible, 500,000 acres would have to be charged $1.25 per acre water rent. Every single acre already cultivated in the valley would have to join in this scheme, as well as a significant amount not in cultivation (probably close to 300,000 acres). The difference between the county bonding plan and a privately sponsored reclamation program was simple to the committee: the people would be in control. The Water Storage Committee believed that "corporations [were] not given to laying awake nights devising ways and means for alleviating the conditions of its patrons." Sounding very populist, the committee wrote that "if any corporation has the control of our water supply we may rest assured that the people will be required to pay about all the traffic will bear."[40] However, these farmers and landowners were really less antagonistic to business than they were to an unfair deal; the Hudson Company's failure to begin construction until rates were doubled suggested the latter.

The optimistic plans of the committee spurred hopes of irrigating half a million acres for a potential population of one million, yet brushed aside the difficult problems of uniting the farmers behind the bonding proposal and the enormity of the proposed indebtedness. "A little energy and determination," the committee said, was all that was needed to sell the bonds and begin work within a year. There was, however, a small, but by no means assured, maneuver which had to be completed before the Water Storage Committee could exercise its large amount of determination: Congress had to pass enabling legislation in order for Maricopa County, located as it was within a federal territory, to be able to bond itself.[41]

That nothing much was accomplished between April, when the Board of Trade's Water Storage Committee issued its report, and the fall was not unusual, given both Congress's summer recess and valley residents' own proclivity to spend their summers in cooler climes. Another citizens' meeting, held in the fall of 1900, selected a permanent Salt River Valley Water Storage Committee composed of thirty-six men, "representing every canal, every section, and every industry in the valley."[42] The enthusiasm of the first meetings abated, however, when the rains began to fall and the need for water became less immediate. Conflict also appeared among groups of landowners. "There was talk, talk, talk, and inaction," the *Arizona Republican* reported, "and grumbling accusations. Motives were impugned and cliques were formed and some determined if the plan they advocated were not adopted no plan would be."[43]

Part of the problem had to do with old rivalries between lands under the north-side canal system and those under the south-side system; another aspect was divergent self-interests. Farmers in

Tempe were fiercely protective of their vested rights, much like the
Old Settlers' Protective Association. Large landowners like Dwight B.
Heard, who owned all the lands irrigated by the San Francisco Canal
(approximately 8,000 acres), and Alexander J. Chandler, with about
18,000 acres on the south-side irrigated with water from his profes-
sionally developed Consolidated Canal and power plant, sought to
increase their own advantages. And the canal companies, always concerned with profits, proposed complicated and expensive plans for
their sale or use. Trying to manage both the water-storage efforts and
the committee's strong personalities was Benjamin Fowler, a newly
transplanted Yankee who was president of the sometimes quar-
relsome committee.44

Like many newcomers to Arizona, Fowler probably moved to the
valley for health reasons. Particularly for those with lung ailments,
Arizona's mild climate was advertised as being all the medicine one
needed for a complete recovery. In 1889 Fowler, with his wife, Ella
Francis Quimby, abandoned his successful career as a book publisher
(first with Dodd, Mead and Company in New York and later with his
own firm of Powers, Fowler and Lewis in Chicago) for a new career as
a rancher and businessman in the Salt River Valley. Fifty-six years
old, and scarcely in town long enough to assess the potential of the
area, the Massachusetts-born Fowler soon became a leader within the
community. Perhaps because he had received a classical education at
Phillips Academy at Andover and at Yale University, Fowler
appeared to the valley residents to be a skillful negotiator and per-
suasive enough to smooth over the rough feelings between many of
the existing political factions. He was quickly sought after to participate in committees and clubs, and was elected president of the Arizona Agricultural Association, the Phoenix Board of Trade, the Associated Charities of Phoenix, and the Phoenix Chamber of Commerce
soon after his arrival. People in the valley offered him the opportunity to be a director of their future; he responded eagerly and with
a sense of mission.45

Since the county bonding proposal was the one selected by the
Board of Trade's committee, the Salt River Valley Water Storage
Committee asked Fowler to go to Washington, D.C., to introduce the
necessary enabling legislation. Armed with a general idea of what the
committee envisioned in the way of a bill, Fowler traveled to Washington, at his own expense, in the fall of 1900. Once in the nation's
capital, Fowler lobbied hard for the Salt River Valley. He was interested in persuading the Congress to pass legislation favoring the
bonding plan, and in presenting the valley's situation to government

Benjamin Fowler was the first president of the Salt River Valley Water Users' Association. A skillful negotiator, Fowler was able to manage politics both locally and in Washington, D.C. He considered federal reclamation "a magnificent experiment" that would make the desert bloom. One of the Reclamation Service's loyal friends, Fowler traveled throughout the West on behalf of the reclamation movement, sharing the experiences of the Salt River Valley with other landowners who hoped to secure a government project.

officials, particularly Frederick Newell. Also on Fowler's list of people to see was George Maxwell, the foremost irrigation propagandist in the country. Director of the National Irrigation Association (which was financed largely by railroad and mining interests) and a former California water lawyer, Maxwell was a proponent of government reclamation. Convinced that reclamation of the arid lands would solve the nation's social problems by decentralizing population from urban centers, Maxwell approached national irrigation with a crusader's zeal.[46]

Fowler asked Maxwell for advice on how the Water Storage Committee should proceed, and Maxwell responded in great detail. Suggesting that the citizens of the valley organize themselves into a Landowners' Co-Operative Water Company which would take control of water rights and the land under the canals (thus eliminating the disruptive problem of floating water rights and the questionable support of the canal companies), Maxwell saved his most important recommendation for last. The new organization should acquire "full and complete control" over both the Tonto site and a second damsite at McDowell, near the confluence of the Salt and Verde rivers. The Co-Operative Company should build a reservoir at the first site over which it gained control, probably through a bonds-financed project,

George Maxwell, the foremost irrigation propagandist in the nation in 1900, advocated federal reclamation with a crusader's zeal. Convinced that reclamation of the nation's arid lands would solve American social problems by decentralizing population from urban centers, Maxwell used his influence with Congress and President Theodore Roosevelt in order to secure government approval of the Salt River Project.

and then "concentrate all the influence and energy of the valley to secure the construction of a reservoir at the other site by the National Government."[47]

Maxwell had also recommended that Fowler have the United States Geological Survey begin to make preliminary surveys for the McDowell reservoir, to bore for bedrock, and to prepare the maps, plans, specifications, and estimates of cost, "so that it can be known accordingly and in detail just what the reservoir will cost."[48] The same work should be completed for the Tonto site. Maxwell suggested to Fowler that the committee offer to pay half of the investigation costs if the Survey would perform the work. Fowler wrote Secretary of the Interior Ethan Hitchcock on November 20, 1900, asking that United States Geological Survey engineers examine the McDowell and Tonto reservoir sites, and offered $1,500 on behalf of the Salt River Valley Water Storage Committee as a contribution to the effort. Charles D. Walcott, who had been director of the Survey since 1894, accepted Fowler's offer and authorized the beginning of the Arizona work.[49]

During November and December, Fowler talked with Newell and Maxwell often, taking lunch and dinner with both men and visiting at Maxwell's home in the evening. Since both Newell and Maxwell were supporters of government reclamation, Fowler must have heard all the arguments in favor of that policy, and despite his continuing effort to secure the Maricopa County enabling legislation so that local control of the storage works would be insured, he began to lean toward a federal project in the Salt River Valley. Both Fowler and Maxwell left for Phoenix in late December 1900, and although Fowler was somewhat discouraged by the lack of progress in Congress, he hoped Maxwell would buoy the Water Storage Committee and valley citizens with his infectious enthusiasm for federal irrigation. Important developments in the bonding bill, however, made him return to Washington from Chicago; Maxwell would wait for him before going to Arizona.[50]

Fowler was unaware of the degree of dissent in Phoenix over the bonding bill he had submitted to Congress. Few could agree on what provisions should be included within the bill, but most could agree on what they disliked. In particular, many disapproved of the provision by which the Maricopa County Board of Supervisors would administer the sale of the bonds. An amendment was included which provided for the election of a commission to administer that aspect of the storage project. Other areas of concern included tightening the voting requirement so that owning taxable property would become an additional criterion. But it was not just the bonding bill to which local citizens objected. When Arthur P. Davis arrived in the valley to begin the Geological Survey's investigation of the Verde River damsite, valley residents complained that he should be investigating the Tonto site, the storage-dam location for which Fowler was supposedly lobbying Washington. Dwight B. Heard, another transplanted Yankee who had come to Arizona for his health and acquired a great deal of wealth in the process, suggested that a subscription movement raise the necessary funds for the Survey to continue its work at the Tonto site, and that a request be directed to Frederick Newell for this purpose.[51]

Fowler, meanwhile, was back in Washington and, despite a newspaper story which indicated that he had some "pull" in the Capitol, he was unable to move the enabling bill through committee; there was no chance Congress would guarantee the interest on the bonds, nor would it allow a government engineer to work under an advisory board of civilians.[52] Of no help was the Water Storage Committee's sending Fowler a new bill to introduce in January 1901. Arizona was a territory with little enough political clout, but Fowler had also to contend with the charge that Maricopa County could not make up its mind on its own proposal. If there was no agreement in the valley, Congress felt little obligation to authorize the scaled-down, two-million-dollar bonding plan. Rumors abounded that Arizona's own delegate to Congress, Marcus Smith, did not favor the bonding proposal, and Arizona Governor Murphy believed that it would be difficult to have the legislation passed by Congress during the current session. Murphy suggested that the Water Storage Committee draft a bonding bill for the territorial legislature, so that Congress could then simply affirm that decision. The committee selected a subcommittee to draft yet another bonding proposal.[53]

By March 1901 the Water Storage Committee had nearly disbanded; disgruntled farmers wondered whether a bonding bill was the best idea after all. The *Arizona Republican* editorialized that:

> The insidious hope of federal aid has stolen in and adulterated the usual judgement of our people and they have fallen. In the hope of getting something for nothing, they, like our Indians, are willing to sit and dream and hope.[54]

Arizona was a territory, the paper reminded its readers, and because of that fact "stands no chance of securing favors." In addition to the political reality of territorial status, the only federal reclamation bill which could possibly be successful in Congress was the Newlands Bill, which provided federal funds for reclaiming the public lands of the arid West. There was no place for the private lands of the Salt River Valley under such an arrangement. The valley newspaper implored local residents to forget their differences and unite in order to "build the dam ourselves and own it and control it."[55]

Benjamin Fowler did not give up in his effort to secure a storage dam for his adopted home. Elected to the territorial legislature, Fowler succeeded in passing a water-storage commission bill in April 1901, which enabled the counties to institute a small tax for two years solely for the purpose of creating a working fund for water storage. The Maricopa County Board of Supervisors quickly availed itself of the opportunity offered by the Fowler Act, and asked Judge Webster Street of the Third District Court to appoint five water-storage commissioners. Charles Goldman, Dwight B. Heard, and William D. Fulwiler of Phoenix; J. T. Priest of Tempe; and Jed G. Peterson of Mesa were selected to oversee the $15,000 annual fund; Fowler could not be appointed because he was a member of the legislature which had passed the bill.

The chief goal of the Board of Water Storage Commissioners seemed to be acquiring title to the Tonto reservoir site, which was held by the Hudson Company. Arguing that the 1891 revision of the Timber Culture Act instituted a five-year time limit within which work on an irrigation canal, ditch, or reservoir had to be completed, the water-storage commissioners asked General Land Commissioner Binger Hermann to award the filings for the Tonto site to Maricopa

County. This initial attempt by the Board, however, was not successful, probably because the Hudson Company continued to assert
its intentions to build the dam.[56]

THE NEWLANDS BILL

While Fowler worked in the territorial legislature and the Maricopa County Board of Water Storage Commissioners tried to gain
control over the Tonto site, George Maxwell and Frederick Newell
lobbied the Congress throughout 1901 for passage of the Newlands
Bill. Designed to overcome the limits of private enterprise in the
construction of irrigation works, the Newlands Bill provided for the
creation of an arid-land reclamation fund, consisting of receipts from
the sale and disposal of public lands in the sixteen states and territories of the arid West. The Secretary of Interior was to have sole and
complete discretion over the use of this fund and, upon the recommendations of the United States Geological Survey, over selection of
the projects which would provide water only for public lands. Repayment for federal construction of these storage works and canals was
to be complete, although no interest would be charged on the
principal.[57]

The Newlands Bill was supported, in part, by large landowners in
the West, by railroad and mining interests, and by the McKinley
Administration. Secretary of Interior Hitchcock, influenced by Newell, sent to the House Committee on Public Lands, which reviewed the
bill, a letter in strong support of federal aid to irrigation; the letter
said, in part:

> In some respects, the case is comparable to that of a city whose
> harbor has been improved. The land values are increased, but the
> work [as] carried out by private enterprise may not be
> remunerative to the builders. It is evident that if further reclama-
> tion is to take place it must be through governmental action.[58]

Although the Newlands Bill provided for construction of much-
needed reclamation works in the West, it also effectively circum-
vented regional policies and traditions regarding irrigation and cor-
rected what Representative Francis Newlands of Nevada perceived to
be poor administration by the states; it advocated a more closed system of decision making than had previously existed in internal
improvement legislation. Representative of the "Progressive" sentiment sweeping the nation at the turn of the century, in which reformers tried to inject rational system and organization into American
political, economic, and social life, this piece of legislation stressed the

spirit of science and technology in developing the arid lands of the West for the nation as a whole, not for local interests.

Notwithstanding this national approach, regional conflict over federal irrigation was very much at the heart of congressional debate. Many westerners distrusted federal controls over the natural resources of their region and favored the "Wyoming Plan," which placed control over reclamation projects in the hands of a state engineer, rather than the federal government. Easterners saw this spirit of incipient rebellion, along with greater western productivity brought about by federal reclamation works, as a threat to their economic predominance. As a result of these attitudes, neither the West nor the East came out in strong support of the Newlands Bill.[59]

President William McKinley and Secretary of Interior Hitchcock supported the natural-resource policies of national reclamation and forest conservation articulated best by Frederick Newell and Gifford Pinchot, chief forester of the Department of Agriculture's Forestry Division, but they did not actively work for them. Newell, Pinchot, and Maxwell met almost every evening during the congressional session to discuss the Newlands Bill and perhaps plan a lobbying strategy, but their efforts were unsuccessful in the 56th Congress. The Newlands Bill was narrowly defeated on March 1, 1901.[60]

It seemed only a matter of time, however, until the reclamation bill or some version of it would pass the Congress, and Newell, Pinchot, and Maxwell continued their lobbying on Capitol Hill. Maxwell had rented a house next door to Newell in order that he might commit all of his efforts to securing a reclamation act. In September 1901 President McKinley was assassinated by Leon Czolgosz, an anarchist, and Vice-President Theodore Roosevelt assumed the office. Roosevelt, a friend of Pinchot, and, through him, of Newell and Maxwell, committed himself to the natural-resources policy they advocated, and in his first message to Congress outlined a plan of action which they had largely written. The reintroduced Newlands Bill was a priority piece of legislation for the new and popular president.[61]

Benjamin Fowler, upon the request of the Water Storage Committee and a group of local citizens concerned about Arizona statehood, returned to Washington in January 1902 to continue his efforts to secure passage of the enabling bill for Maricopa County that had long been stalled in committee. Even though the Newlands Bill provided only for reclaiming public lands, Fowler must have had some indication from Newell and Maxwell that a change in emphasis to include private lands was possible. Newell had said as early as 1893 that private landowners would have to be taken into consideration in any big project, since they held much of the irrigable acreage, and President Roosevelt stated the following in his message to Congress:

> Whatever the nation does for the extension of irrigation should harmonize with and tend to improve the condition of those now living on irrigated land . . . . Our aim should not be simply to reclaim the largest area of land and provide homes for the largest number of people, but to create for this new industry the best possible social and industrial conditions.[62]

It seemed probable that Fowler would be swept along with Newell and Maxwell to fight for the Newlands Bill.

Throughout the winter and spring of 1902, Fowler met with Newell, Pinchot, and Maxwell to discuss Arizona, irrigation, and the Tonto project. He was joined in February by Sam McCowan of the Phoenix Board of Trade and in April by Dwight B. Heard of the Board of Water Storage Commissioners and Dr. E. W. Wilbur of Mesa. All four of the men from the Salt River Valley were eager to talk about the Tonto project, and by all indications Newell and Maxwell were happy to hear them out. Fowler and Heard, in particular, became good friends with Newell and Pinchot, partly because they were Republicans and Progressives, and partly because they were both from the East and of good standing; Fowler had graduated from Pinchot's alma mater, Yale.[63]

The rest of the Salt River Valley contingent left Washington in April, but Fowler stayed, perhaps inspired by crumbling resistance to the Newlands Bill, as Maxwell's dream of home-building on the lands to create new communities and markets for the nation, and as the political persuasiveness of Roosevelt seemed to take hold. Finally, on June 17, 1902, Congress passed Francis Newlands's National Reclamation Act. The bill as originally passed, however, made no provision for private lands. Alert to the problems imposed upon western development if an amendment including private lands was not adopted, and perhaps as a salve to those who had advocated a program with more state and private control, Maxwell, and presumably Fowler, lobbied both Congress and their friends in the Roosevelt Administration. Consistent with his earlier-stated philosophy on reclamation and private lands, President Roosevelt instructed Secretary Hitchcock to secure an amendment so that stored water could be developed for private lands, and this the Secretary "somewhat grudgingly" did. The Salt River Valley provided a model for a government reclamation project constructed on the public domain to serve mostly private land, although no projects had as yet been selected.[64]

President Roosevelt signed the National Reclamation Act into law, and the United States Geological Survey quickly proposed to Interior Secretary Hitchcock that he create a new Reclamation Service from within the Survey's own hydrography branch. Partly to insure that the Department of Agriculture's Irrigation Division and the Army Corps of Engineers would not be involved as an operating agency, and partly to solidify control of the program in the hands of the engineers, this initiative was successful; and Newell was appointed chief engineer of the Survey's Reclamation Service on July 9, 1902.[65]

Fowler, who had paid little attention to the enabling legislation for Maricopa County while the fight for the National Reclamation Act remained to be won, now rejected that path for the Salt River Valley altogether. Close to the center of national reclamation policy-making, Fowler realized that Salt River possessed all the attributes of a successful project. He and Newell spent a considerable amount of time together throughout June and July of 1902, and Newell arranged to go to Arizona. Fowler and Maxwell met him in Chicago, and then again in Los Angeles. While in California, Maxwell, Fowler, Newell and another Survey engineer, Joseph Lippincott, took a small vacation together at Terminal Island. Throughout the summer, Fowler must have discussed with Newell what the people of Salt River Valley needed to accomplish before they could successfully compete for a reclamation project. Although the technique for determining project eligibility had not been fully determined, Newell considered it important that a project fulfill the financial provisions of the Reclamation Act, that the technical engineering and hydrologic aspects be good, and that the water rights be adjudicated.[66]

The Salt River Project, as it was coming to be known, fit the technical profile perfectly, but the other two provisions would be difficult for the valley to fulfill. The long-held traditions of prior appropriation, of individual determination of beneficial use and the duty of water, and of reluctance of the old settlers with vested rights to share with the newer residents of the valley were part of the irrigation heritage handed down since the days of Jack Swilling's community ditch. To be successful in securing a federal irrigation project, people would have to overcome petty differences, which they had been unable to do despite three attempts at organizing for water storage, and to unite in creating both a common water-rights policy and an equitable means of financing the project. Benjamin Fowler took up this challenge as his own. With the support of Newell and the aid of Maxwell, he did not intend to fail.

Forming the Salt River Valley Water Users' Association

The national government provided a great opportunity for Salt River Valley landowners to build their long-awaited water-storage project. The National Reclamation Act of 1902 promised financial subsidy through the use of interest-free federal money; the absence of adequate capital for construction had been the primary obstacle to a locally sponsored project. But what initially seemed an act of national benevolence to the arid region became, upon closer examination, federal largess with strings. Local control of the water-storage project, an issue of some importance in the 1890s when landowners solicited private investment, ran counter to the Reclamation Service's and President Theodore Roosevelt's belief in the importance of centralized authority. Local water-use practices would now be judged against the conservation credo of the greatest good for the largest number of people over the longest period of time, a progressive maxim reflected in the 1902 reclamation law. Local water politics became embroiled in the movement for national social reform, as Frederick Newell's Reclamation Service sought to make reclamation of the arid lands the keystone for change in natural-resource policy. Government subsidy of local reclamation projects also meant federal control.

ADJUSTING LOCAL INTERESTS AND FEDERAL LAW

Circumstances placed Benjamin Fowler in the role of leader of the Salt River Valley water-storage movement. A friend of Newell's,

[25]

Fowler was inclined to let the Reclamation Service's concept of reclamation shape the local institutions required to allow for selection of
Salt River as a federal project. In contrast to Fowler's approach,
Dwight B. Heard, who challenged Benjamin Fowler for leadership of
the water-storage movement, recommended local control of water
politics and practices that were not dominated by federal lines of
authority. Benjamin Fowler was on his way home from Washington,
D.C., and the successful lobbying for the National Reclamation Act
when Dwight Heard invited "a representative gathering of gentlemen from different parts of the county" to meet with him to discuss
his plans to secure a government project for the Salt River Valley.[1]
The differences between the two men and their followers suggested
that creating a local reclamation plan based upon consensus would
not be easy. That Heard was apparently questioning Fowler's position
as leader of the local water-storage movement insured personal
conflict.

Dwight Heard, one of the largest landowners in the valley, as well
as the most significant source of local investments, had a financial
pipeline to Chicago and a political one to the White House. A Progressive in the Roosevelt mode, Heard counted himself both friend
and political ally of the President and of TR's most trusted adviser,
chief forester Gifford Pinchot. Heard's family was well established
(his ancestors had settled in Wayland, Massachusetts, in 1623), and he
had married the daughter of Adolphus Bartlett of Hibbard, Spencer,
Bartlett and Company of Chicago (the nation's largest wholesale
hardware concern), so he had family standing in the East and financial connections in the Midwest, through his father-in-law.

Heard moved to the valley in 1895 for personal reasons: to
recover his health and to establish his own financial empire. Because
of this quest for success, the depth of his community spirit was often
suspect. Heard's earlier efforts (1898) to help privately finance the
storage dam at the Hudson site linked him with those who wanted to
build the reservoir for personal gain; he could not rid himself of this
association after he switched his allegiance to a project financed by the
government. Similarly, in 1910, Heard's lobbying for a substantial
bridge across the Salt River to improve development in south Phoenix
coincidentally linked his property to the city. If Heard used "steam-
roller tactics," as his opponents sometimes charged, he clung to his
ideas and beliefs tenaciously.[2] He was a principled man, as many of
the Progressives were, who sincerely believed that the community's
interests and well-being depended upon his own; his success often
resulted from convincing others that this was true.

Heard presented his ideas on satisfying the government reclama-

Dwight B. Heard, one of the largest landowners in the Salt River Valley, challenged Benjamin Fowler for leadership of the project. Heard recommended local control of water policy and practices and was intially opposed to the methods of the U. S. Reclamation Service. He was a principled man who sincerely believed that the interest and well-being of the community were linked with his own.

tion requirements in a simple and uncomplicated manner. His plan called for (1) the formation of a water-users' association which would secure title to the reservoir site and then turn it over to the government; (2) an engineering commission (primarily from the Geological Survey) to determine stream flow and then "adjudicate" the priority of receiving water for lands under cultivation; and (3) repayment of the construction debt in ten payments. The essence of the plan was speed in packaging it for Washington and implementing it locally.

This plan, while covering some of the basic conditions of the Reclamation Act, was typical of Heard's style; he was "an impatient, energetic person who often annoyed fellow committee members with his determination to get on with business."[3] Yet his style was in harmony with the Progressive spirit epitomized by Gifford Pinchot, who believed the letter of the law should be stretched to accommodate that which was best for the people. Like Pinchot, Heard believed he understood, better than most, what was best for the people. Where Frederick Newell and Benjamin Fowler seemed more modest about their personal accomplishments, Pinchot and Heard were cut from similar egotistic cloth.

Benjamin Fowler, therefore, had to combat both the simplicity of Heard's proposal to secure government support and his rising ambition to take charge of the water-storage movement. Tired after his long trip across the country, with only a few days at home before he would leave again to see Newell and Maxwell in Los Angeles, Fowler irritably insisted that the government would not help landowners sort out their problems. It was up to the water users, Fowler believed, to construct the right situation for government selection of Salt River as a reclamation project. He suggested four general points as a basis for discussion of a federal reclamation plan for the valley:

(1) Water must be appurtenant to the land; vested rights should be allowed to stand, but enforcement of territorial irrigation law, particularly the Kibbey Decree which sought to eliminate the "floating rights" of the canal companies, was essential;

(2) Private corporations must not reap the benefits intended for settlers: ostensibly this would include both canal companies and the large land organizations like the Arizona Improvement Company and the Bartlett-Heard Land and Cattle Company;

(3) The government must be provided with a reservoir site;

(4) Repayment must be completed within ten years.[4]

These conditions could not be met at once, Fowler said, and need not be done immediately. "The government itself is not going to move with startling rapidity," Fowler told the *Republican*, "nor is it going to distribute reservoirs throughout the arid region on the plan of giving them to those who happen to apply first."[5]

The difference between Fowler's and Heard's plans lay in each man's view of what was required to implement national reclamation at Salt River. Heard thought essentially all that would be required was to secure title to the reservoir site; the government would decide the priority of lands receiving water. Under Heard's plan, the government would make the hard decisions for the water users. Fowler, on the other hand, knew the government would not come to Phoenix to negotiate or settle any of the existing differences, nor would it participate in the litigation on the water question or engage in condemnation procedures. Ground had to be cleared, according to Fowler, so the government could participate under the Reclamation Act at Salt River. Rather than the government's deciding to build a project at Salt River, Fowler believed it was chiefly up to the water users to pool all the water-related issues, adjust their differences, and, thus, create the conditions he thought necessary for Salt River to become a national reclamation project.

The Salt River Valley had an excellent chance to be selected for a project because its physical conditions were more favorable than other sections of the country, and the new Reclamation Service needed an initial success to stimulate the irrigation movement. Both Fowler and Heard believed, as their friends in Washington did, that Salt River "would be taken as a model for the work the government would perform in other arid parts."[6] If Fowler was irritated with Heard's preemption of the reclamation issue, he was more concerned with taking the necessary steps to unify valley landowners.

A mass meeting of all the citizens interested in water storage was called for August 3, 1902, to organize yet another water-storage committee. Landowners under the various canals, the canal companies, and the City of Phoenix determined the criteria for committee selection: the canal companies would have one representative per canal, the water users under the canals would have two representatives per canal, and the City of Phoenix two representatives. Benjamin Fowler was again chosen as the committee chairman. The new Water Storage Conference Committee was charged with the task of adjusting all differences between local interests and federal reclamation law. While having a vague idea of what should be investigated, the committee really had no clear vision of how to proceed. Fowler, sensing the confusion of the committee, wisely invited George Maxwell to return to Phoenix to address both the committee and local residents on federal reclamation requirements.[7]

The National Reclamation Act, while providing specific information regarding when land was to be withdrawn, the maximum acreage to be irrigated from a federal project, and what was to be included in the issuance of public notice, did not offer legislative details on what a group of landowners should do to apply for project consideration. Section Two of the act was vague in its criteria for project selection, assigning responsibility for determining "all facts relative to the practicability of each irrigation project" to the Secretary of Interior.[8] Frederick Newell (who, as director of the Reclamation Service, dominated reclamation concerns within the Interior Department) briefly outlined what he considered important elements in choosing a federal project: economic stability, good technological and hydrological conditions, and the settlement of water rights. Yet within these broad guidelines was room for many interpretations, as Heard had demonstrated in his plan and as the new Water Conference Committee illustrated in its rough start toward developing its own plan.

George Maxwell, director of the National Irrigation Association, was the nation's primary spokesman for national reclamation. He came to Phoenix on August 9, 1902, with a simple message for the landowners and the Water Storage Conference Committee: gain control of the irrigation systems; eliminate from the water-storage project those people (other than farmers) who would benefit; and form one association of all the landowners in order to put the project on an economically sound basis and to settle disputed water rights. Maxwell's plan was really no different from the plan he had proposed to Fowler in 1900: a merger of interests into a landowners' cooperative association, so that the "men who own the land and till the soil control the irrigation systems," was Maxwell's chief recommendation to valley landowners.[9]

While aware of the difficulties involved in uniting all the landowners in the valley on this question, Maxwell firmly believed it could be done. But it would take time and careful consideration, and he warned against "the man who tries to find a short cut and leaves out of sight difficulties which will arise up and confront him when half-way across which he ought to have foreseen and got out of the way at the beginning."[10] In a subtle slap at Dwight Heard, who had rushed to publicize his plan for water storage, Maxwell advised the people of the valley that Benjamin Fowler had been indispensable to the irrigation movement. Since Fowler had the "confidence of the eastern people," it was necessary that he be sent back with the valley's proposal to the Secretary of Interior.[11]

The Water Storage Conference Committee, enthusiastic after Maxwell's spirited talk on what they had to do for selection as a federal project, formed an executive committee to develop a plan of action. Composed of eleven men, including Judge Joseph Kibbey as legal adviser, Benjamin Fowler as chairman, and George Maxwell as consulting reclamation adviser, the executive committee released its report October 2, 1902. It called for the formation of an association of all landowners, with no more than 250,000 membership shares to be "perpetually and inseparably appurtenant to the land to which they are issued."[12]

This proposed merger association, based upon land ownership, thus eliminated the canal companies from participation in the water-storage project. All landowners wanting rights to stored water, the committee reported, should become members of this association, which would have a central governing board to deal with the federal government on behalf of all the members. This board of governors would also have control and management over all matters of common interest, such as the construction and operation of pump plants, protection of the water supply, and prevention of appropriations on either the Salt or Verde rivers above the canal systems of the association. It was not, however, to assume control or manage any of the separate canal systems or the distribution of water from them. This would be accomplished by a local board selected by landowners under each system; water would be delivered by the merger association from the reservoir to each canal's headgates in proportion to their respective rights.

The portion of the year's supply of stored water to which each landowner was entitled would be fixed in proportion to his acreage shares. This amount would be reserved for his discretionary use until, but not beyond, the end of the reservoir year, subject to the plan of distribution fashioned under each canal. A water entitlement could not be carried over into the next reservoir year; if the landowner did not take all his water, he lost his right to it. The committee recommended construction of a reservoir with a storage capacity of 1,478,750 acre-feet to irrigate no more than 200,000 acres. Estimated cost for the reservoir, including power facilities for pumping, was $2.5 million, with a flat price of $12.50 per acre due in ten annual installments.[13]

Within this plan were most of those provisions which Maxwell had advocated so strenuously two months earlier; the landowners would have control over the irrigation systems. Not included, however, was any provision to separate those owning land for speculative purposes from those who farmed the land. The National Reclamation Act specifically limited use of government-stored water to 160 acres for land in private ownership of any one landowner residing on the land or in the neighborhood of the land. It did not mention, though, that the landowner must "till the soil," as George Maxwell had told the Salt River Valley. While supporters of the national irrigation movement had envisioned new farms built on reclaimed lands for migrating settlers from the East, the law itself simply provided a maximum limitation on acreage to be irrigated with government water and a vague residency requirement; residing in the neighborhood of the land and the terms of residency were not well defined. Perhaps eastern congressmen were less concerned with who would comprise the new markets in the West than with the actual creation of the markets. The executive committee unanimously approved and the whole committee of twenty-six supported this general framework, although the plan did not provide for adjudication of valley water rights. While solving one part of the federal reclamation requirements by forming a merger association, the water users in the valley were neglecting others.[14]

Still, the executive committee's plan was a beginning. The Water Storage Conference Committee wanted to test the merger plan on valley landowners, and offered a mock "sign-up" of land to determine interest. By October 19, 1902, the subscription book had been signed for about 30,000 acres, but the *Republican* editorialized that "it should be twice that."[15] Perhaps landowners were reticent to sign up, even if it cost nothing and was not legally binding, because there was no certainty that the Water Storage Conference Committee's plan would be acceptable to Washington. "There was no official interpretation, no court construction, no authorities to be consulted," Fowler wrote two years later, "only the law itself—new, untried; a magnificent experiment."[16] By the end of the year, about 150,000 acres had been signed up in support of the preliminary agreement, enough land to guarantee repayment to the government. The executive committee resumed its regular meetings to draft the legal articles of incorporation for the new merger association; Joseph Kibbey, with the aid of George Maxwell, did most of the work.[17]

Maxwell had returned to Washington after his brief visit to the valley in August, staying, however, abreast of developments in Phoenix. In November 1902, he wrote Frank Parker, secretary of the executive committee, that he wanted to see President Roosevelt:

> . . . to confer fully with him as to the splendid effort that is being made by the people of the Salt River Valley to not only harmonize all the conflicting interests in the valley and solve their own local problems, but to create a magnificent object lesson of what can be done to unite irrigation communities . . .[18]

Maxwell believed, and told Parker "in the strictest *personal confidence*," that the Tonto project would be the first reservoir built by the national government. The National Irrigation Association, Maxwell's vehicle of support, was increasing its influence, and the "whole strength of our splendid organization goes behind your project the moment we get the local situation adjusted."[19] While Maxwell did not commit the National Irrigation Association to the Salt River Project until he was satisfied with the landowners' organizational plans, he certainly took a personal stand in support of the executive committee's draft and worked for its successful implementation. He returned to Phoenix to help construct the articles of incorporation in late November 1902.

In Washington the Reclamation Service was busy making preparations to survey and examine potential reservoir sites in the West. Although surveys of the Salt River Project had been done in 1897 and 1900, the Reclamation Service planned the most specific one to date for 1902–1903. While claiming that no project would be granted special preference, the Service was encouraging the valley in ways the water users thought were indicative of support. In August 1902, after much discussion with Frederick Newell, Fowler had said that the reservoir "is just as certain as the sun shines," even though Maxwell suggested he was a bit too optimistic.[20] When, in November of that year, Dwight Heard thought that a duplicate of the Geological Survey's model of the Tonto reservoir would help local education efforts, the Survey, "in its desire to help along the preliminary work," sent the original.[21]

Certainly the personal relationships among Fowler, Newell and Maxwell accounted for much of the Service's unofficial support for the Salt River Project, but the excellence of the physical site also captivated the engineers' imagination. "The gorge on Salt River offers an especially favorable site for a masonry dam," wrote Newell, "the most permanent, conservative and secure form of construction for a high dam that is known to engineering science." Similarly, the sedimentary formation, with the strata inclined about thirty degrees to the horizontal, dipping toward the reservoir, was "a most favorable condition for retaining stored waters and for the stability of the dam." The foundation and rock abutments were "all that could be desired."[22] If there was a perfect damsite on which to begin the experiment of national reclamation, the Tonto seemed to be it.

Local opinion regarding the government project was mixed. Because the engineers were excited about the damsite and because a water distribution system already existed in the valley, some landowners waited to see if the government would compromise any reclamation requirements before signing up their lands. The *Republican* warned that those people waiting to be coaxed into joining the merger association were making a mistake, since the government insisted that reclamation projects be done on a fair, businesslike basis. ". . . The government does not propose to give anybody 'forty acres and a mule,'" wrote the *Republican*; "neither will it give 'forty acres and an assured water supply'; the idea of any gift in the transaction must be wholly eliminated."[23]

Part of the confusion about the requirements arose from the absence of communication between the executive committee and the water users during the months after the plan was announced in early October. Intended to prevent harmful rumors from circulating throughout the valley, the executive committee's news blackout may have prevented the continuing reclamation education of landowners. Still another reason may have been that both Fowler and Kibbey, two of the most effective spokesmen for reclamation locally, were engaged in other issues during the fall of 1902. Kibbey, a Progressive Republican, campaigned successfully for election to the Council of the Twenty-second Territorial Legislature. Fowler was busy with Arizona's unsuccessful bid for statehood (the Oklahoma-New Mexico-Arizona statehood omnibus bill went before the Senate in late November), and was chairman of a Board of Trade committee responsible for securing a sugar beet factory for the valley. Yet the heart of resistance to the executive committee's plan lay in the unspoken belief that the Salt River Project could be constructed with little change in local conditions.[24]

THE ARTICLES OF INCORPORATION

Fowler and Kibbey knew that selection of Salt River as a project depended upon government acceptance of its organization, and, as a result, the executive committee carefully considered its proposal for incorporation. Based upon the following principles, the Articles of Incorporation of the Salt River Valley Water Users' Association sought to reconcile reclamation law with territorial vested rights:

(1) The association should include all water users with vested rights;

(2) Those vested rights include the following conditions:
   a. The basis of an appropriation from public sources—the Salt and Verde rivers—is land ownership and residency;
   b. Beneficial use of the water shall be the measure and limit of the appropriation;
   c. The right to the appropriation is appurtenant to the land;
   d. The rights to appropriation are severally prior—first in time is first in right.

(3) The natural flow of the Salt and Verde rivers should be under the same rules of use and distribution as stored water, uniform and subject to priority;

(4) The proportionate costs of the government works, and the cost of operation and maintenance, should be equal to all;

(5) The powers of administration should be centralized in the association, although the water-users' members should provide as much supervision and direction as possible, subject to approval by the Secretary of Interior;

(6) The powers of the association should be so distributed that there is a maximum of responsibility and a minimum of peculiar personal benefit;

(7) Ample security should be provided for the government by making the assessment charge a lien on the land.[25]

The articles subordinated local interests to national ones by making every subscriber for stock in the water-users' association subject to the rules and regulations of Congress or any Executive Department of the federal government. Completed in early January 1903, the articles were circulated among Phoenix lawyers for review and then submitted to the whole committee for approval.[26]

The articles of incorporation were masterfully drawn, anticipating problems between local custom and federal reclamation law where no precedent existed to guide the way. Specifically, Kibbey and Maxwell tackled the thorny problems of water rights. By using beneficial use, in this case meaning that amount of water required for proper irrigation, as the measure and limit of the water right, the articles attempted to limit the possibility that a landowner with prior rights to the natural flow would waste water by taking both that water and project-developed water. For example, a farmer with prior rights to five acre-feet of natural-flow water would not be able to take an extra acre-foot of project-developed water to irrigate his alfalfa crop if the amount of water required for its proper irrigation was five acre-feet. Similarly, priority of right lost its singular importance in determining water rights, as the articles attempted to create the conditions for equality of water use among old and new settlers. Kibbey explained how this would come about:

> If the amount of water available from all sources shall be sufficient to properly irrigate the number of acres of land which the Secretary of Interior shall estimate can be irrigated therefrom, then all distinctions between the rights of the shareholders cease and become of no importance.[27]

Yet there was no guarantee that the available water supply would always match the acreage to be irrigated, and so the articles also provided that priority of appropriation should govern if there were nothing but natural flow.

Frederick Newell and the Reclamation Service were impressed when they saw the final guidelines for the new Salt River Valley Water Users' Association in February 1903, and recommended them as models for other projects;[28] in this way the valley water users set the precedent for others. But for landowners with old water rights, particularly under the Tempe and Mesa canals, the articles of incorporation radically changed local practices. The idea of prior appropriation lost much of its power, as did the notion that the individual should determine his own beneficial use of water. Where floating water rights existed before, the Salt River Valley Water Users' Association prohibited its members from transferring shares in the association unless the corresponding land was also transferred. The suggested cost per acre of $12.50 payable over a ten-year period did not include the initial subscription charge to the water-users' association; thus, the price of stored water was substantially higher than the average $1.50-per-acre charge most landowners with vested rights were accustomed to paying for delivery of the natural flow.[29]

Opposition to the articles of incorporation formulated by Kibbey and Maxwell arose within the executive committee. If some of the landowners resisted the initial plan for storage because they believed they could get more for less, Dwight Heard, with the support of E. W. Wilbur and J. W. Woolf of the conference committee, disputed what he saw as an abrogation of reclamation principle. The minority group of the Water Storage Conference Committee issued a report containing basically five points of contention with the articles:

(1) The possibility that too few acres in cultivation would subscribe to the association, placing the burden on those who do subscribe, or that too many would subscribe, providing for inadequate water distribution;

(2) The articles failed to adequately protect existing water rights;

(3) Centralizing power in the association would eliminate local autonomy of the several canals;

(4) Assessments for construction should not be shared equally, but apportioned according to benefits derived from the dam;

(5) Instead of being assessed equally for maintenance and operation of the entire system, members of each canal district should pay the upkeep for their own canals.[30]

Clearly, Heard and the minority objected to subsidizing landowners in any way.

The minority group of the Water Storage Conference Committee did not dispute the need for a water-storage dam. Even landowners with the earliest and best normal-flow water rights saw the clear advantages of regulating the river. Severe flooding in the valley in 1891 had been followed by nearly a decade of drought, and few farmers were left untouched by the Salt River's capricious nature.

Their main objection to the draft articles of incorporation was that the costs of the dam would not be distributed according to the level of benefits received from it. What the minority group sought in 1903 was a kind of benefit-cost ratio for each member of the Salt River Valley Water Users' Association, although they did not clearly define it in those terms. Those landowners receiving only benefits derived from regulating the river would pay only that portion of the total construction relating to river regulation. Those landowners receiving benefits derived from both regulating the river and water storage would pay more. And those landowners who received all the benefits, including "new" water developed from storing flood water, would pay the most.

The minority group also objected to the centralization of power in the Association. They believed that each canal company and ditch association should maintain autonomy over their respective canals and ditches and that the Association should not be given control over operational and maintenance decisions. Essentially, the minority group did not want the articles to change too drastically the irrigation status quo, whereby landowners did not either share the costs equally or lose control over their ditches. Their quarrel with the articles of incorporation of the Salt River Valley Water Users' Association was not directed against the project, but against the method by which it would be administered and managed.

Fowler, however, saw these protests by Heard and the others as selfish and concerned only with personal interest. He viewed the minority report as exhibiting both a reluctance to adopt new methods and general unwillingness to accept several reclamation principles, including the appurtenance of water to the land and the limitation of federal water to 160 acres. Heard's persistent argument for the establishment of a "regulation right," in which the flood waters would be held back in the government reservoir and the normal flow regulated for landowners with vested rights and good land in excess of 160 acres, seemed to Fowler a complete denial of the acreage concept.[31]

The dispute between Fowler and Heard over the question of appropriate conditions for association membership illustrates one conflict within the larger conservation movement. Fowler seemed to view reclamation with a reformer's eyes, seeing with it possibilities for society to conform to the ideals of correct human conduct. For him, the 160-acre limitation on federal water put the government on the side of the little farmers, who would be protected from land speculators and water monopolists by centralizing authority in the hands of those who could best protect their interests—that is, the Salt River Valley Water Users' Association and the United States Reclamation Service. Heard, on the other hand, saw reclamation as a business manager might, as an opportunity to rationalize water distribution for the production of better crops. Heard was for the little farmer, too, as long as the land he worked was productive, not marginal. To provide water for small farmers just to have small farms seemed to Heard a waste of a precious resource. He believed local control of the canal systems would provide better service than consolidation under a central authority. Both men were Progressives and proud of the label, both had friends within the national conservation movement, yet each looked at the other with some suspicion and resentment even while they worked for resolution of the reclamation problem in the Salt River Valley.

On January 7, 1903, Maxwell gave a speech calling attention to what he termed the "sectionalism" of the valley. Using the National

Irrigation Association's fight to have the Reclamation Act passed as an analogy, he urged greater understanding by all competing elements within the valley; just as the East had to be shown how it might benefit from the West's prosperity, so those with advantages under the present system had to be shown how federal reclamation under the Salt River Valley Water Users' Association would be profitable for them. When the minority report of Heard, Woolf, and Wilbur circulated throughout the valley just ten days later Maxwell was furious. This, he thought, was a threat to the valley's chances for securing the government project. If the landowners of the Salt River Valley could not unite under one plan, it was quite possible they would be passed over in favor of a project that could. Should this happen, Maxwell believed Heard would be at fault.[32]

The *Republican*, as well as the majority of the Water Storage Conference Committee, was quick to criticize the vagueness of the minority report and its motivation. An editorial in the *Republican* stated:

> As nearly as can be ascertained, the opposition is based upon the alleged fear that somebody would get the best of somebody else should the articles be accepted—the fear, in short, that some of the interests which now consider themselves in a position of advantage against their neighbors, would surrender some of their rights or privileges or advantages, should the government take up the work on the lines laid down by the committee.[33]

The *Republican* editorialized, sounding much like Maxwell, that the articles as drafted were in strict harmony with "unofficial and friendly suggestions" of officers of the government; radical departure from the plan would not meet with their approval.[34]

On January 20, 1903, the Water Storage Conference Committee voted against every minority plank by a two-thirds margin, and the Articles of Incorporation of the Salt River Valley Water Users' Association were approved. The rush to enroll land with the Association would demonstrate the public's acceptance of the articles.[35] Kibbey and Maxwell scheduled three mass meetings, in Tempe, Phoenix, and Mesa, to explain the articles of incorporation to valley landowners.

For many on the south side of the river, the obstacle to signing up was merging their canals with the association. Many of the landowners using the Tempe Canal, for example, did not want the financial responsibility of maintaining other valley canals, some of which were in various states of disrepair. Judge Kibbey advised them that they did not need to merge their canal with the Association if they chose not to do so. They could join the Association and continue to receive their water at the head of their canal if they wanted. He did not tell them, however, that the articles required the Association to supervise all the canals participating in the Salt River Project. In Mesa, landowners wanted to know how much time they had to attach their floating water rights to land in case they decided to become members of the Association. Maxwell believed three years was the minimum amount of time for this purpose, since certification of ownership in the water-users' association would not be issued until the reservoir was completed.[36]

While the Tempe people seemed initially convinced of the opportunities available under the Association, by February 10, 1903, they had decided *not* to become members since their lands were least in need of stored water. The Tempe withdrawal actually worked to unify some landowners waiting to join, since it temporarily quieted Heard and Woolf, both of whom had stock in the Tempe Canal.[37]

The Salt River Valley Water Users' Association officially incorporated under Arizona law on February 9, 1903, but Fowler and the Water Storage Conference Committee had given Newell a copy of the preliminary articles when he was in Arizona in early January to meet with the survey crews in the field. On a train from Albuquerque to La Junta, New Mexico, he read the final draft of the articles. They were really no surprise to Newell, as the main points were those Maxwell had argued since the fight for national reclamation began in the 1890s. Newell found them acceptable, and, with Maxwell back in Washington with him in February, he moved quickly to select the preliminary projects for Secretary Hitchcock's approval.[38]

SELECTION OF THE SALT RIVER PROJECT

On March 6, 1903, Newell and Charles Walcott of the Survey presented five projects to Hitchcock for selection: Milk River, Montana; Gunnison, Colorado; Sweetwater, Wyoming; Truckee, Nevada; and Salt River, Arizona. Of Salt River, Walcott wrote Hitchcock that:

> The conditions are typical of those which must be made elsewhere, and in considering this project and determining upon rules and regulations, it is necessary to create such precedents as will be desirable for other parts of the U.S.[39]

The clarity of the articles of incorporation and the committee's adoption of the reclamation plan embodied within them succeeded in showing Washington that Salt River was ahead of every other section of the country in its preparation for federal reclamation.

Ample funds (well over ten million dollars) existed in the revolving reclamation fund for construction without drawing upon the fixed fund for any state. Both Charles Walcott, director of the U.S. Geological Survey, and Frederick Newell, director of the Reclamation

Service, advocated using the floating fund, at Hitchcock's discretion, for Salt River. This idea was crucial, for the Salt River Project had an estimated cost of $2.8 million, and Arizona had fixed funds (through the sale of public lands) of only $62,565. Newell believed that Secretary Hitchcock knew and cared very little about the matters of federal reclamation, and beyond "some feeble protests," the head of the Interior Department authorized the decisions put forth by Newell and Walcott. On March 10, 1903, Newell dictated a letter to Fowler and Maxwell, presumably telling them that Salt River would be selected; official acknowledgement of the initial choices came four days later.[40]

Despite this official notification of the selection of the Salt River Project, Dwight Heard and others in the Tempe area continued to battle the adoption of the Salt River Valley Water Users' Association Articles of Incorporation. Although Fowler had presented the articles to Washington officials as "the people's plan," Heard thought a better title would be "Maxwell's Speculative Plan:"

> . . . legitimate farmers with well-developed places and valuable water rights are asked to put up the bulk of the security and apparently will receive the least benefit, while the speculative holders of idle lands (the class who now so enthusiastically endorse Mr. Maxwell's plan) put up the least security and receive the greatest benefit.[41]

Heard attempted to delay construction on the reclamation project until he could present alternative organizational plans to the Secretary of Interior.[42]

The Reclamation Service and George Maxwell nervously watched the "fierce fight" between the minority on the water- users' association committee and the majority. The minority, especially Heard, charged Maxwell with many things, including corruption; Walcott told Hitchcock that "if the water users follow Maxwell's advice the minority will not profit—which is sufficient reason for their hostility." The Board of Governors of the new Salt River Valley Water Users' Association also supported Maxwell by inviting him to sit with them whenever he was able to attend.[43]

Walcott received from Heard a copy of the "Tempe Plan," in which the minority combined their notions of local autonomy and regulated rights with the requirements of the Reclamation Act. Heard hoped Walcott would thus amend the association articles, which Hitchcock had accepted on April 17, 1903. Walcott took Heard's plan to Hitchcock in May, but the Secretary decided not to take the matter up. In writing Heard of this decision, Walcott noted that the Reclamation Act's author, Senator Newlands, who was quite influential regarding national irrigation, had also reviewed the Salt River articles and considered them fair, both to landowners and the government. The national irrigation establishment supported the blueprint for the Salt River Project drawn up by Fowler and Maxwell. Commenting upon the bitter split between Heard and Maxwell, Walcott told Heard: "knowing you both, I think that if you had come at this problem through the same training and point of view as Maxwell, you would hold as tenaciously to the views he advocates as you now do to those you are supporting so strenuously."[44]

The *Arizona Democrat* urged Tempe farmers to look carefully into the motives of Heard, "this man with a Chicago father-in-law," and see to it that they were not trapped into a scheme which would "injure them in the future."[45] Maxwell worked hard to destroy what he termed the "Heard-McClatchie-Woolf-Ivy" influence, and believed in early June 1903 that he had been successful everywhere but in Tempe. "He [Heard] will continue to make trouble—lots of it," Maxwell wrote Walcott, "but he can no longer delay us...[since] this community as a whole [is] now ready to follow your lead and do anything you want done." The right thing for the government to do, Maxwell thought, "for the protection of its own interests," was to begin construction of the reservoir works.[46]

Dwight Heard, believing in his cause, did not really seem to understand why he was subject to so much personal abuse in his efforts to modify the articles. In a lengthy explanation to the *Phoenix Enterprise*, he tried to tell valley landowners that more land was patented in the Salt River Valley than the 200,000 acres provided for in the water-users' association and that the water supply was simply inadequate for those inferior lands without vested rights which would be included within the project under the articles. Heard felt that landowners like himself, with vested rights and improved lands, were being asked to carry too heavy a burden for the benefits they could expect to receive under the articles. Because one's land would be subject to a lien for repayment of the reclamation project, those with the better and improved lands would take a substantially higher risk than those with unimproved and uncultivated land. Still, it was hard for Heard to escape the charge that the Barlett-Heard Land and Cattle Company would benefit more than others under his proposed changes.[47]

After receiving Walcott's letter in May, Heard went to Washington to see both Walcott and Hitchcock personally. According to the director of the Geological Survey, Heard presented his views "in relation to the situation at Phoenix in a very gentlemanly, quiet manner, and did not open up detailed discussion on the minority amendments with the Secretary at all." The Salt River Valley landowner was "most dispassionate and reasonable in presenting his views," and Walcott believed that Heard left Washington planning to assist in the work of securing the Tonto reservoir for the benefit of the Salt River Valley. Walcott told Maxwell that "if this same spirit is shown on his return to Phoenix, I trust that you can all get together, bury the hatchet and go ahead."[48]

Secretary Hitchcock's refusal to modify the articles of the Salt River Valley Water Users' Association effectively stopped Heard from pursuing that path of changing the fundamental direction of the water-users' organization. Although he fought the articles desperately, Heard never considered himself anything but a friend of the water-storage movement. Others found this notion somewhat ironic; when Heard wrote Frederick Newell in 1922 for a letter of support on this issue (to be used in a political campaign), Newell responded that he remembered Heard's participation differently:

> I am impressed with the fact that the Salt River project at various times was on the verge of being abandoned, and that it was only by the almost superhuman persistence of B. A. Fowler and some of his colleagues that the project was finally kept alive against what at the time seemed a very irritating opposition from the minority . . . I make the mental reservation that in your statements you naturally do not and cannot explain how nearly the minority committee came to upsetting the work in hand, nor could you then appreciate the intense feeling aroused within the Reclamation Service.[49]

Heard was not among the initial subscribers to the Salt River Valley Water Users' Association, nor were any of the lands under the Tempe Canal. Charles Walcott did convince him, however, that he would have more influence in securing reforms in the articles as a member than as an outsider, and in July, Heard personally subscribed 720 acres, and 640 acres of the Bartlett-Heard Land and Cattle Company. Still, under Fowler's leadership, he was excluded from the initial decision-making of the new water organization.[50]

Others who had opposed or wanted to delay the selection of the Salt River Project were chiefly those in Pinal County south of Phoenix, who wanted the San Carlos Project for that county to be constructed instead. Those supporting government selection of the San Carlos Project over the Salt River Project did so primarily on the basis that it would benefit both the Gila River Pima Indians and, because of the great amount of public land in the project area, the small homesteader. Established landowners who wanted the government project at San Carlos were so confident that these two characteristics would insure their project's selection by the Secretary of Interior that they neglected to organize and lobby their cause. Combined with unsatisfactory engineering specifications, this lack of local coordination made Salt River look like a better prospect and persuaded Newell and the Reclamation Service to relegate San Carlos to a list of secondary projects. Those supporting the San Carlos Project lost further momentum as Secretary of Interior Hitchcock approved, in June 1903, the withdrawal of federal lands needed for the Salt River Project. Concurrently, Secretary Hitchcock authorized the construction of roads, the purchase of required lands, and the preparation of contracts for the main structures of the Salt River Project. Geography, engineering design, and now organization were all on the side of the Salt River Project, and nothing would be able to stop its construction.[51]

SECURING SUBSCRIBERS FOR SHARES IN THE ASSOCIATION

From February 9 through July 17, 1903, the subscription book of the Salt River Valley Water Users' Association was open to those who owned land within the boundaries set by the articles of incorporation (see map, below). For a small initial assessment of ten cents per acre, landowners could subscribe for stock in the water-users' association. This did not, however, make them stockholders, nor did it insure that stock would ever be allotted to them. What it did provide was an opportunity to *become* stockholders.

The articles of incorporation provided that only those who initiated, and finally perfected, a government reservoir right could become shareholders. This provision meant that only those landowners who fulfilled the government requirements of residency and maximum acreage to be irrigated with government water (160 acres) would be eligible for Association membership. Judge Joseph Kibbey described the reasoning behind this point:

> The Irrigation Act provides for the Association of the owners of the lands irrigated by the Government and this we deemed to be exclusive of others. We further deemed it unwise to associate those together whose interests might be so diverse as to eventually disrupt the Association . . .[52]

The water-users believed that to extend membership in the Association to anyone other than holders of rights from the government might make a speculative or monopolistic combination possible.

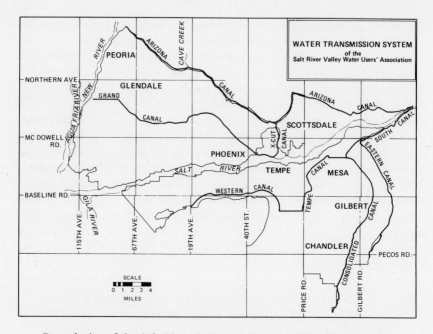

Boundaries of the Salt River Project, as determined in the articles of incorporation in 1903 (the boundaries were unchanged in the mid-1980s). The map shows the Phoenix-area towns served by the various canals within the project. Map drawn by Cartographics Department, Salt River Project.

For those who "purposely or negligently" failed to initiate and perfect their government rights, and in the event more shares were subscribed than the Secretary of Interior authorized, a forfeiture clause was included which allowed the Association to exclude certain subscribers; however, subscribers could not withdraw voluntarily. Subscribers generally had several years before the government would complete project construction and begin water distribution. During that time they could perfect their reservoir rights; for most, this meant simply selling any excess acreage.[53]

If all of this sounded terribly uncertain, it was only because the requirements for membership were necessarily vague until government surveys could be completed regarding the maximum amount of irrigable acreage from natural and stored sources of water, the amount of underground water which could be developed, and the most beneficial duty of water. One could be fairly confident of becoming a member, however, if the land subscribed was 160 acres or less, was within the project boundaries as defined within the articles of incorporation, and had been previously cultivated.[54]

Benjamin Fowler headed the new water-users' association committee charged with soliciting subscriptions for stock. With the help of William Christy, treasurer of the Association, he canvassed the valley to secure these subscriptions; when Christy died in April 1903, the Subscription Committee was expanded from two to five members, drawn from the association's Board of Governors. Although they began their efforts in early February, the committee signed up fewer than 60,000 acres by the first of May 1903. Concerned because the subscription rate was less than anticipated, the Board of Governors authorized the committee to use any methods it thought best which "will hasten the securing of subscriptions for shares in the Association."[55]

A. J. Chandler, also a member of the Subscription Committee, believed the main trouble in securing subscriptions lay with the canal system; if a majority of those farmers using the Utah Canal, for example, came into the Association, they all would join. To achieve this end, Chandler thought it best for the Association to conditionally subscribe the land and to allow voluntary withdrawal if desired. Despite Chandler's view of the problem, the Subscription Committee members did not approve of conditional subscriptions, and they continued to sign up land gradually within the valley until June, at which time forty percent of the total acreage subscribed was secured. By June 22, 1903, the Board believed the 142,620 acres signed up allowed the association leeway to restrict further subscriptions. From that day forward, no subscriptions for shares in the Association would be received for any part less than the whole of all irrigable lands owned by the applicant in any one quarter-section, nor would they be received for lands lying outside the reservoir district as defined within the articles of incorporation; in addition, those lands already subscribed that lay outside the district would be rejected.[56]

By the end of June 1903 enough acreage had been pledged as collateral for the government project, although it was roughly 60,000 acres short of the projected maximum of 200,000 acres. Of this total acreage subscribed and listed in the 1903 stock book, eighty percent consisted of land held by individuals; twelve percent by companies, banks, and municipalities; six percent by land agents and trustees, and the remaining two percent by small groups of individuals signing up parcels of land and by subscribers with incomplete names. Fifty-two percent of the total acreage signed was in holdings of 160 acres or less. Acreage subscribed in excess of 160 acres, or forty-eight percent of the total, belonged solidly to individuals (seventy-seven percent) rather than to banks, companies, or municipalities.[57]

Although the government placed great emphasis upon the 160-acre requirement for federal water, landowners in the Salt River Valley were not discouraged from signing up more than that amount to the Association; perhaps the Association encouraged this to secure enough member lands while anticipating several years in which members could dispose of their excess holdings. Those landowners subscribing land in excess of 160 acres did so to raise the value of the land for its eventual sale. They knew they would not have to sell the excess land until the government completed the project, and subscribing the land to the Association allowed the land the opportunity to participate in the project; land without good water rights was worth little. The water-users' organization in the Salt River Valley illustrated the individual subscriber's domination of federal reclamation there in spite of the oft-expressed fear in the late nineteenth century of large companies monopolizing stored water.

Primarily farmers, the individuals signing up their land in the Association in 1903 were young men (between twenty and forty years of age), married, with families, who had come to the area from the Midwest.[58] About eighty percent were born in the third quarter of the nineteenth century, and the largest group came from the north-central states.

In 1903, when they signed up, more than half of the subscribers lived in the rural areas of the Salt River Valley—areas defined as outside the limits of Phoenix and Mesa—on farms. Of those lands subscribed, forty-six percent were in the Phoenix area, nineteen percent in the vicinity of Mesa, and twenty percent in the Glendale-West Phoenix area. Perhaps it was their age or midwestern heritage that made many of the individuals eligible to subscribe their lands cautious about joining the new water-users' organization; more probably it was that (in 1900) forty-two percent of them owned their land free from mortgage. Signing up meant pledging their land as collateral for a large, expensive project.

Only seventeen percent of the sample signed up their lands in February, when the subscription books opened: while twenty-five percent more signed in March, when the project was selected by the government, the numbers decreased significantly in April and May. The Subscription Committee of the Salt River Valley Water Users' Association had good reason to be concerned when it suggested in May that any method be used to increase the number of subscribers. Heard and the minority who opposed the legal organization of the water users might have discouraged valley farmers from joining. It was not until June, when construction of the project began and Heard resigned himself to the Association, that a wave of new subscribers enabled the Board of Governors to breathe a sigh of relief, knowing that they could meet the government requirements.

There did seem to be a relationship between the location of a landowner's property and the date it was subscribed. More than fifty percent of those signing up land in Phoenix did so in February and March; in Mesa, more than half signed up their land in June. In the smaller rural ares, such as Laveen, Tolleson, Peoria and North Phoenix, landowners also signed up their property in June. Land subscribed in Glendale and the Chandler-Gilbert area was generally subscribed throughout the five-month period.

A relationship also seems to have existed between the location of property and the amount of acreage subscribed. Fifty-eight percent of those signing up land in Phoenix subscribed 60 acres or less; sixty-five percent of those landowners in Mesa also subscribed 60 acres or less. The outlying areas seemed to contain the larger acreage subscriptions: eighty-one percent of Chandler-Gilbert landowners alone signed more than 120 acres each.[59]

Holding title to the land subscribed was a prerequisite for membership in the water-users' association. In 1900 nearly half of the individuals selected for study owned their land outright; another thirty-two percent owned their land with some sort of mortgage. It is not surprising that the amount of land signed up in 1903 by more than half (fifty-seven percent) of those who owned their farms free of mortgage was 60 acres or less, since most family farms in 1903 averaged 40 acres. Forty-two percent owning mortgaged farms subscribed 60 acres or less, as did thirty-six percent of those owning homes without a mortgage. Clearly, those members of the water-users' association who owned farms did not own much beyond the average farmer. Those sample members listed as renting a house or farm in 1900 must have purchased some land (although not necessarily the same house or farm) before signing up in 1903.

Thirty-three women in the group of sample subscribers signed up for stock in the water-users' association in 1903; most of them were from the Midwest, were between thirty and fifty years of age, and were married to farmers. Most women subscribed less than 60 acres, with the model statistic between 10 and 20 acres. In this sample population, many of the married women signed up land and their husbands did not, although there were several cases when both husband and wife signed up separate parcels of land. The application for stock in the Association did require the signatures of both spouses if the applicant was married, and more than one landowner was delayed while fulfilling this condition because many wives were visiting in cooler climates to escape the valley's summer heat. These women could ostensibly vote in the water-users' elections seventeen years before general suffrage for women and nine years before Arizona statehood provided the vote for women. There is little evidence, however, to indicate that women, single or married, exercised their prerogative to become involved in water-users' business.

Although the new Salt River Valley Water Users' Association made no membership provision for farmers over speculative landholders, it seems to have been, nonetheless, an organization of cautious, small-acreage-holding farmers. As such, they took a risk in following Fowler into the untried experiment called national reclamation and becoming association members. Yet they seem also to have been exactly the population toward which reclamation was directed: self-supporting farmers. Frederick Newell wrote of this reclamation ideal:

> The home is the foundation of all that is best in the State . . . . Its preservation and the perpetuation of its ideals are duties for the Nation. There can be none higher than to furnish opportunities for homes for self-reliant citizens, particularly those of the pioneer type, whose past achievements stand out on the pages of American history.[60]

Thomas Jefferson's agrarian ideal of the sturdy yeoman farmer building up America suited the Reclamation Service director's image of government reclamation in 1903. The differences between Fowler and Heard, and between each leader's brand of conservation, however, would raise questions regarding that image's appropriateness for the Salt River Valley in the twentieth century.

The organizing Committee of the Salt River Valley Water Users' Association designed a new water-users' coalition to manage, in concert with the Reclamation Service, the water resources of the Salt River Project. Authority would be centralized, flowing from top to bottom; little attention was publicly paid to the position of the farmer at the bottom. As the Association asserted its command of both local water institutions and policies, the question of what constituted local control became a subject for debate. At the heart of the matter was the developing alliance between the federal government and the Salt River Valley Water Users' Association.

Institutional Framework for
Federal Reclamation

The increase in the number of landowners subscribing to the Salt River Valley Water Users' Association in June 1903 insured the predominance of Benjamin Fowler and Joseph Kibbey's vision regarding what shape the new water-users' organization would take. This predominance did not mean, however, the end of controversy for the Salt River Project. The Salt River Valley Water Users' Association, formed under the auspices of Frederick Newell's Reclamation Service, represented a new way of irrigating in the valley: water resources were to be managed centrally, and the decision-making role of the individual farmer was to decline in relative importance.

Federal reclamation at Salt River had its advantages and disadvantages, but it affected everyone, regardless of his position on the subject. Issues which were not easy to resolve emerged from reconciling federal reclamation principles with traditional irrigation practices. From 1903 through the remainder of the decade, questions arose involving the Tempe lands, the acreage limitation provision of the National Reclamation Act, and the criteria for membership within the Salt River Project, and answers to these questions continued to be elusive. On the other hand, Benjamin Fowler and Frederick Newell demonstrated what centralized management of the valley's water resources could look like by taking over the privately owned northside water system for the Salt River Project. The result proclaimed, at the very least, the Salt River Valley Water Users' Association ascendancy over water issues in the valley; at the same time it also suggested the difficulties Fowler and Newell faced in asserting reclamation's "gospel

[49]

of efficiency" over the slow, ponderous method of decision through local debate and majority rule.

"All has been said, all has been done that is possible to make the matter plain," editorialized the *Phoenix Enterprise* on July 15, 1903. "If any want to come in they have two more days in which to sign up."[1] The water-users' association had subscribed 186,000 acres by the middle of July (out of a maximum limit of 250,000 shares, or acres) and, although Reclamation Service engineer Arthur P. Davis predicted that the area to be irrigated would be only 180,000 acres, many members of the Board of Governors were anxious to bring the Tempe lands into the reservoir project. There were approximately 20,000 acres in Tempe with vested rights to the natural flow of the Salt River, and the water-users' association wanted to make water distribution and the determination of irrigable acreage simpler by including those lands within the project. Similarly, the cost of the project would be less per acre if all land with vested rights participated. By excluding such lands, the water-users' association (1) would not have the same control over the duty of water on the Tempe lands as they had over their own Project lands, (2) would have to subtract the Tempe normal-flow water supply from the total water supply for the valley instead of "pooling" all the valley's normal-flow rights, and (3) would have a higher cost per acre to repay.[2]

Despite their extensive efforts, the members of the Board of Governors were not successful in persuading large numbers of Tempe landowners to subscribe for stock in the Salt River Valley Water Users' Association. Considering Heard's argument that many of them would pay for benefits they would not receive, most landowners under the Tempe Canal chose to remain within their own system of water supply and delivery. Thus, the Association's problem of having too many acres with inadequate rights persisted, and the issue of which lands would be included within the government project seemed to threaten the earlier momentum.

THE QUESTION OF MEMBERSHIP

Disappointed at Tempe's refusal to join, but not dissuaded, the Salt River Valley Water Users' Association closed its subscription books on July 17, 1903, and submitted them to the Secretary of Interior. The decision to accept all or part of the landowners subscribed as stockholders in the government project rested within that office. However, the Secretary could not decide what the amount of irrigable acreage under the Salt River Project would be until the Reclamation Service prepared the necessary reports on water supply, distribution,

and land classification. This was not something the Service was prepared to do soon, as it was burdened with administrative and preliminary construction details on several projects at once. Putting the
proverbial cart before the horse, the Reclamation Service commenced
its construction plans without providing the projects with a maximum
number of acres which could be irrigated from the dams. As a result,
confusion and vagueness continued to dominate, and questions of
who was and who was not a member of the Association persisted,
generating the impression that the project was founded on something
less than business-like principles.

Compounding the problem was the great desire of the Reclamation Service to sign up as much land as possible, to ensure that the
federal government would be repaid for its project costs. Even
though the Salt River Valley Water Users' Association had closed its
subscription books, Frederick Newell advised creating a "waiting list,"
in which additional acreage could be signed up and considered in case
the original subscriptions proved unacceptable.[3] Taking Newell's
advice without question, even though more acres were already subscribed than could be supplied water, the Board of Governors
reopened subscription of shares to the Association, via the waiting list,
in early 1904.

This waiting list provoked Dwight Heard once again to complain
to Charles Walcott of the Geological Survey regarding the direction
federal reclamation was following in the Salt River Valley. Heard
believed an immediate determination of the irrigable acreage of the
project was necessary, because 198,587 acres had been subscribed,
5,000 acres were on the waiting list, and 30,000 acres with well-established rights remained outside the Association as of April 1904.
(Fowler's figures were 190,000 acres, 10,000 acres, and 20,000 acres
respectively.) With the water supply of the valley adequate to irrigate
an estimated 180,000 to 200,000 acres (this included use of underground water), Heard's concern seemed genuine. More important,
perhaps, was his practical realization of the problems of irrigating
land subscribed before the final acreage had been determined. Heard
wrote Walcott the following:

> It seems to me that of the 198,587 acres which are subscribed to
> the association, those who have paid assessments in the association
> and continue to do so will steadily strengthen their equitable
> rights to the use of water the longer this question of the location
> of the acreage to be served is left undetermined.[4]

After paying non-refundable assessments of ten cents per acre for
maintenance of the water-users' organization, for operation and

maintenance charges related to the upkeep of the water-distribution system, and for water rental charges involved in the right to use project water until the project was completed and member lands determined, a landowner who had inadequate prior rights but who had profitably cultivated his land with project water would hardly be consoled with the idea that he had paid his fees, for a *chance* to become a member. This was the official line of the Salt River Valley Water Users' Association, and Heard had reason to be concerned.

By 1905, the question of how much acreage would be served water from the reclamation project had yet to be resolved. The stated policy of the Association was to continue to apply pressure on those landowners with vested rights outside of the project to sign up. If all the land with vested rights belonged to the water-users' organization, the Board of Governors believed there would be no water supply problem and that the repayment burden would be manageable. Concurrently, if membership shares were allotted by priority of right—the date when water had first been put to a beneficial use on the land—the speculative and marginal lands which had heretofore subscribed for shares would be rejected.

With these two goals before them, the Board of Governors proposed to the Secretary of Interior in July 1905 that all the lands on the waiting list be put on the regular subscription list, that all lands with vested rights be solicited to join the Association without a delinquent payment, and that a friendly suit (Hurley v. Abbott) be initiated in the Third Judicial District Court to determine priority rights within the Salt River Valley. On November 11, 1905, Secretary Hitchcock approved the request from the Board and accepted all contracts for subscription of stock that were on the waiting list. The Tempe landowners, however, still refused to sign up for shares, and the sentiment of the majority of landowners in the valley favored the dismissal of the friendly suit because of its great cost in time and money. As construction began on the storage dam itself, the solution to the problem of how much and whose acreage would be included within the government project seemed even further away. "We agreed upon the principles of selection," wrote Kibbey of the water-users' policy to Fowler, "but of course we could not and never will agree upon a specific application of those principles."[5]

At the same time that valley water users were considering how to determine which lands would be included within the project, the Reclamation Service was pressing Fowler and Kibbey for compliance with the 160-acre limitation on the Salt River Project. The 160-acre limitation for private lands on reclamation projects was designed to prevent monopoly in the West, both on new lands brought into productivity through government reclamation projects and on old lands held by private interests. By restricting the use of federal water on private lands to the Homestead Act precedent of 160 acres per landowner (with restrictions on the amount a family could hold as well), the federal government hoped to create the conditions for increased growth of small, profitable, family farms. In order for this growth to occur on government reclamation projects, those subscribing excess acreage to the Association needed to divest themselves of all but 160 acres in order to receive stored water. Coincidentally, those qualified to apply for government water rights needed to know which excess lands would be included within the Association, because there was little public land available on the Salt River Project. Conveyance or sale of excess lands had to proceed, according to the Reclamation Service, along with the final determination of acreage to be included within the project boundaries.[6]

Conveyance of excess lands to the Salt River Valley Water Users' Association was the method of compliance suggested by the government. In this way, landowners would convey "in trust" their excess lands to the Association, which would then sell the land at a fair price on behalf of the landowner either at the time of, or subsequent to, delivery of water from the project. If the landowners did not want to convey their land to the Association, they had to sell the excess acreage themselves before they could become members. The Reclamation Service intended that this conveyance process eliminate any element of inflated land prices which might occur due to the government irrigation project.

Judge Joseph Kibbey believed that conveyance of excess acreage on the Salt River Project would be very unattractive without a determination of which lands would be included within the project; Kibbey did not think any landowner would convey to the Association land which might not be entitled to water anyway. The Association itself would be "embarrassed" by accepting such a trust, knowing that the lands conveyed would never benefit from that trust. Unlike other reclamation projects, which had a surplus of water for a limited amount of irrigable acreage, the Salt River Project found itself in the opposite situation. Therefore, Kibbey reasoned that

> . . . the disqualification of the present holders (by reason of excess) is of very much less importance than the fact that the land may not under any ownership be entitled to share in the water . . . . The disqualification of the owner may be remedied—the legal status of the land to the water supply cannot . . . .[7]

Conveyance of excess land to the Association, according to Kibbey, would put the water users in the rather equivocal position of offering lands for sale in order to allow the owner to subscribe for shares of stock "when in fact the land is in no case entitled to water (or shares)."[8]

A better alternative, Kibbey thought, would be to allow the subscriber to choose which 160 acres he wanted to subscribe, and if he did not choose to designate it, the Association would decide, based upon compactness, uniformity, and symmetry of the ultimate district. Kibbey argued the case well for the Association, and the Reclamation Service somewhat grudgingly followed his reasoning. Realizing that different conditions on each project prevented uniform solutions, the Service dropped its pressure for compliance with the 160-acre rule early in the construction of the Salt River Project. The majority of subscribers to the Association had signed up 160 acres or less, anyway, so the 160-acre limitation rule was less controversial in the early years on Salt River than it was on some of the other reclamation projects.[9]

Uncertainty over the acreage to be included within the project, coupled with the levying of assessments for maintaining the water-users' association, prompted Dwight Heard and several other land-owners on the north side of the river to form, in April 1904, a committee to elect "public-spirited, conservative and business-like" men to the Board of Governors and the Council of the Association. The time for water-boosting was over, they thought, and the Salt River Valley needed to prepare for the economic consequences of reclamation. Although Heard noted a "considerable hesitancy" on the part of certain districts within the Association to elect Benjamin Fowler president, he and his followers believed Fowler deserved a chance to demonstrate "if he has the business capacity to handle the practical business questions which now confront us."[10]

Heard and his group were remarkably successful in the 1904 campaign, which had surprisingly low voter turnout, considering it was the first election of the Association. His group won 25 out of the 30 seats on the Council (the legislative body), and 8 out of 10 seats on the Board of Governors (the policy-making arm of the Association). The group was also successful in electing E. W. Wilbur vice-president, forcing Fowler to work closely with a former antagonist from the minority committee.[11]

Heard wrote Charles Walcott of the U.S. Geological Survey that, with the election, the "sectional and personal distrust and prejudice aroused by Mr. Maxwell while here will soon be entirely eliminated from the situation . . . ." Perhaps hoping to repair some of his damaged credibility with the Reclamation Service and Frederick Newell by shifting blame for Salt River Valley antagonisms on Maxwell,

Heard also wrote that he was sure that time would dissipate what he believed was Maxwell's campaign against him within the Service; by all accounts, Newell did not change his mind about Heard.[12]

While Heard was exhilarated over the election results, which may have restored to him some of the leadership he lost in the battle over the articles of incorporation, Fowler was outraged at his organized effort to take over the Association. Fowler wrote Morris Bien, Newell's chief assistant and legal officer of the Reclamation Service, that

> . . . the element headed by Heard . . . made an aggressive campaign at the last election, while my friends took no active part, thinking to secure a fair expression of the wishes of the people. In this we were mistaken, as the scheming and aggressiveness of the other side secured the election for selfish purposes of a sufficient number of the governors . . . .[13]

Fowler believed that his friends felt a "hearty disgust" for what had transpired, but did not want to bother Bien with the details. "It is enough that I am annoyed by local details," wrote Fowler, "and not you."[14]

Frederick Newell gave Fowler a boost, however, when he told the Association's Board of Governors in a June 1904 trip to Phoenix that "the government and the officials of the United States Reclamation Service have unbounded confidence in Mr. Fowler and Mr. Kibbey, and the present advanced position of the Association is due largely to that fact."[15] Newell successfully deflated Heard's group, which sought greater control over the Salt River Project, with his unqualified support of Fowler and Kibbey, despite Heard's electoral victory and the persistence of unanswered questions. Salt River had already been selected as a federal project, and most landowners and farmers there remained acquiescent to the views of the Reclamation Service.

The election came at a critical juncture in Fowler's administration, because the water users were scheduled to vote in May 1904 on the contract with the United States. Newell had thought that a contract with the Salt River Valley Water Users' Association was necessary to prevent individual members of the organization from withdrawing, thus jeopardizing government investment in the reclamation project. Because the Association was "purely voluntary," Newell had sought some measure by which the lien against project lands could be enforced. To satisfy this concern, a contract had to be ratified by the shareholders (or by those subscribing for shares) in the Association.[16]

Technically, the contract did little more than give the government and the water-users' organization a legal tool to enforce repayment of the construction debt. It also reiterated those provisions within the articles of incorporation requiring appurtenance of water to the land, determination of prior rights and acreage to be served water under the project, and retention of title to the storage works by the government until provided for otherwise. Section Eleven, however, proposed a new twist to government reclamation on the Salt River Project:

> . . . When the Secretary of Interior shall make, approve, and promulgate rules and regulations for the administration of the water to be supplied from said proposed irrigation works, such rules and regulations, and such modifications thereof as the Secretary may, from time to time, approve and promulgate, shall be deemed and held to be obligatory upon this Association as fully and completely and to every intent and purpose, as if they were now made, approved, promulgated and written out in full in this memorandum, and are to be read and construed as if so done.[17]

As Gifford Pinchot had struggled to centralize control of the nation's forests within his bureau of the federal government, Frederick Newell had quietly taken steps to consolidate authority over the uses of reclamation-project water, at least on Salt River, in the hands of the Secretary of Interior.

The contract of 1904 was one which favored the government, although the water users on Salt River had no criticism of this. The earlier concern of owning and controlling the storage works "for ourselves" seemed to dissipate in the anxiety about receiving stored water. Submitted to the water users in May, and lobbied for hard by Fowler, the contract was ratified by more than the required two-thirds of the small vote cast, winning 24,662 votes out of a total of 24,902 (one acre = one vote). Heard and his group may have taken control of the Board of Governors, but Fowler seemed to still engender confidence in his administration, as indicated both by ratification of the contract and by the low voter turnout.[18]

If the contract with the United States favored the government, it also offered advantages to the Association, for it committed the Reclamation Service irrevocably to the successful construction, operation, and maintenance of the Salt River Project. Fowler, who advocated the conservation principles set forth by Pinchot and Newell of the Roosevelt administration, welcomed the centralized authority of the Service, and saw in it the end of water problems in the West. So committed was Fowler to this set of principles that he was often asked by Newell and others in the Reclamation Service to travel with them to other projects, so that he could give the many water users in the West his first-hand experience with federal reclamation. In fact, the Reclamation Service requested, over the course of almost a year, that Fowler visit some of the northern projects to explain government requirements for federal reclamation and to assist the water users there in preparing the framework of organization. He was, as the *Reclamation Record* reported, "one of the loyal friends of the Service."[19]

Fowler understood what the Reclamation Service was trying to create on the arid lands west of the 100th meridian, and in many instances he brought the Service the support of the Salt River Valley Water Users' Association when no other group of landowners would step forward. His relationship with Frederick Newell had been critical to securing the selection of Salt River as a reclamation project; it would remain important for expansion of the original plans. Yet the close relationship between Fowler and the Reclamation Service—focused as it was on the large, national picture—excluded others in the Association who were more concerned with the local situation at Salt River. As a result, few within the Association understood just what the Reclamation Service might expect of them. As long as construction of the project proceeded smoothly and the cost remained low, most valley landowners had no quarrel with Fowler or his philosophy, and seemed content to let him lead as he wished.

Title to the Tonto damsite still belonged to the Hudson Reservoir and Canal Company, and before actual construction could begin on the project, it had to be purchased by the water users for the government. Henry H. Man, president of the Hudson Company, demanded $200,000 for the site; when the Reclamation Service refused, he reduced this to $100,000. In early 1904 the government appointed a board to appraise the holdings of the company at the Tonto site; the appraisal board recommended $40,000 as the purchase price, and the Hudson Company accepted this figure. Many landowners in the valley, however, thought this amount generous:

> Few people believe that the Hudson Reservoir Company has a moral right—as to the legality they know nothing—to a single dollar of the money raised by mortgaging the farms of the Salt River Valley; few people can be induced to believe that these New Yorkers with a Phoenix assistant have any moral right to recover from the people of this section the money they spent in promoting a scheme of which they made a failure; few people will appreciate the generosity which prompted them, when they were flatly told they could not have $200,000 or $100,000, to accept $40,000 "rather than delay construction of the reservoir."[20]

In a deed dated July 19, 1904, the Hudson Company conveyed to the United States all of its rights associated with the Tonto damsite.[21]

Most of the land within the flood lines of the reservoir had been purchased by 1905, and the remainder, estimated to be about fifteen percent of the total, would be condemned because of bad title or excessive price.[22] Finally, the Tonto reservoir site which Maricopa County surveyor W. M. Breakinridge had reported upon so favorably in 1889 belonged to the government. Those who complained about the amount paid to the Hudson Company forgot the tremendous excitement generated when the company had first come to the valley. Although there had been great disappointments, the company had completed valuable hydrology and engineering studies without which the government would not have been able to start construction of the project as quickly as it did, and without which the Salt River Project might not have been selected in the first place.

BUYING THE NORTHSIDE CANAL SYSTEM

With the reservoir land and the title to the damsite out of the way, discussion within the water-users' association centered upon the restructuring of the canal companies. As early as May 1903 the Board of Governors had suggested that preliminary steps be taken to adjust each water-user's respective rights to the carriage of water and to apportion individually the cost of the canal from which each took his water. This was necessary so that the Salt River Valley Water Users' Association could begin its supervision of all the canals in the valley as required by the articles of incorporation. The great obstacle to this effort was the private canal company which controlled most of the northside water distribution, the New York – based Arizona Water Company (successor to the Arizona Improvement Company and the Arizona Canal Company).[23]

While Fowler, Kibbey, and the Reclamation Service had discussed government purchase of the northside system during the writing of the articles of incorporation and the 1904 contract, both documents had been ratified and adopted without seriously planning for that possibility. The water users left the question of purchase of the northside system to those provisions in the articles which called for the levying of special assessments. In this manner, water users under the various canals to be purchased—not the Association—would bear the cost of their acquisition.[24]

Probably because the price was too high, the water-users' organization made no effort to purchase the Arizona Water Company's interests in the northside system, including the Arizona Dam, until the floods of 1905 made the need for their inclusion in the Association more immediate and the price more negotiable. As the Salt River raged during the months of January and February 1905, a section of about 100 feet washed out of the 1,100-foot-long Arizona Dam, the timber-crib diversion dam 28 miles northeast of Phoenix which normally sent water into both the northside and southside canal systems. Damage to the dam and to the canal headworks made irrigation of lands under the Arizona Canal difficult. The cost of repair to the dam alone would be great, and the Arizona Water Company hesitated. After conferring with Joseph Kibbey and George Christy of the Board, Fowler asked the Arizona Water Company if it would sell to the Association.[25]

Sometime during the spring Benjamin Fowler, in the East on Association business, suggested to Newell that the government appoint a commission to appraise the value of the northside system and the Arizona Dam. Although the water company had mentioned no price, it was clearly struggling to recover the amount of its indebtedness—nearly a million dollars. Since the Arizona Water Company was a nonresident corporation, most people in the valley resented its lack of consideration of local interests and needs; an independent view of the appropriate purchase price was thus necessary to persuade the water users to buy. Similarly, the stockholders in the Arizona Water Company received from its management an inflated view of how much the company was worth; even though the company was in receivership, they, too, needed an independent opinion on what was a fair price.

Fowler believed that a permanent, masonry, diversion dam needed to be constructed as soon as possible for the benefit of the whole valley, and that the Arizona Water Company should not assess the northside for repairs to the 28-year-old Arizona Dam prior to an Association assessment for permanent construction at a later date. On May 6, 1905, Fowler formally requested that Frederick Newell consider the possibility of appointing a competent board "to study the situation, investigate the conditions, measure the rights and equities of both parties, appraise the property and fix the price and terms which are reasonable and just and within our power to meet."[26]

In his response Newell ignored Fowler's suggestions regarding the appointment of an advisory board to determine the value of the Arizona Water Company, focusing, instead, on the question of a permanent diversion dam. Noting that Salt River had already received more money from the reclamation fund than it should have been allotted under Section 9 of the Reclamation Act (which stated that the Secretary of Interior should expend money derived from each state or territory within such state or territory), Newell hedged as to whether the Reclamation Service could construct a new dam. He next reasoned that the Salt River Valley Water Users' Association still needed to determine judicially the water rights within the valley, and that a "proper adjustment of these rights [is required] before any new expenditures are undertaken in the Valley or any stored water is furnished for irrigation."[27]

For those who had dragged their feet on the friendly suit to determine water rights in the valley—the *Hurley v. Abbott* suit—here was yet another reason (besides determining the basis for allocating membership shares in the Association) to push forward with the adjudication. Newell had linked further construction on Salt River to this resolution of valley water rights and, by requesting that the service engineers investigate the feasibility of a masonry dam, he had also hinted that the Reclamation Service could come through for Salt River despite Section 9. Debate over the best means to secure the adjustment of water rights—through continuation of the *Hurley v. Abbott* suit instituted in 1904 or by contract—persisted throughout 1905 – 1906.

Newell must have informally relayed Fowler's request to Charles Walcott, director of the Geological Survey, because Walcott asked Interior Secretary Ethan A. Hitchcock to consider appointing a disinterested commission to appraise the property of the Arizona Water Company; Hitchcock agreed just twelve days after Fowler's request to Newell. Writing Fowler in New York, Walcott told the president of the association that the Secretary had agreed to appoint the commission upon the "distinct understanding that the United States does not at this time assume the obligation to pay the amount appraised nor to purchase the property at any price or in any event, this question left for future decision when the value of the property . . . shall become known."[28]

The Department of Interior suggested to Fowler, in a letter to him dated June 1, 1905, that he prepare a formal request, and Fowler and Judge Hiram Steele, vice-president and receiver of the bankrupt Arizona Water Company, responded on June 7. In their request they asked the Secretary to appoint three disinterested engineers to appraise the property of the Arizona Water Company, including:

(1) the Arizona Canal, with all dams, headgates, cross-cuts, laterals, equipment, and all vested rights;

(2) the franchises and established businesses of the company;

(3) its controlling interest in the capital stock of the Grand, Salt River, Maricopa, and Water Power Canal Companies;

(4) all water rights owned by the company, with a complete description of all its land.

Hitchcock formally approved the request on June 10, 1905.[29]

The commission members suggested to Hitchcock by Charles Walcott were three engineers of the United States Reclamation Service: George Y. Wisner, W. H. Sanders, and A. E. Chandler (both Wisner and Sanders were members of the Salt River Project consulting board of engineers). Believing all three men to be well qualified to appraise the property of the Arizona Water Company, Hitchcock designated them as the commission on June 14, 1905. Testimony to the great degree of confidence that both Benjamin Fowler and Judge Steele had in the Service and that the Nation as a whole had in the impartiality of the engineering profession during the first decade of the twentieth century is the fact that no one questioned the ability of Reclamation Service personnel to judge fairly the value of a crucial element in the success or failure of their own reclamation project.[30]

Fowler presented the commission plans to the association's Board of Governors on June 26, 1905, nearly one month after Charles Walcott had secured Secretary Hitchcock's approval. It is probable that since Fowler was in the East during most of the spring, he waited until his return to present the proposal for the Board's consideration. The board members unanimously supported Fowler's activities on behalf of the water users; although they expressed concern about having the intangible "vested rights" of the Arizona Water Company determined by the courts (particularly the company's claim to water rights) and they restated the water-users' policy about having the cost assessed to the northside lands, they endorsed wholeheartedly the members of the appraisal commission.[31]

While Benjamin Fowler returned to Washington to work out details of the commission and to receive advice from the Reclamation Service, Judge Joseph Kibbey maintained close communication with him regarding events occurring in the valley. Kibbey had come to Arizona from the Midwest in 1893 and shortly thereafter became the attorney for the Florence Canal Company. Throughout his career, Kibbey held many positions within the territory's political structure: as an Arizona Supreme Court Justice, a Territorial Councilman, Territorial Attorney General, and Governor in 1905. While many in Arizona—and, indeed, Secretary Hitchcock himself—wondered whether Kibbey's roles as governor of the state and as attorney for the Salt River Valley Water Users' Association presented a conflict of interest, Kibbey was quick to deny the charge. Furthermore, he was outspoken regarding the importance of his role as the association's attorney, considering that job both his source of pride and lifework. The time that he devoted to the purchase of the northside distribution system and the Arizona Dam while serving as governor is indicative of his commitment. Kibbey and Fowler agreed in principle on what needed to be done in this effort, but they differed remarkably as to how to do

Judge Joseph Kibbey came to Arizona from the Midwest in 1893. Throughout his career, he held many positions within the political structure of the Arizona Territory: he was an Arizona Supreme Court Justice, a Territorial Councilman, Territorial Attorney General and Territorial Governor in 1905. The time that he devoted as attorney for the Salt River Valley Water Users' Association was indicative of his commitment to solving the problems of water use in the area.

it. Fowler followed closely advice from the Reclamation Service, while Kibbey, in Phoenix, attuned his ear to the opinions of the Association's Board of Governors. The fact that they were guided by these two different viewpoints created some tension between the two men on how the Association should proceed in purchasing the canal system.[32]

Although the commission had been appointed in June 1905, engineering commitments on other reclamation projects kept the three men from meeting in Phoenix until November 1905. During the interim six months, while the Reclamation Service gathered data concerning the canals, Fowler and Judge Hiram Steele, of the Arizona Water Company, attempted to carry on their own negotiations. Little was done between June, when the commission was authorized, and September, when Fowler again returned to Washington. Fowler believed that time was the most critical element in the sale; the Reclamation Service had many demands from other projects to consider besides those of Salt River. If the Association was unable to come to terms with the Arizona Water Company quickly, Fowler feared that the Salt River Valley group might be passed over in its request for additional funds. Of some significance, too, was the threat of winter storms as severe as the preceding years, and the importance of starting repair work immediately.[33]

Complicating the situation was the ambiguous position of Judge Hiram Steele. As the receiver of the Arizona Water Company, Steele complained that he had no authority to make a deal and, because of his precarious position, he would not commit himself to a potential asking price for the assets of the company in the Salt River Valley. He accused Fowler of being "timid and unwilling to assume responsibility" because the president of the Association did not feel it his place to suggest a price which the Association might be willing to pay. Fowler believed the company was "up against it" and that it was the association's role simply to protect its own interests. "The investment was theirs," he wrote Judge Kibbey; "if unwise they must suffer, not you and I."34

Fowler was willing to discuss the price with Steele, however, whereas Kibbey stoically believed that the Association must be prudent and indifferent to the entire sale. When Fowler wrote Kibbey that he had some idea what price would be acceptable to both the government and the water company, but could not give an exact figure, Kibbey was irritated that the Board of Governors had been left out of the discussion. Kibbey wrote Fowler that it seemed "strange to us that it could be made known to you about what price Judge Steele would accept, and what price the Department would approve, and that could not be made known to the Board."35 Judge Steele had hinted, when he was in Phoenix in October, that $700,000 would be acceptable to the company; this was an amount equal to their first mortgages and defaulted interest, plus fifty percent of the income bonds, and repairs to dams. Kibbey thought this figure absurd. "The Board is entirely indifferent about further negotiations," the Association's attorney wrote Fowler, for "it has lost confidence in them and will not renew them, or even encourage their renewal . . . ."36 Expedition of the sale was more advantageous to the company, Kibbey thought, than to the water users.

Fowler answered Kibbey on October 23, 1905, with confidential information he had received that $350,000 would secure the water company's interests (he did not tell Kibbey that he had met with Hiram Steele and Frederick Newell). Fowler seemed to view his role as more educator than negotiator; he tried to inform both the bondholders of the Arizona Water Company and officials within the Geological Service of the depreciated conditions of the physical property of the company. He believed that if the water company shareholders were given a little time "to adjust themselves to the new conditions in which they are so unceremoniously plunged," they would treat the Association fairly. Fowler, who understood Steele and the conditions he faced in New York, wrote Kibbey that the water users were "just at the crucial moment; . . . everything looks favorable for our interests."[37] Instead of closing off negotiations, as Kibbey suggested, Fowler believed that it was in the Association's power to close negotiations soon at favorable figures. Still, Fowler, the man in Washington, was providing little detailed information to the group in Arizona that he represented.

If Fowler was confident and cheered by the $350,000 figure, the Board of Governors and Kibbey were not. The Arizona Dam should be considered a liability, rather than an asset, Kibbey argued, and the Association should pay no more for the system than what it might cost to replace it, an amount Kibbey estimated at $250,000, exclusive of the dam. The only positive element Kibbey and the Board saw in purchasing the system from the water company was "the advantages we may obtain by ease of terms of payment if the Government should buy . . . ."[38]

Coupled with the general problem of treating with the water company were the demands of the minority stockholders in three of the canals on the north side controlled by the Arizona Water Company: the Grand, Maricopa, and Salt River canals. Led by Phoenix attorney Louis Chalmers and Dwight Heard, these local shareholders believed that they should also be paid for their minority interests in the canals; they were, thus, demanding compensation if the sale proceeded.

On November 6, 1905, Judge Hiram Steele wired Phoenix's Home Savings Bank and Trust Company (C. F. Ainsworth, president, was attorney for the water company) that $350,000 was an acceptable purchase price, provided that the government would take immediate charge of the works. The bank made an effort to promote the fairness of this price, and Ainsworth tried to persuade the Association's Board of Governors to pay it. Fowler advised just a few days later that the Board should wait for the results of the engineering commission, which was scheduled to meet in Phoenix on November 25, 1905, before agreeing to the sale. This behavior seems somewhat odd for Fowler, committed as he was to a quick sale and to his previous belief that $350,000 was acceptable to the Reclamation Service as a purchase price. It is not improbable that his friends in the Service, possessing information collected for the commission, suggested to him that the $350,000 figure might, indeed, be too high. Perhaps Fowler now also felt less rushed to complete the sale, as the Service surely would have indicated to him by this time whether Salt River retained a chance to secure further appropriations from the reclamation fund.[39]

The report of the commission was submitted to U.S.G.S. director Charles Walcott on December 8, 1905, after the three engineers had heard testimony in Phoenix and had reviewed engineering reports prepared by Jay Stannard for the Reclamation Service and H. F. Robinson, a local civil engineer employed by the Arizona Water Company; interestingly, the estimates were similar. Because of Judge Kibbey's decision in *Wormser v. Salt River Valley Canal Company*, which stated that a canal company is a carrier of water but does not have rights to the water it carries for other appropriators, the commission considered the claimed water rights of the company nonexistent; that the Arizona Water Company possessed no water rights had always been the Association's position. All franchises and contracts were termed liabilities for the government, rather than assets. As a result, the only items appraised were physical properties. The commission recommended that the value of the Arizona Water Company holdings be set at $304,161.[40]

Not surprisingly, Benjamin Fowler and the Reclamation Service strongly supported the report of the commission as "being fair and just." It would now be the Secretary of Interior's decision whether the government would accept the price for the purchase of the northside water system. Floods in November had further damaged the headworks of the Arizona Canal and washed away even more of the Arizona Dam. Lands under the northside system were now without effective irrigation, and many cultivated farms were endangered as a result. The need for a new, permanent, diversion dam was never more apparent, and Fowler wrote the Association's Board of Governors that Salt River's chances of success were about even. Relating that their prospects "would surely have gone aglimmering at this time had not the matter been brought to the Secretary's attention last May and the Government in a measure committed to the purchase," Fowler believed that this commitment alone was "the peg on which our hopes now hang."[41] Other projects had been making "great and special demands on the reclamation fund and bringing powerful influences to bear on the Secretary which would undoubtedly have resulted in leaving us entirely out in the cold but for our timely action over seven months ago."[42]

Secretary of Interior E. A. Hitchcock's legal assistant had several questions regarding the validity of certain aspects of the proposed contract between the Arizona Water Company and the government; as a result of these questions and of other pressing government business, a final contract from Interior was delayed until February 17, 1906. Part of the delay stemmed from the water company's position that it could not give a complete and perfect title to the government (which was necessary before the Reclamation Service would begin construction work on the new diversion dam, approved by Walcott and Hitchcock January 9, 1906) without the cooperation of the minority stockholders. The water company contended that this group—the

Chalmers-Heard group—should contribute *gratis* its interests in the northside canals, and that the entire appraisal sum of $304,161 should be paid to the New York corporation. The government's position was that the sum should be paid to both groups, with any adjustment left to them. Judge Steele also argued that the company's alleged water rights should be made a part of the assessment, although Fowler, the Reclamation Service, and even Judge Steele knew that under Arizona law this claim was preposterous. The Arizona Water Company further argued that insufficient consideration had been given its right-of-way along the Arizona Canal. After much discussion, Charles Walcott, Arthur Powell Davis, and Morris Bien, along with Fowler, agreed to pay $10,000 more to the water company in order to expedite matters, for a total price of $314,161.[43]

W. J. Murphy, the original contractor for the construction of the Arizona Canal, a shareholder in the earlier companies controlling the northside system, and the owner of a sugar-beet factory served by the Arizona Canal, came to Washington late in the contract negotiations to urge the government to pay the water company $50,000 more to hurry things along. Fowler vowed to pay no more than the appraised price, and told Murphy he was ruining things; rather than pay more, the government was prepared to institute condemnation proceedings against the Arizona Water Company. Hiram Steele was irritated that he was forced to accept terms which he considered unfavorable to the company, but was prepared to sign the contract, as the company really had little choice in the matter. Yet the night before the contract was to be executed, Murphy offered to trade the company 200 unspecified acres of his land, with a paper value of $40,000, in exchange for the nonexistent water rights of the company. In this offer Steele saw a means to save face with his people in New York, and he accepted Murphy's proposal; Murphy perhaps saw a way to enlarge his own position at home.[44]

As for Murphy, Fowler wrote the Board of Governors that before the contract was executed "a dispatch was sent to Phoenix saying that the 'Government had closed contract by W. J. Murphy putting up the difference.' " The facts of the matter were, Fowler explained, that Murphy's name did not appear in the documents, "and so far as the Government is concerned they did not know of this trade until agreement was reached with the Water Company." The contract had already been struck, and the Arizona Water Company had little choice but to sign; Murphy's deal simply allowed Steele to report to his people a larger dollar figure than before.[45]

On March 7, 1906, Secretary of Interior Ethan A. Hitchcock approved the contract for government purchase of the northside canal system for the Salt River Project, although the water rights in the valley had yet to be adjusted. Combined with the promise to build a new diversion dam at Granite Reef in place of the deteriorating Arizona Dam, this contract provided a $700,000 additional allotment to the project from the reclamation fund, bringing the project total to $4.5 million. The government did not include any provision within the new contract to change that part of the 1904 contract calling for equal assessments among all members to repay the costs of the facilities. As the matter stood, the cost of the northside system would be included in the total government costs, rather than be assessed only against landowners within the northside system.[46]

THE 1906 ELECTION

Benjamin Fowler's success had been complete. He had managed to turn a 1905 springtime thought into reality. Like Frederick Newell and the engineers at work building the project, Fowler had thought of the possibilities for efficient reclamation on Salt River. The Salt River Project would function more efficiently with control of the northside system and a new diversion dam, and he had managed to convince the Reclamation Service of their necessity. He had done this alone, often at odds with the association which he represented, and despite Murphy's unsolicited efforts to help close the sale of the Arizona Water Company. Yet what seemed to Fowler to be his most successful achievement nearly cost him the presidency of the water users' association in 1906. His tendency to focus on the big picture of national reclamation led many in the valley to believe he ignored local concerns, particularly the issue of project cost and repayment.

To Fowler's surprise, he and his administration were the key issue in the 1906 election. Dwight Heard, Fowler's main antagonist throughout the early years of the Association, had decided, after two years, that Fowler did not have the businesslike acumen necessary to carry the Association past the water-promotion period. Heard again helped line up a slate of conservative candidates headed by Dr. E. W. Wilbur as the presidential candidate, to defeat Fowler's friends. In a 1906 pamphlet distributed to the Association's members, Heard stated that:

> Mr. Fowler's supporters, in their efforts to change the conservative character of the Board of Governors, and to dictate to the farmers of the valley, have forced this contest for the presidency, and it should be clearly understood that a vote for Dr. Wilbur is a vote in favor of the Farmer's Ticket.[47]

Heard, Wilbur, and others opposed to Fowler's administration charged that Fowler had aligned himself with "speculative interests," rather than with genuine farmers with irrigation experience. Also high on their list of complaints against the water users' president was the *fait-accompli* manner in which Fowler had handled the negotiations with the Arizona Water Company.[48]

Some characterized the 1906 election as an honest difference of opinion concerning the direction the Salt River Valley Water Users' Association should take, but Fowler viewed it as a continuation of the problems caused by Heard and Wilbur during the writing of the articles of incorporation:

> Heard, Wilbur and the old minority interests have never been reconciled to the basis upon which the Association has been incorporated and consequently they have never been reconciled to my election as president.[49]

Rumors regarding the negotiations with the Arizona Water Company for the purchase of the northside system had Fowler advising the association to pay $1 million, then $900,000, then $650,000; the $10,000 added to the purchase price for right-of-way compensation was said to be Fowler's commission. If Fowler knew who had started the gossip, he did not say, but he did believe that "if six years' work in this Valley along these lines is not sufficient to justify the people in reelecting me, I will step to one side and let someone else take up the work."[50]

Of course, Fowler had no intention of stepping aside, even though there was significant opposition to his way of doing things; he had come to regard the Salt River Project almost as his own, and he felt proprietary about it. Not all of Fowler's supporters agreed with him, but they did believe it would be more trouble for the Association to change the established program. The Reclamation Service, which was encouraging this sentiment, was said to have telegraphed Judge Kibbey that "to defeat Mr. Fowler would be a very dangerous proceeding to swap horses while crossing the stream."[51] Frederick Newell even wrote opposition candidate E. W. Wilbur that it would be a great mistake to change presidents at that point:

> Mr. Fowler has been very effective; has won the confidence of the present administration, and even though a man of larger experience might be had, yet I feel personally that the work of the Salt River Valley might be set back very seriously by making a change.[52]

Despite Heard and Wilbur's much publicized opposition, members of the Association heeded the Reclamation Service's advice and their own predilection to leave things as they were; they gave Fowler

60 percent of the vote on election day. Wilbur ran strongest in the southeastern portion of the valley (an area of old water-rights), while Fowler swept Phoenix and the northwestern and southwestern districts of the Association.

As Fowler reflected upon the election of 1906 and his own strong showing, despite an organized attempt to replace him, he must have felt a great deal of satisfaction with the progress of the Association. By 1906 the water users had worked out in the articles of incorporation their legal basis as a government reclamation project, signed a contract with the government for the construction of the water-storage dam, persuaded the Reclamation Service to enlarge the project by including both a permanent diversion dam and ownership of the northside distribution system, and begun the tedious process of adjudicating the water rights of the valley. Wilbur's campaign against Fowler was more than a paper one, yet both he and Heard underestimated the extent to which valley landowners hesitated to change the reclamation program already established; many believed it might be better, but felt comfortable with what they knew. Fowler would have been incorrect, however, in correlating this reluctance to change with approval of his style of leadership. Valley landowners were beginning to concern themselves with the ultimate cost of the project, and they cared little for the larger national picture of frontier homebuilding; they wanted Fowler to direct his attention more to Salt River than to Washington.

While the process of laying the institutional framework for federal reclamation in the Salt River Valley had been controversial, there was little argument from Frederick Newell's Reclamation Service that it had also been successful. Considering that the "human element" of reclamation engineering was, as Newell often stated, the most difficult and important of the Service's tasks on the projects, the relationship between Fowler and the Service perhaps made this an easier chore on Salt River Project.

The problems involved in forming the Association and centralizing water-resources management in the valley seemed to diminish in intensity once construction of the project's water-storage dam at the Tonto site began. The physical isolation of the damsite, the wild and barren terrain through which roads had to be built, and the hot summer temperatures in which construction would take place suggested to many the need for some engineering miracles. Although the Reclamation Service engineers claimed no divine intervention, the resulting physical structures for the Salt River Project attested to some extraordinary engineering skills.

Building the
Roosevelt Dam

Just as no precedent existed for the farmers' organizing the Salt River Valley Water Users' Association under the Reclamation Act of 1902, no large-scale irrigation works precedent existed for the engineers of the United States Reclamation Service. Instead, they had to develop original plans for each large system. Frederick Newell placed dam stability and economy at the top of the Service's list of engineering criteria, and the consulting board of engineers planning the Salt River Project under Newell's general supervision attempted to follow his standards carefully.[1]

Plans for the project included several components in addition to the dam. Preliminary construction work consisted of building roads and a base camp for the engineers and workers. A cement mill and sawmill were added to exploit natural resources. A power canal and permanent power-producing facility were designed to take advantage of the abundant possibilities for inexpensive hydroelectricity. The dam itself required a sluicing tunnel, an outlet tunnel, and a coffer dam before the foundation could be excavated. Stone had to be quarried in large pieces before the masonry could be laid.

The water-storage dam, named the Roosevelt Dam in honor of President Theodore Roosevelt, was planned as a simple gravity structure composed of uncoursed rubble masonry. The total height of the dam above the lowest foundation was to be 245 feet; since the damsite favored a curved form, the proposed structure was to be built on a circular curve, convex upstream, with a backside radius of 400 feet. This simple gravity structure, with its curved form, would greatly

The west end of the town of Roosevelt, Arizona, as it was in March 1906, during construction of the dam. Located on the south side of Salt River approximately one-half mile upstream from the damsite, the town had a population of about 500 during the peak of construction. After the dam was completed and the reservoir began to fill, the town was abandoned and eventually inundated.

increase the stability of the dam; the masonry dam was the most conservative and permanent design yet devised.[2]

Louis C. Hill, supervising engineer on the Salt River Project, Arthur Powell Davis, chief engineer of the Reclamation Service, and Fred Teichman, design engineer on the Salt River Project consulting board, calculated this engineering design with an eye toward economy. The solid, fine-grained, sandstone cliffs, which the dam would abut, provided the stone necessary for constructing the dam and, thus, eliminated freight and other quarrying charges. Initially, the estimated cost of cement purchased in the open market, shipped by rail to the point nearest the dam, and then hauled to the damsite by wagon was a prohibitive $9 per barrel. Before deciding on a less expensive dam, the Service investigated the possibility of manufacturing its own cement at the damsite. Good limestone and clay deposits at the site produced a quality Portland cement at an estimated $3.14 per barrel, and despite protests from the "cement trust" about government interference in the marketplace, the Service proceeded to build a cement mill at the damsite. Similarly, freight charges for hauling oil to the town of Roosevelt to produce electricity to power construction machinery were too high (usually more than 30 percent of the cost), so the consulting board of engineers designed a power canal to produce cheap hydroelectricity at the construction site. Plans for a government sawmill to cut construction timber in the Sierra Ancha Mountains (about thirty miles northeast of Roosevelt), for a permanent construction headquarters with modern conveniences to attract long-term labor, and for its own shorter and better freight road to minimize the most expensive hauling were other signs of government concern for economy.[3]

PREPARING FOR DAM CONSTRUCTION

Between 1902 and 1904, the Service completed a series of cadastral maps of the Salt River Valley, which showed not only land contours, but canal and road systems in great detail. Working through the hot summer months in the most rugged and desolate of canyons, the engineers and workers on the project glimpsed the problems that climate and terrain would make for construction: temperatures ranged from 20 degrees to 120 degrees Fahrenheit, and the reservoir site was virtually inaccessible by wagon. Sixty miles separated the reservoir site from the town of Mesa, and it was forty miles from Globe, a mining town southeast of Roosevelt. Both towns had railroad connections, but no freight road existed from the construction site to Mesa (which had the advantage over Globe of two railroad connections), and the road to Globe was treacherous, winding through several mountain ranges. Frederick Newell wrote in his Third Annual Report that few reservoirs had been constructed in locations where the natural conditions were so favorable and the transportation facilities so meager. The Reclamation Service needed to build good connective roads to these transportation centers. In addition, roads were needed to link those natural resources available near the damsite: a lumber road to the Sierra Ancha Mountains and a road to the clay flats that were three miles away from the proposed cement mill. The first construction on Salt River was, thus, rather mundane: road-building and permanent camp construction.[4]

The 372-square-mile area of the Salt River Project (shaded) receives its water from the 13,000-square-mile watershed of the Salt and Verde rivers. Located in the central part of Arizona, the Salt River Project was designed to provide irrigation to its member lands within the greater Phoenix metropolitan area. Map drawn by Cartographics Department, Salt River Project.

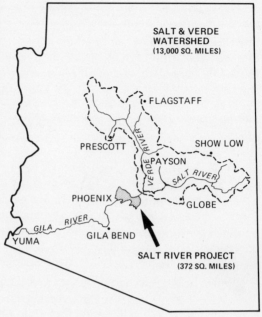

The road to the sawmill was quickly carved out in early 1903 and was completed by December of that year. With the sawmill plant in place, upon completion of the road, contracts for cutting and sawing lumber were let in early 1904. The Reclamation Service, unhappy with the performance of the two private contractors at work in the sawmill during the first half of 1904, took over management of the mill itself in July; average monthly output increased from 119,500 to 214,000 board feet. By mid-September 1905 all the timber which could be conveniently reached had been cut, and the excess lumber was hauled in to the damsite in November. The lumber road was, by necessity, the first piece of construction on the project; wood was needed for construction of the permanent camp, culverts and bridges for the roads, tunnel timbering, and building forms for concrete structures.[5]

On the north side of Salt River were the clay hills necessary for the production of cement. The cement mill was located on the south side of the river, and a three-mile-long road was built across the river connecting the two in 1903. Usually the ford across the river was inconsequential, but, when the river was high due to rain or snow on the 13,000-square-mile watershed, getting the clay to the cement mill was more difficult. After an excellent-quality clay was discovered on the south side of the river, during excavation for the power canal, little use was made of the clay hills across the river or of the road to these deposits, although the lower one and one-half miles of it formed the lower part of the regular freight road to Globe. This road was simple to construct, probably requiring only dredges to even out the land.[6]

The high-line freight road to Globe, located on the upper side of the power canal, ran twenty miles from the cement mill to the old road from Globe to Livingstone. Construction was difficult, since much of the road was cut out of the hill; it required heavy sidehill work and strongly cemented gravel. Initially the road crossed the power canal about a mile from Roosevelt, but rising water and convenience of delivery caused the engineers to reroute the road higher on the side of the hill. The direction of the heaviest loads was toward the damsite, and the greatest adverse grade built into the road in this direction was about 6 percent; grades as great as 10 percent were permitted in the opposite direction. Since the road to Globe was the only freight road in existence when preliminary work began, all machinery (for the cement mill, the temporary power plant, and the sawmill), oil (for early operation of the cement mill), lumber, feed, and supplies came over this forty-mile road by wagon to the reservoir site. The high-line road to Globe, begun in December 1903 and completed in May 1904, allowed for easier delivery of these supplies from the Globe and Northern Railroad terminus.[7]

Mesa had the advantage of two competing railroad lines—the Santa Fe, Prescott and Phoenix, and the Maricopa and Phoenix; freight rates were also competitive. Since freight charges accounted for so much of the final cost of supplies, and since twenty-two miles of the sixty miles from Mesa to Roosevelt were desert and comparatively level, the Reclamation Service wondered whether a new road from Mesa might not be worth the expense. Calculation of the difference in freight rates was $15 a ton in favor of Mesa, and so work began in October 1903, near Goldfield, Arizona, located on that part of the proposed mountain road nearest the valley; in December road construction began at Roosevelt, on the upper end of the road in the canyon below the dam.[8]

To avoid the spillway on the south side of the river, the new freight road was located in the mountain, high above the dam itself. It descended to the river around the walls of a rocky side canyon with nearly vertical cliffs. Following the river for about seven miles, the road was deep inside the canyon; because some parts of it in this section were built along steep cliffs, solid-rock cuts twenty to sixty feet deep were necessary. A classic understatement described this area as one of the most difficult parts of the road; lifelines were essential to protect the workmen and, even with them, there were fatalities. Another problem-filled part of the road was that at Fish Creek Hill, where the road climbed the hill toward Mesa at a 10 percent grade, primarily along the foot of a vertical cliff several hundred feet high. The sheer cliff in this section required rock fills seventy-five feet high to achieve the recommended width of the road and rock cuts sixty to seventy feet deep.[9]

Only three miles of the road near Goldfield had been completed when work was temporarily discontinued, pending the outcome of a bonding plan by the valley to contribute toward the cost of the road. Because the cities and towns would benefit more from the new freight road than the landowners of the association, many town boosters, who wanted the road built as soon as possible, believed they should help shoulder the cost. Congress passed enabling legislation in early 1904 so that Phoenix, Mesa, and Tempe could bond themselves, at $65,000, $3,500, and $4,000 respectively; Mesa passed the bonds unanimously, Phoenix by 94 percent, and—to no one's surprise—the bonds barely carried in Tempe. Local banks agreed to secure the money and Phoenix and Mesa sold most of their bonds; as a result, the work force on the Mesa-Roosevelt Road increased to four hundred by the middle of June 1904. Tempe had not yet "taken the trouble to sell her bonds," and most believed the project would realize nothing from that subscription.[10]

The Mesa-Roosevelt Road was first used in early 1905, but it was heavily damaged by flooding that spring and fall. It seemed that "flood followed flood, each succeeding one greater than that before it, with hardly enough time intervening to permit repairs to be made before work was again swept away;"[11] these conditions delayed the road's completion until 1909.

Thirty to fifty Apache Indians built the last major road; the 1907 Tonto Road replaced the old Tonto Road, which had been submerged by the rising reservoir. It, too, was expensive and difficult to build, requiring a 3,700-foot-long crossing over Tonto Creek and the removal of rock and other material eighteen to twenty miles, primarily by hand; over 500 feet of 30-inch concrete pipe culverts were laid, and 4,000 cubic yards of dry wall were put in. The Indians were separated from the rest of the large labor force at work on the Salt River Project, and available evidence does not indicate whether they were also accorded the eight-hour-day and pay equal to the others. They were, however, a consistently productive labor group, responsible for many aspects of the construction and greatly depended upon by the Reclamation Service for much of the heavy work.[12]

Of all the roads built by the Reclamation Service on the Salt River

Project, the Mesa-Roosevelt Road was by far the most difficult and expensive. The Service told the Congress in its Third Annual Report that:

> The construction is as expensive as heavy railroad work, the cost of some short portions reaching $25,000 per mile; in others it fell as low as $500 per mile . . . . [However,] the reduction of rates on oil for burning cement, on food, on machinery, supplies, hay, grain, etc., will nearly pay the full cost of the road.[13]

The U. S. Reclamation Service constructed a total of 112 miles of permanent roads at a cost of over half a million dollars, or about $5,000 per mile on the average. Temporary construction roads, such as those to the cement mill and the clay beds, cost another $44,000, charged entirely to the cost of the project.[14]

Since most of the preliminary work on the project consisted of road-building and surveying, there was little need for a permanent headquarters camp at the damsite throughout 1903. The town of Livingstone, a short distance away, provided temporary quarters for Reclamation Service personnel and the labor force until 1904, when construction on the reservoir site itself necessitated a permanent camp. Preparations, which had been made during the previous year, included a small water system, built for the Roosevelt community, and, in anticipation of the summer heat, a refrigerator plant of two-ton capacity to produce ice. Situated on a high bluff overlooking the reservoir were the office building and reading room, cottages for the engineers, tents for the workers, and a corral.[15]

Because the camp was located so far from any other settled community, the Reclamation Service built a small hospital and hired a Phoenix doctor as camp physician. Sanitation was provided by a septic-tank sewage system, and electric and telephone lines were strung throughout the burgeoning village. A small vegetable garden provided fresh food for the laborers and engineers on the project, and bathhouses were built for their comfort. Completing the picture of civilization at Roosevelt was the jail, used mostly to confine those who had violated the strict anti-liquor rules imposed by the Reclamation Service.[16]

Supervising the work on the Roosevelt Dam was Louis C. Hill, a former railroad engineer and professor of hydraulic and electrical engineering at the Colorado School of Mines. Hill was thirty-eight years old when he took charge of the Salt River Project in 1903, and, although he had been a divisional manager of the Great Northern Railroad, he had never before directed an irrigation project. Perhaps because few engineers had extensive irrigation experience on large-scale projects, Frederick Newell assigned the design for the Roosevelt Dam and the Salt River Project to Hill, Davis, and Teichman, retaining final approval, however, as director of the Reclamation Service. Hill's education in civil and electrical engineering at the University of Michigan made him a good choice for engineer-in-chief. He assembled a team of engineers to direct, under his supervision, the various construction aspects of the project. J. D. Stannard was administrator of the Phoenix office, Howard S. Reed of the canal system, W. A. Farish of the roads, and A. M. Demrich of the electric plant. When Hill was appointed supervising engineer of all Reclamation Service work in Arizona, southern California, New Mexico, Texas, and Utah in late 1904, Chester W. Smith was chosen as the new engineer-in-charge for project construction. Smith was the engineer responsible for implementation of the project design, and for improvisation when things did not work out as they should.[17]

Chester Smith arrived at Roosevelt late in the afternoon of December 22, 1904, and over the few days remaining in the year learned generally the direction of the work and plans. The pace of work on the project increased under Smith, as he took little time from his duties for anything else; unlike Hill, who lived in Phoenix with his wife and children, Smith was alone at Roosevelt. He was an engineer totally involved in his work, who believed in conservation and viewed engineers as key elements in it. Publishing extensively in technical journals, Smith enjoyed solving engineering problems and sharing solutions with his fraternity of fellow engineers. His workday began at sunrise and lasted well into the evening, and this routine stopped only when illness forced him to his bed. While some men might have hesitated to take the challenge of supervising construction of the Salt River Project, given the difficulties of location, economy, and the completion goals, Smith never seemed to waver. He was completely devoted to making the Salt River Project a success, and he expected the same from every other worker there; he seemed to have little regard for those less committed.[18]

During January 1905 Smith reviewed the proposed power-canal lines and the sawmill site and road; he also showed various representatives of national construction companies the reservoir site. Through February and March, he started construction of the temporary bridges and auxiliary cables necessary for hauling material across Salt River (the rock quarry was located on the north side of the river, and almost everything else was on the south side), had two Italian stonemasons at work on stone samples to determine the specific gravity of

the rock, and designed and worked out the lumber fill for the temporary dams necessary to divert the normal flow of the river from the
various construction sites.[19]

Bids for construction of the dam opened on February 23, 1905.
Twenty firms from all sections of the country submitted detailed estimates. Included within these estimates were prices for three classes of
excavation, for construction of the masonry dam, coping, wing walls,
bridges, bridge piers, and overhaul, and for the time necessary for
completing the work. John M. O'Rourke's firm from Denver, Colorado, builders of the Galveston seawall, submitted the winning bid of
$1,147,600 for construction of the Roosevelt Dam in two years. Smith,
however, preferred the bid of a St. Louis Company, Broderick and
Ward ($1,187,200 for a completed dam in seventeen months), and he
listed them first in his notes and O'Rourke second; whether economy
was the only deciding factor is unknown.[20]

O'Rourke needed cement before he could begin foundation work
or the necessary construction of the coffer dam, which would divert
the river from the foundation site, and Smith prodded the crews that
were completing the problem-riddled cement mill. Although excavation for the foundation of the cement mill began in November 1903,
delays—due to slow delivery of equipment and to the floods of early
1905—left the cement mill unfinished until the water receded in February 1905. The rain-soaked road from Globe caused one shipment
of cement to take eleven days in January 1905, before reaching the
damsite; workers were able to deliver only two loads of oil in February. Smith discovered that no oil-storage tanks had been constructed
near the mill; this oversight further decreased productivity, and design of a 2,000-barrel tank began late in 1904. Output increased by 50
percent when he built a second tube mill for grinding cement in
November 1905. With an adequate amount of oil stored to fuel the
temporary steam plant (prior to completion of the power canal), the
cement mill began to run with only minor interruptions. Although
the government price of $3.14 per barrel of cement was less than all
the others, the use of oil for fuel in the mill accounted for more than
50 percent of that cost.[21]

PLANNING FOR HYDROELECTRIC POWER

The high cost of using oil as a fuel source during construction was
but one of the reasons that the Reclamation Service designed Salt
River as the first multi-purpose reclamation project in the nation.
Other arguments supporting the added hydroelectric capacity were

chiefly of local interest. Farmers in the valley who were not located under one of the project canals depended upon the pumping of groundwater to irrigate their crops; the power canal and power plant located at Roosevelt would provide inexpensive hydroelectricity for pumping. Several copper mines, located within the Globe-Superior-Miami triangle, about fifty miles from the damsite, also needed cheap power for rock-digging equipment. Still another potential customer of the hydroelectricity produced at the Roosevelt Dam was the City of Phoenix. George Maxwell wanted to develop "every atom of electric power" for the irrigation of the Salt River Valley; Frederick Newell agreed with him. For these reasons, the original plans for the project included a 19-mile-long power canal, which would produce 4,400 horsepower (3,282 kilowatts) in a temporary unit to be used in constructing the dam and in pumping water for irrigation, and a permanent power plant of 4,400 kilowatt capacity.[22]

The power canal, with its head at the upper end of the reservoir, skirted the reservoir basin along the water level when the basin was full, passed around one end of the dam in a channel cut in the rock wasteway, dropped several feet through a hole in the rock, and then went out and over the precipice to the temporary powerhouse. Contracts for excavation were let in March 1904, but the difficulties of digging out 600,000 cubic yards of rock and dirt and of driving 9,000 feet of tunnel were sufficient for Smith to bet a new suit of clothes that excavation would not be finished within the estimated time. He won; excavation was completed in November, three months late.[23] The work was heavy, but the complications of the canal project centered mostly on the construction of the reinforced concrete pressure pipes that carried a capacity water flow of 250 cubic feet per second underneath Pinto Creek, a tributary of Salt River located upstream from the damsite.[24]

The use of pressure pipes to carry water underneath water was not new; municipal waterworks in Europe and in the eastern United States had included them for several years. What was new about the work at Roosevelt, and considered quite timely by other engineers at work in developing water systems, was the use of reinforced concrete pipe, (which could carry water at high pressure) instead of the wood and cast-iron pipes which dominated water-system technology at that time.[25]

Work on the Pinto pressure pipes for the power canal involved a labor gang of about thirty men continuously laying concrete around steel reinforcement rings. The primary reason for continuously laying the concrete was to avoid irregular transverse joints; if the joints were not smooth, the pipe would leak, pressure would devolve upon the concrete rather than the steel, and the pipe would crack. A specially designed movable form facilitated continuous work. Problems arose, however, with cement peeling off its steel plates. Soft soap and oil were used as remedies, but even so the government-produced Portland cement was slow to set, requiring more time and labor than originally anticipated. For this reason, labor was the highest cost in construction of the pipes.[26]

Temperature also adversely affected the pipe's construction. On the first of the two Pinto lines there were few interruptions to continuous work, and most of the pipe was built in comparatively cool weather, so transverse joint problems were minimal. But the second Pinto line was built entirely during the hot, summer months with several interruptions to continuous work, and, when it was first filled during cold weather, at least forty perceptible cracks developed in the transverse joints; the result was severe leakage.[27]

Smith seemed to enjoy diagnosing the problem on the Pinto lines. In his words, he believed the pipes cracked because "the concrete shrank in the process of setting; this was resisted by the steel rings, thus producing a condition in which the steel was in compression and the concrete in tension, therefore on filling the pipe, the concrete took the entire load."[28] He worked on this problem after dinners, until one evening, after dining with Hill and some other engineers, he realized the problem and the solution. Repairs were made by cutting the cracks out, inserting oakum caulking, and then putting stiff mortar over the joints; grout was run into the crack from the outside.[29]

The Reclamation Service constructed the 2,600-foot-long Pinto pipes at a cost of nearly $106,000; similar pipes at Cottonwood Creek cost less than half that amount. Smith acknowledged labor as the principal cost of the Pinto pipes, calling the labor employed in Arizona, "inefficient and high-priced."[30] Yet even with the construction problems and the labor costs, the reinforced concrete conduit pipes for the Salt River Project's power canal received accolades from Thomas Wiggins, an engineer on the New York Board of Water Supply: "The engineers of the Reclamation Service deserve great credit for the way the pipe was built and its cheapness under rather adverse conditions . . . it illustrates what can be done by ingenious engineers who are also practical."[31]

Water was diverted into the power canal intake by a boulder and concrete overflow dam, and the entrance to the intake was governed by gates designed to exclude sand and other material from the canal. Although the intake gates kept much of the heavier debris from flowing down the canal, Teichman designed a novel rotating screen, located at the penstock (where the water flowed into the guide buck-

ets of the powerhouse turbine), to keep grass and sticks from lodging
in the buckets and breaking the turbine runner. Settling basins above
the entrance to the Pinto pipes and in front of the penstock also
removed silt from the water in the canal. The power canal was first
put into operation April 1, 1906, but it was plagued with breaks in the
banks in September, so that water was kept out of the canal and no
power was available. These breaks were quickly repaired, however,
and the operation of the canal proved quite satisfactory to the Service.
Final cost of the power canal, including all excavation, tunnels, pipes,
gates, settling basins, and repairs, was approximately $1.5 million.
The Reclamation Service had initially estimated its construction costs
at $91,000, but even the engineers did not attempt to justify the
expensive overruns; the high labor costs and quirks of nature, as
well as the untried character of the work itself, contributed to the
inflation.[32]

The permanent power plant was, in a sense, an extension of the
temporary plant designed by the project's engineering consulting
board. Although the temporary unit was needed immediately, the
engineers (George Y. Wisner, W. H. Sanders, O. H. Ensign, and
Louis C. Hill) decided to install it in a recess cut out of the canyon wall
about thirty-five feet above the low-water mark, which would also
house the permanent plant. The temporary unit was enlarged in 1907
to include a second penstock which would connect to the dam (the
first connected with the power canal), and the installation of additional turbines (there would eventually be three units producing
power). Upon construction of the permanent stone powerhouse,
Smith discovered that the waterwheel had been badly cut due to cav-
itation (the hydraulic erosion of steel due to high velocity flows); he
immediately ordered a new one, since that was about the only solution
to the problem at the time.[33]

High velocity flows posed other problems in construction as well.
At the same time that excavation on the power canal began, the government was at work blasting out the approaches to the sluicing tunnel on the south side of the river, which would carry the water around
the damsite during construction. The tunnel, driven by a private
contractor beginning in May 1904, was 13 feet wide, 11 feet high, and
480 feet long, and passed through a solid mountain wall of quartzite
and sandstone before exiting above the dam spillway. Construction
was difficult and uncomfortable; a small rise in the river flooded both
portals with mud and debris, and several hot springs were struck,
forcing temperatures inside the tunnel to 130 degrees Fahrenheit.
Apache Indian and Mexican laborers poured concrete on portions of
the tunnel floor, from the entrance to the hydraulic gates, and on the
sides and top of the section below the gates, as the engineers had

instructed, although the design called for a steel and concrete floor. After completion in September 1906, when water was turned through the tunnel under high pressure, the deep cuts produced required complete reconcreting of the tunnel floor; this was finally finished in 1909.[34]

The hydraulic gates in the sluicing tunnel were unique in that "no other instance [was] known where gates of this size [were] operated under so high a head."[35] A combination of steel and bronze, of the stony type, the six gates moved on rollers and were operated by hydraulic cylinders electrically controlled. Set in two groups of three, the gates were used for both service and emergency purposes. The service gates were designed to regulate the amount of outflow from the reservoir, and the emergency gates were to control water in case of accident or repair to the service gates. Although designed to handle a head of water of one hundred feet, an increase in the head imposed operation limitations on the hydraulic cylinders. When the high flow in September 1906 caused a large amount of damage to the tunnel, it also attacked and damaged the upper battery of gates and carried away a portion of the bronze roller trains. Although repaired with the tunnel, the gates never functioned as they should have.[36]

CONSTRUCTING THE DAM

All of this construction—the roads, permanent headquarters, cement mill, power canal and powerhouse, and sluicing tunnel—was simply a prelude to the main act at Roosevelt—building the dam itself. John O'Rourke's construction company signed a contract with Secretary of Interior Ethan A. Hitchcock in April 1905, agreeing to finish the dam in two years; the company immediately began preliminary work. During the remainder of 1905 O'Rourke's crew established camp on the north side of the river, secured equipment, installed the machine plant, and began stripping the quarries for stone and driving piles for a coffer dam and flume. They were the builders, putting together the pieces designed by the engineers.

The contractor's work was closely monitored by Chester Smith. Although the two men seemed amiable toward each other in the early days of construction, by the end of the first year their relationship was strained; O'Rourke must have wondered what he had involved himself in, and Smith quite candidly believed the government could do all the work better and faster than O'Rourke's group. The central problem between the two was quality of construction. Smith was quite concerned with dam stability, as were the other engineers, and insisted on performing the work methodically to insure its safety; no step was to be eliminated and no unauthorized shortcuts would be allowed. O'Rourke, on the other hand, saw before him a contract with a two-year deadline; his goal was to push the work as rapidly as possible. In attempting to meet their respective goals, a certain amount of tension developed between the engineer and the builder.

That the strain between Smith and O'Rourke did not automatically transfer to the men working under their authority was due primarily to the very clear delineation of the work to be performed on the dam by the Reclamation Service and by the contractor. O'Rourke and his men were responsible for building the coffer dam, the flume, and the cableways (from the quarry to the damsite and from the damsite to a spot upstream where waste was hauled), for cutting the stone and spalls (small fragments of stone) from the cliffs for the dam, for excavating the foundation, and for laying the masonry. The Service was to provide power, cement, and sand and to build the toolhouse, gatehouse, reinforced bridge on top of the dam, outlet tunnel, and sluice gates. Accountability for the tasks of building was clear.[37]

In addition to working on separate jobs, the men on O'Rourke's crew worked out of a different construction area from those in the Service, although they all ate together in the mess hall and presumably were housed in the same bunkhouses. There is little evidence to suggest that workers were concerned with the differing philosophies of the contractor or the Service.

It was the vagueness of Smith's instructions—to supervise O'Rourke's construction—which left the contractor somewhat unsettled about his own function. Their relationship was not one that each had embraced, but rather one mandated by the Department of Interior. Latent difficulties between the two men were perhaps unfairly accentuated during the 1905 floods. Rain began to fall at noon on November 26, 1905, and between 6:00 P.M. of that day and 11:00 A.M. of the 27th, the river rose thirty feet at the damsite; the discharge increased from 2,000 second-feet to nearly 130,000 second-feet. All the work done on the coffer dam and flume was washed away, as well as some of the necessary machinery for continuing construction.[38]

Minor flooding occurred throughout the remainder of 1905 and into 1906, preventing renewal of construction until March. When the river receded to a point at which O'Rourke's crew could begin anew on the coffer dam, the contractor requested that the flume be dispensed with and the sluicing tunnel alone carry the river. While Smith and Louis Hill agreed to this change in construction plans—probably in an attempt to hurry the work along—Smith was not entirely pleased with the prospect of the tunnel's carrying the entire flow of the Salt River; the river had already shown its erratic nature, and the tunnel carried a maximum of only 1,300 second-feet. Concern over the sluicing tunnel as the only source of water carriage around the damsite proved well founded, as very minor floods washed over the coffer dam delaying construction several times throughout 1906 and 1907.[39]

While O'Rourke's initial construction delays resulted mainly from flooding during 1905, he was slow to respond to the flood emergency. His company left machinery on the riverbanks and did not quickly rebuild the coffer dam with flume, nor did it employ an adequate number of workers to pump the water from the foundation site. This lack of preventive activity led Smith to believe the contractor from Denver was inexperienced in large construction, despite O'Rourke's Galveston seawall. Construction problems on the dam throughout 1906 gave further credence to his earlier impression. For example, in February 1906, the man scheduled to do the pile driving was ready to start, but the hammer was not available. In addition, O'Rourke had not hired a sufficient number of skilled quarrymen, probably because he underestimated the inaccessibility of skilled labor in Arizona and because he did not pay very well. Although O'Rourke insisted that recently recruited quarrymen from California would arrive by June 14, 1906, Smith was forced, by the end of September, to ask two stonemasons he knew in Pennsylvania to come to work on the dam and to bring masons and laborers with them; Smith even offered to pay railroad fare for the two men.[40] The coffer dam O'Rourke was rebuilding throughout the spring of 1906 remained incomplete by June, and Smith thought the construction crew was "not making any energetic attempt to back up the gap or to make the dam tight by depositing fine material on the upper side."[41]

The gap in the coffer dam allowed as much as 20 percent of the river to flow through, flooding the excavation pit for the foundation of the permanent dam and preventing the use of the hydraulic excavator. The "entire progress [of the dam] is depending on the closing of the upper [coffer] dam," Smith wrote on June 18, 1906, disturbed by the slowness of O'Rourke and his crew. He outlined a plan for the contractor in which the construction workers would work nights, use fine material and rock to fill the gaps in the upper dam, and then concrete the lower one. Even with these instructions, O'Rourke continued to place scarce labor on work projects that could wait; this practice delayed the cutting of stone and the completion of the coffer dam, and generally set back the date at which laying masonry could begin.[42]

In all fairness to O'Rourke, no contractor had experience in building large irrigation works such as those envisioned at Roosevelt; just as the landowners and engineers experimented with new ideas and forms, so the contractor relied on his ingenuity to solve unanticipated problems. Because the coffer dam did not hold all the water expected, more of the river flowed into the damsite than the hydraulic excavator could handle, so the construction crew built a sump just below the upper coffer dam to cut off the water which would normally fill the pit. Although Smith did not believe that the work of lowering the hydraulic excavators was pursued as energetically as it should be, O'Rourke did manage to begin laying the foundation masonry for the permanent dam on September 20, 1906—more than ten days ahead of the schedule Smith pessimistically thought possible.[43]

By the fall of 1906 the coffer dam held a sufficient amount of the river (there were fortunately few rains) so that work of building the dam progressed nicely. Excavation along the dam line to the solid bedrock was completed with little use of explosives, so that the rock would not be weakened. The foundation was thoroughly cleaned of all gravel, sand, and earth, and all fissured or disintegrated rock was removed; the dam would rest on solid rock throughout. Once the foundation was cleaned, the stone could be laid. The aim of the Reclamation Service was to use the largest proportion of stone and the smallest proportion of mortar and concrete in the dam that could be practically secured. For this goal to be accomplished, the Service provided facilities for handling stone weighing as much as ten tons, and large stones were used almost exclusively. To facilitate the drying of concrete during the hot season without cracking, all masonry was kept wet during the time of construction and until the work was at least six days old by piping water by gravity from the power canal to cover the face of the dam with a thin wet film. The temperature of the masonry was, thus, kept as much as 75 degrees below that which it would otherwise have reached.[44]

Chester Smith, other engineers of the Service, and John O'Rourke's crew also developed a faster and better method of laying masonry. In the classic method used on other masonry dams, a dam's vertical joints were filled with comparatively stiff mortar and then spalls were "laboriously laid up by a mason with a trowel." The new method involved filling the vertical joints with quite wet concrete (largely placed by dumping it), churning and spading when necessary, and throwing spalls in the joints. Not only did the new method increase the amount of masonry which could be laid (from an average

Excavation for the foundation of Roosevelt Dam went down to solid bedrock and was accomplished with little use of explosives, so that the rock would not be weakened. This photo, taken in September 1906, shows excavation at the base of the abutment wall. Excavated materials were removed from the pit by large metal buckets, which were transported by cableways; a bucket hook is visible at upper left. Materials were excavated by manual labor, using pick axes, sledge hammers, and shovels.

of six cubic yards per derrick-hour to an average of sixteen cubic yards), but it also resulted in masonry that was more watertight than that produced by the classic method.[45]

Despite these new, faster methods of laying masonry and O'Rourke's readiness to begin setting the stone for the dam, Smith remained dissatisfied with the work's progress. He considered the contractor's crew to be unorganized and, as he had done for the construction of the coffer dam, Smith outlined a plan for the builder to follow. All the power drills were to be placed in the excavation pit and work was to begin immediately on the cut-off trench; all the trimming and cleaning of the stone must be performed in the quarry, not at the damsite; no more stone was to be stored in the excavation pit, where it would be in the way of excavation; night work would begin October 1, 1906; the stone would be crushed finer; and more men must be trained to perform the skilled masonry work. Smith's evident displeasure with the contractor's work generated rumors around Roosevelt that the government wanted to finish the job, rather than extend another contract deadline to O'Rourke.[46]

Although Smith denied that the government would finish the dam itself, it is probable that he would have muttered something concerning the wisdom of replacing O'Rourke with a more competent Reclamation Service crew. O'Rourke tried to hurry the work along not by hiring more workers or by paying a wage that would entice skilled labor to remain at the isolated construction site but by trying to evade the eight-hour work day mandated by law. When Smith refused to allow the contractor to ignore this legal provision, O'Rourke, in October 1906, appealed to Louis Hill. The contractor insisted that Hill should declare a state of emergency, a situation that would suspend enforcement of the labor provision. Hill refused; the eight-hour law was to remain in effect.[47]

In November seven skilled workers left the contractor's camp right in the middle of important excavation work because, as Smith noted, "O'Rourke would only pay $3.50 per day instead of $4." On another occasion (November 18, 1906), water was low in the power canal, and the power and lights were shut off from 9:00 P.M. until 12:30 A.M., so O'Rourke's watchman shut down the hydraulic lifts and went home. When water then came in, there was no one there to start the pumps, the bottom of the pit filled with water, and no masonry could be completed for several days until it was pumped out. As Smith remarked, "this need not have been the case."[48]

The problem of diverting the river had not been solved by the coffer dam and sluicing tunnel. High water throughout the winter of 1906 and spring of 1907 continued to flood the excavation of the foundation, so, in 1907, O'Rourke's crew began building a rock-fill dam to supplement the concrete coffer dam in driving the river into the tunnels. By May 6, 1907, more than two years after the signing of the government contract, the rock-fill dam extended completely across the river, and O'Rourke's men were at work making both the rock-fill and concrete coffer dams tighter, so that laying the main body of masonry for the permanent dam could proceed uninterrupted. Even with this bit of progress in taming the river, Smith

When high water came in the spring of 1908, the southern part of
the dam (left) was high enough to cause the river to flow over the
north end only. About two months after this photograph was taken
in April 1908, construction crews began laying masonry at the north
end. The wooden, stiff-arm derricks on top of the dam were used to
move the quarried stone into position. A temporary walkway
stretches across the floodwaters to the north end of the damsite.

continued to find the contractor and his men inept. On May 8, 1907,
Smith went down to the coffer dam and found O'Rourke's crew "fid-
dling around, doing nothing but [getting] their mixing plant in shape
to run."[49] Continual mistakes by O'Rourke's crew in dumping concrete into water that was not still led Smith to report the next day that
"the job is not being conducted with energy or brains."[50] Breakdowns
in the hydraulic pipes, inadequate provision for steam pumps to
power the contractor's centrifugal pumps, and the persistent problem
of maintaining an adequate labor force produced postponement after
postponement for setting the stone for the main dam.[51]

Although George M. Steinmetz, manager of O'Rourke's crew, promised Smith that setting the stone for the main dam would begin June 1, 1907, water in the pit prevented this. When the contractor wanted to lay new masonry on top of the masonry laid in the fall of 1906, rather than at the low point, as Smith required, O'Rourke angrily declared that he would appeal to Washington. Because he was many months behind schedule in building the dam, O'Rourke was in a hurry to get several layers of stone laid as an indication of his progress. Smith knew, however, that stone laid at the low point of the excavated foundation would prevent movement, particularly in the event of flooding, which had plagued the construction of the dam since 1905. Louis Hill supported Smith, of course, and O'Rourke fussed and fumed throughout the summer at what he considered persecution by the two engineers.[52]

In August 1907 Smith and O'Rourke had a long talk about "things generally." The contractor did not feel that he was getting "a square deal"; Smith tried to explain government regulations concerning waste, dumping, and payment for goods produced. The results of this talk were not entirely satisfactory, and O'Rourke continued to go over Smith's head to Louis Hill for permission to do things differently; Hill continued to side with his engineer in charge of construction. This problem continued until the final stone was laid February 5, 1911.[53]

Once the foundation had been cleared, water pumped out, and the masonry set down, dam construction went quickly. There were no floods throughout the winter of 1907 and early 1908 to impede the construction progress. When high water did come in the spring of 1908, the southern two-thirds of the dam were at a sufficient elevation that the excess water passed over the north end of the dam only, without delays to the contractor. In June, O'Rourke's men began laying masonry at the north end of the dam, and from this month forward, the south end of the dam was kept from eighteen to fifty feet higher than the other. On November 29, 1909, the contractor brought the elevation of the lowest part of the dam to 150 feet, the elevation which was supposed to have been reached by April 1907.[54]

Construction of the Roosevelt Dam and its ancillary structures, completed in February 1911, was marked both by new technological features and by inefficient and inexperienced contractors. While the introduction of reinforced concrete pressure pipes, advanced methods of laying masonry, and innovative hydraulic sluice gates helped to spur the pace of building the dam, as well as to characterize it as a modern piece of construction, the problems between John O'Rourke and the U.S. Reclamation Service hindered its progress. The more

The downstream face of Roosevelt Dam, February 1909. Water elevation behind the dam is 73 feet. The completed power house is located just below the dam (center right), and part of the transformer house is visible at the lower left of the photo. The building on the hill in the background is Apache Lodge; built by contractor John M. O'Rourke, it served as the residence for his engineers, foremen, and inspectors. White water at the lower center of photo is discharge from the sluice tunnel. Cableways, which were used to transport material from one side of the river to the other, are visible at top right.

time and men it took O'Rourke's company to build the dam, the more costly it was to become to the landowners of the Salt River Valley Water Users' Association, both in irrigation water lost and in project dollars to repay; the same was true, of course, for the Reclamation Service's expensive overruns on the power canal.

Yet throughout the period 1904–1908, when construction problems peaked, visitors to Roosevelt did nothing but praise the work and its creators. Benjamin Fowler, Dwight Heard, A. J. Chandler, and

W. J. Murphy were just a few of the prominent members of the Association who ventured up the winding road from the valley to check on the dam's progress. More often than not, Chester Smith would personally lead them through the labyrinth of tunnels, canals, and proposed dams, so that these men felt they were informed about the project they would eventually call their own. From across the nation came important politicians, such as William G. McAdoo (a power in the Democratic party who would become Secretary of the Treasury in 1913) and Secretary of Interior James Garfield, to check on the nation's reclamation program at Salt River. Often led by Frederick Newell, Louis Hill, Joseph Kibbey, or Benjamin Fowler, these men also followed Smith over the Roosevelt project, seeing for themselves the conditions which they had previously known only through Reclamation Service reports.

Few, if any, of the visitors to Roosevelt were aware of problems, other than the 1905 floods, which were pushing back the date of completion of the dam. Newell, Hill, and Smith considered these problems to be engineering concerns which could be solved by the practical, rational men of the Service. They knew that compared to other reclamation projects, the problems at Salt River were minor ones with predictable solutions. If the private contractors on the sawmill could not produce, the government would take over; if the concreted portion of the sluicing tunnel broke away during high flows, it could be replaced; if the hydraulic gates malfunctioned, they could be fixed. O'Rourke's construction company made mistakes which delayed the final date of the dam's completion but did not mar its ultimate success.

Officials of the Reclamation Service considered the Roosevelt Dam a magnificent achievement, and a "monumental triumph of the skill and genius of [its] scientist creators."[55] Residents of the Salt River Valley and the nation joined them in their praise. The magnitude of engineering and construction accomplishments—and this still cannot be lost on the visitor rounding the final turn up Roosevelt Road to see a dam of solid rock looming between the Mazatzal and Sierra Ancha Mountains—dominated other issues.

The Business of Irrigation

The original plans for the construction of the Salt River Project depicted a reservoir of half the capacity of the one eventually built, with no provision for the development of a permanent hydroelectric power supply. An increase in the federal funds available for construction, through growth of the reclamation fund, led to more comprehensive plans; the power canal and power plant, northside canal system, and Granite Reef diversion dam led the list of additions. Most landowners in the Salt River Valley Water Users' Association approved of enlarging the Salt River Project to include the extra features, and the Association lobbied the U.S. Reclamation Service to build them; however, many of the landowners seemed unaware of the mounting costs. The initial estimate for project construction of $3.75 million increased to $8.9 million by 1909, and to $10.5 million by 1912.[1]

As the project neared completion and repayment was due to begin, farmers and other landowners questioned both the projected costs and the lack of financial information which had been furnished them. In 1912, dissident farmers concerned about repaying the reclamation debt to the government charged that more money had been spent in the construction work than was necessary. They chastised the leadership of the water-users' association for not making the Reclamation Service more accountable to the landowners who would pay the construction charges. They called also for a federal investigation of the government's role in the Salt River Project, and joined other water users nationally in demanding a change in the repayment section of reclamation law. They wanted not only a different repayment schedule, but also an alternate method of assessing construction charges and greater federal subsidy.

The Association's Board of Governors, meanwhile, also questioned the ten-year repayment schedule set forth in the 1902 Reclamation Act, advocating instead extension of the repayment period to twenty years. Other water-users' associations on federal reclamation projects made the same request for an extension of time for repaying the costs of the projects, and the national movement for extension gained momentum. To the chagrin of the U.S. Reclamation Service, their pioneer yeomanry was in revolt.

The noisy call for a federal investigation of the Salt River Project by one group of angry landowners clashed with the Board of Governors' effort to avoid controversy in order to secure congressional legislation allowing for extension of time for repayments. Additionally, a small group of landowners—some with old water rights and others farming modest plots of land under a well-established canal— renewed the Old Settlers Protective Association and challenged the democratic basis upon which the Salt River Valley Water Users' Association was formed: that a secure water supply was of equal benefit to everyone.

The conflict which arose between the two points of view soon became a serious one in the valley. While the construction costs and repayment schedule were the immediate issues to be solved, complete resolution of the breach among Salt River Valley water users on the project required an evaluation of the Association's relationship with the Reclamation Service.

The water users' disenchantment with federal reclamation stemmed from three sources: (1) concern with the increased costs of the project, due to expansion of the system and cost overruns; (2) realization that some would benefit more than others, although all would pay the same rate; and (3) a belief that the Reclamation Service did not care about local conditions. Opposition to the Service was by no means universal, however, and the tension between those within the Association who backed the reclamation principles as they were stated in the Reclamation Act of 1902, and those who believed the time was right for change, dominated local water-user politics from 1909 to 1914, when the reclamation issue was also examined nationally.

THE EXTENSION OF REPAYMENT ISSUE

Because reclamation legislation and the 1904 contract between the government and the water-users' association clearly stated that repayment of the project debt was to be borne equally by water users and paid in ten annual installments beginning a year after the project's completion and the issuance of public notice, the Reclamation Service—its director, Frederick Newell, in particular—was surprised that the rebels questioned who should bear the costs of irrigation. Congress plainly intended that the direct beneficiaries, rather than the government, shoulder the cost of the irrigation system. Newell believed that federal irrigation was "a challenging political experiment to test and validate the belief that government could provide services on a businesslike repayment basis."[2] In all cases, the federal government believed the works must pay for themselves.[3]

The water users who were challenging the government position advocated an approach that was growing in popularity in the West: greater federal subsidies for the reclamation projects. The capital invested nationally to irrigate one acre grew by 100 percent from 1900 to 1910, and by 226 percent from 1910 to 1920; because this increase was due, in large part, to purchase of expensive storage and pump facilities for land already under irrigation, the money spent did not increase the number of acres cultivated. Since many assumed that the government intended the reclamation of the arid lands as an internal improvement for the country as a whole, they believed the nation should pay the costs of the main structures or, barring that, the difference between the initial estimate and the final costs. Where the Reclamation Act failed to specify who should pay for a particular element, this group considered the government liable.[4]

An added point of contention on Salt River was really the continuation of an old complaint raised earlier by some landowners with well-established water rights: assessments should not be equal, but structured, so that those landowners with the greatest need of the project and, therefore, with the greatest benefit from it, would pay accordingly. Mrs. J. W. Stewart of Mesa wrote President Roosevelt in 1908 of the problem of equal assessments:

> We think as do hundreds of others that we ought not to have to pay the same price for the Roosevelt Dam as do those who have no water rights, or that our ditches and rights shall be thrown into the common fund and we will only be paid whatever Mr. Hill thinks the canals are worth at present.[5]

The Stewarts were both past the age of fifty-five; they had three daughters and a forty-acre farm, and Mr. Stewart also taught in the common schools for $600 per year. The costs of the federal project, equally borne, meant that the Stewarts would have to pay between

$1,200 to $1,600 for project repayment, plus water dues ($50 to $100 per year), irrigating expenses, regular farm labor, and taxes. Despite the lively propaganda of the early years, in which national reclamation was seen as a panacea to the problems of immigration from the East, irrigated farming was not a poor man's proposition.[6]

The Stewart story was fairly typical for small landowners with vested rights in Salt River: farming would initially cost them more with federal reclamation than without it. Landowners holding large amounts of land for speculative purposes without an assured water right, however, would profit quickly from the development of an additional water supply; land without water was worth little in the arid West. A. J. Chandler and Dwight Heard, who both owned land in excess of one thousand acres, could sell their surplus holdings for far more than would be possible without a reclamation program: non-irrigated lands were valued at $50 to $75 an acre in 1909, while irrigated lands were appraised at $75 to $750 an acre, depending upon their location.[7]

Clarence J. Blanchard, the statistician for the Reclamation Service, sensing the growing disillusionment with the repayment terms in the arid West, wrote Benjamin Fowler in early 1909 that the time for reckoning was not far distant. Completion of the Roosevelt Dam would signal the end of construction on the Salt River Project, and Blanchard warned Fowler that the government would demand payment. He also told the president of the Association that there would be little sympathy from the Service if the water users requested more time, as the Salt River Project was the most favorably situated of all.[8]

Dissatisfaction with the principles of federal reclamation and the Reclamation Service was raised nationwide in 1906, when a spin-off group from the 1905 meeting of the National Irrigation Congress organized to promote changes in the repayment and acreage-limitation provisions of the law. This group, which had been loosely organized, formally became the National Federation of Water Users' Associations in September 1912. Frederick Newell personally advised Benjamin Fowler to send some "good delegates" to the September 1906 National Irrigation Congress meeting in Boise, Idaho, writing that "I think it would be in the interest of Arizona to try to head off attacks along this line."[9] Newell also confidentially wrote Louis Hill to lobby this cause further with Fowler and Joseph Kibbey, as "unfavorable action at Boise might result injuriously to Arizona."[10] Whether these admonitions from Newell were threats or not, the Salt River Valley Water Users' Association sided with the Reclamation Service and did not join the proposed national organization of water-users' associations, even though nearly half of the other federal projects sent delegations;[11] perhaps it was no coincidence that the Salt River Project was allocated additional money to purchase the northside canal system that year.

Lobbyist George Maxwell cautioned Charles Walcott (by then director of the Smithsonian Institution) in the spring of 1909, however, on the state of affairs at Salt River and voiced concern about repayment. "In a nutshell, I think the people in the Valley are living in a fool's paradise," Maxwell wrote Walcott, "and the officers of the Reclamation Service are facing the probabilities of a great catastrophe there without an adequate conception of its possibilities."[12] The fundamental problem, according to Maxwell, was that an "$8 million irrigation project to reclaim an area larger than the entire irrigated area of Southern California, outside of the Imperial county, is being built and the cost charged to a community of only 35,000 people."[13]

The projected charge per acre for repayment had increased from $20 in 1903 to $45 in 1909, and the reduction of land holdings to facilitate new landowners was very slow. Congress had passed legislation in 1906 allowing the receipts from the sale of hydroelectric power on a project to apply to its reclamation fund debt, and Maxwell feared that Salt River Valley landowners were relying too heavily on this method of repayment. Selling power to the mines as a source of revenue was "being diligently dwelt upon by the land speculators in the Valley," and Maxwell believed it created the impression that "the landowners will never have to pay the debt to the government."[14]

Visiting the valley in April 1909, Frederick Newell, perhaps taking Maxwell's view to heart, warned landowners that the dam was nearly finished, and asked if they were ready to accept their responsibilities. "The long period of construction work that moves slowly at first, accustoms the people to delay," Newell told the *Arizona Republican*, "and when at last things begin to hum, it is finished before the community is hardly aware of it."[15] Although the government spent money "right and left" during the construction period, Newell reminded Fowler, Heard, and the others of the association that it "has all got to come back again."[16]

The Reclamation Service was preoccupied with many issues throughout 1909, in addition to repayment. The election of William Taft to the presidency, and his selection of Richard Ballinger as Secretary of Interior, brought with it a change in the direction of national conservation policy. Under Roosevelt, Newell and Gifford Pinchot, director of the U.S. Forest Service, had had an extraordinary amount of authority over the nation's natural resources. Ethan A. Hitchcock· had resigned as Secretary of Interior in 1907, and Roosevelt had appointed James Garfield, son of the former President and a close ally of Newell and Pinchot. The Roosevelt-Garfield policy in conservation had meant, as Frederick Newell later admitted, "doing those things which were necessary and desirable but which were not forbidden by law."[17] The new Taft-Ballinger policy was to do only those things specifically authorized by law.

The appointment of Richard Ballinger to the lead position at Interior was a shock to Newell, Pinchot, and Garfield; the three men on Roosevelt's conservation team had understood that President Taft would reappoint Garfield. The U.S. Reclamation Service, which, under Garfield, had "developed rapidly and gained the reputation of being one of the most effective organizations in the Government, with men and women devoted to the work," was now to be administered by a "practical politician type," anathema to the reformers of Roosevelt's Progressive mode.[18] Newell characterized Ballinger in this way:

> He was not a man of wide views, rather suspicious and secretive. He appeared at first to take some sympathetic interest in the work but never gained a large comprehension of the important features, looking at each detail from a somewhat personal standpoint. His attitude encouraged attack from the various landowners, speculators and investors who were resentful because they had not been able to break through the letter and spirit of the law. Their attacks upon the Reclamation Service instead of being correctly interpreted were permitted to increase.[19]

If Newell did not like Ballinger, believing that he undermined the reclamation program, the new Secretary of Interior reciprocated the feeling. Ballinger floated rumors even before he arrived in Washington that he would "get rid of Newell."[20] He tried to change personnel at the Reclamation Service, on the grounds that Newell had overstepped the bounds of his authority, but Taft, sensitive to the political force of Roosevelt, rejected firing Newell as the best approach for altering the role of the Service. Ballinger criticized Newell for beginning new projects without adequate money in the reclamation fund, questioned his administrative and engineering practices, and openly advocated private irrigation development over federal reclamation.[21]

Rumors over the uncertainty of Newell's remaining as chief of the Reclamation Service persisted throughout 1909. Benjamin Fowler wrote Newell of his concern in December:

> I have been hoping for the best, hoping that you will retain your present position, hoping that the reactionary influence of the present Cabinet would be insufficient to overthrow the wise policies formulated and established by the last Administration.[22]

Fowler feared that with "the turning out of men who have made the Reclamation Service what it is, the Lord only knows what is coming to the arid West in general, and to the Salt River Valley in particular."[23] The Forest Service's Gifford Pinchot believed that anxiety over whether Newell would remain as director of the Reclamation Service and, if not, what path reclamation would take under Ballinger and the new Administration brought Newell "to the verge of a nervous breakdown."[24] Challenged on several fronts—by recalcitrant water users on the projects, by rebellious western legislators, and by the Secretary of Interior himself—Newell held even more firmly to the Roosevelt reclamation principles.

In September 1909 a group of water users from ten federal projects called for a ten-year extension of repayment, for the payment of project operation and maintenance charges from the reclamation fund, and for the payment of construction costs at the original estimate, rather than the actual cost. Even though rank and file members of the local associations did not adopt these resolutions, western Congressmen paid heed to their substance. The U.S. Senate Committee on Irrigation, led by Thomas Carter of Montana, decided to investigate conditions on the federal reclamation projects during the fall of 1909.[25]

Frederick Newell and Richard Ballinger joined the Senate committee on its trip through the West, and all arrived in Phoenix in October 1909. Meeting with the Board of Governors of the water-users' association, Ballinger said that he was pleased with the cooperation exhibited between the Salt River Valley water users and the government. "Unfortunately," the Secretary told the group, "this is not true of some of the other projects; that it is so is an advantage to the people as well as the government."[26] Ballinger was concerned with one issue: whether the people of the valley would be able to meet the payments to the government when due. Judge Joseph Kibbey, speaking for the association, assured the Secretary that they would pay, and they would pay on time; there would be no need for an extension of time on the Salt River Project.[27]

Not every board member agreed with Kibbey, however, and at least one man thought an extension of time would be necessary. Ballinger, in sympathy with this outspoken member of the board, intimated that it was within his authority to retard, rather than hasten, the time when payments should begin. Other farmers at the meeting told the Secretary of Interior that it was only the new landowners who might experience difficulty in repaying the construction debt; they believed the older lands could easily make the payments.[28]

The water-users' association did not really object to the idea of an extension of payments or of reduction of the final construction costs. This flexibility in maintaining two diverse positions was based on self-interest. "The Salt River project is not yet complete as we would like to have it and as we have hoped to have it," Kibbey reported to the Board of Governors October 27, 1909. Both the Reclamation Service and the Association envisioned the installation of additional power plants, so that revenue "to materially reduce the cost to us of our irrigation works" might be derived. The lack of money in the reclamation fund made the possibility for their construction unlikely, but Kibbey had hopes that, if the association placated the government by advocating repayment on time, then $1 million of a proposed $10 million loan from Congress to the reclamation fund might be secured for the Salt River Project.[29] Kibbey laid out the facts before the association's Board of Governors:

> I think it cannot be fairly said that the cost of the project has been either unwarrantably or unfairly increased. It was all done at our own request, and the burden of the cost and acquisition and improvement of the canals and construction of the Granite Reef Dam which were originally our own burden were assumed at our request by the government . . . While we are yet in the attitude of asking the government for further favors, it seems to be the worst sort of policy to offer to repudiate our obligations for those already extended to us.[30]

There were some landowners, albeit a minority, who had other concerns they wanted to take up with the Senate Committee on Irrigation; among these were grievances with the administration of the project by the Reclamation Service and by the water-users' association. While Joseph Kibbey believed that these complaints were important to the individuals making them, he felt that including them within the Association's testimony to the committee would only result in irritating the senators. The committee would go away with "a disagreeable impression of our valley . . . . We want to make a good impression—we can easily make a bad one."[31] Kibbey recommended that the Association's 1910 election campaign would be a better forum for charges of maladministration than the hearings of the Senate Committee on Irrigation. Other landowners agreed with him, and the Salt River Valley Water Users' Association presented a united, if filtered, position in favor of the reclamation principles enacted in 1902.

Benjamin Fowler had been elected president of the National Irrigation Congress in August 1909, and his absence from the valley due to fulfilling that obligation may have diluted the philosophical support for national reclamation that Newell had always expected of the Salt River Project. Joseph Kibbey, while at one time an advocate of those principles, was also an attorney, and he listened to the opinions of his clients, the Salt River Valley landowners. If the association could secure both extension of repayment and reduction of the cost, along with further expenditures for the power facilities, Kibbey believed that was fine; missing was the moral tone that Fowler might have invoked for the repayment principle. The difference in the Association without Fowler became clear during discussion of the water-users' plan to testify before the Senate Committee on Irrigation;[32] pragmatism came to dominate what had been Fowler and Newell's gospel of reclamation.

The Senate committee, chaired by Thomas Carter, traveled for fifty days and inspected nearly all the government reclamation projects; its preliminary conclusions were then released by Frederick Newell: "It [was] impracticable and impossible to make any modifications in the reclamation act without the risk of losing many advantages of the present law."[33] The senators also recommended that Congress expedite unfinished construction with the $10 million advance to the reclamation fund, and "stood their ground on the demand that every dollar that has been spent by the government in the work of reclamation must be refunded."[34]

Secretary of Interior Ballinger wanted to promote a shift in emphasis for reclamation away from the federal government to the states or to private enterprise. The recommendations of the Senate Committee on Irrigation, however, clearly affirmed Newell's positions on repayment and on the importance of the federal role. The Salt River Valley Water Users' Association under Kibbey's guidance had impressed the committee favorably and, while the Association was not the only one to support Newell (the North Platte and Orland associations were among others), it still set an important example for government reclamation projects.

The Secretary of Interior continued, however, to criticize Newell's administration, and requested investigations into many Reclamation Service policies. Ballinger also repealed the highly successful cooperative certificate program which allowed project settlers to exchange labor on irrigation distribution systems for water-user charges. The engineering profession viewed Ballinger's actions as political manipulations to further private business interests; *Engineering News* believed that the U.S. Reclamation Service and Frederick Newell, not the Secretary, defended the public interest.[35]

When Gifford Pinchot of the U.S. Forest Service brought charges of collusion in looting the public lands in Wyoming, Montana, and Alaska against the Secretary of Interior in late 1909, Ballinger's attention turned away from the Reclamation Service. As a result of Ballinger's flagging interests "in the larger affairs," Newell continued to

Construction of Roosevelt Dam was almost complete by early 1910. In this photo, taken in February of that year, a worker sits to the left of one of the large wooden derricks used to place the two- to twelve-ton limestone blocks in position. Scaffolds, used as platforms by the men laying the stone, were erected on the downstream face of the dam because the dam became progressively narrower as it rose (it is only 16 feet wide at the top). The completed power house is partially visible at lower right.

exercise control over reclamation policy.[36] The Salt River Valley Water Users' Association, meanwhile, sought additional federal funds for further construction on Salt River Project.

Construction of the Roosevelt Dam was nearly complete by March 1910, but a cash shortfall of $575,000 prevented the speedy conclusion of the building phase; cessation of work was both "expensive and irritating to all concerned."[37] At the same time, the project was not as complete as the Association would have liked; additional power-producing facilities were desired, as Kibbey had earlier advocated, to reduce the construction debt. The Association worked out a plan with Louis Hill of the Reclamation Service whereby the landowners under the project would assess themselves $2 per acre for two years to raise the necessary money for expansion of the power system. The Reclamation Service would delay opening the project and issuing public notice for those two years, giving the water users enough time to finish the power plants so that revenues from them could be used to reduce the first charges of repayment. Hill successfully persuaded Secretary of Interior Ballinger to provide a cash allotment to finish the dam's construction and to delay the opening of the Salt River Project until the power plants were complete. This arrangement meant that it would not be necessary to wait for Congress to debate and vote on the issuance of $20 million of interest-bearing certificates of indebtedness to bail out the reclamation fund. All that remained was for the water users to approve the assessment against their lands.[38]

Because Frederick Newell, Louis Hill, and other Reclamation Service officials made it known that the reclamation fund contained no additional money for the expansion of the Salt River Project, association members assumed that the only option available was to build the 5,000-horsepower generating plants (located off of the valley's Crosscut Canal) themselves. Although 1910 was an election year for the association, the power plants' assessment was not really at issue. Benjamin Fowler and Joseph Kibbey had originated the assessment proposal, and John P. Orme, who openly declared himself a candidate for the presidency of the Association on March 17, 1910, also advocated the power plan. What Fowler and Kibbey did not say was that they supported the assessment proposal only as a last resort; Fowler believed Congress could be induced to appropriate funds for completion of the reclamation projects, and that he could secure some of them for Salt River.[39]

Although there were signs early in the year of water users' discontent with both Fowler and Kibbey, notably the action by the Association Council to reduce by half their salaries as president and legal counsel, Fowler did not anticipate the wide support Orme would receive upon announcing his candidacy for Association president. Orme was selected by the Committee of Twelve, an organization of water users and valley residents formed to choose candidates for the Association's president and vice-president positions. This committee was less politically motivated than Dwight Heard had been in his earlier attempt to change the composition of the Association leadership, and it enjoyed wide support; the *Republican* editorialized that Orme's selection would be a safe one. While no one openly criticized Fowler's tenure as president, landowners were generally displeased with the unexpected costs of federal reclamation. Although reducing the salaries of the president and legal counsel produced no appreciable savings (the yearly cost to a landowner of eighty acres was 40¢ with the reduction, instead of 80¢), the Board of Governors struck back in frustration where it could. Just as Fowler was associated with the increased costs of the project, he was also a symbol of the national government—the local mouthpiece of the U.S. Reclamation Service, and many landowners within the Association grew skeptical of the idea that he was always pursuing their best interests in the reclamation partnership.

Benjamin Fowler, who had subscribed 440 acres to the Association in 1903, was more of a gentleman farmer than a working one. He, like Dwight Heard, used much of his land for agricultural experimentation. His educational background and his activities in the community reflected a concern for thorough investigation and analysis, and he seems to have focused his efforts largely in these areas. Actual farming on the Fowler place was performed by hired labor. The very qualities that local landowners had admired in Fowler at the outset of reclamation—the penchant for scientific investigation, firm conviction to principles, ability to deal successfully with eastern businessmen and government officials—became liabilities once the project had begun and concern had grown over project costs and local administration. That Fowler was often out of the valley for long periods of time in his work for reclamation added to the general feeling among the Association's Council members that the job could be performed better by someone who understood local farmers' problems rather than national reclamation policy. "It was clear that the farmers did not want that 'city man' Fowler," wrote one reporter of the election; "they wanted one of their own kind."[40] Joseph Kibbey had resigned over the salary dispute, saying that at that salary the position was no longer attractive to him, and Fowler, realizing the considerable opposition to his election to a fourth term, decided to retire.[41]

The *Republican* had come out in support of Fowler on the grounds that his connections with officials in Washington were important for the completion of the project, but the paper also believed John Orme a good choice. With this kind of lukewarm assistance, Fowler bitterly perceived the Association's desire for change as a rejection of his ten years of service to reclamation in the valley.[42] Kibbey had recommended the 1910 election as the proper forum for discussion of poor administration of the Association, and, much to his surprise, it became a vehicle for change as well.

The first president of the Association wrote Frederick Newell of his decision to leave the water users:

Under the circumstances, at the end of a ten years' service of hard, faithful and unselfish work for the Salt River project and

my friends in the Reclamation Service, I thought it a good time
for me to quit when there was something to my credit.[43]

Perhaps Newell saw something of his own fate in Fowler's uncer-
emonious ouster, for he wrote him that "a debt of gratitude is due to
you from the people there, but experience shows . . . that public
services of this kind are rarely recognized by the great body of people." Newell advised Fowler that "faithful devotion is generally followed by neglect upon the part of those benefited."[44] Fowler and
Newell's belief in their own suffering for the reclamation cause is
evidence of the self-righteousness of the conservation movement and
its inability to tolerate different opinions.[45] Newell had hoped that
the Salt River Project, because of Fowler, might be different from the
others in this respect, but now he seemed resigned to the reality of
the situation:

> It is assumed that the Salt River Valley will pass through very
> much the same evolution as other projects—the men friendly to
> the work of the U.S.R.S. being replaced in time by opponents who
> will endeavor to secure some personal advantage by attacking the
> plans and personnel of the Service. This we must expect,
> although I had hoped that the people of the Salt River Valley
> would be too intelligent to permit such a condition.[46]

John Orme, a civil engineer with extensive experience managing
irrigation enterprises and a rancher as well, was by no means one of
the reactionaries Newell feared would come to power. Born in Mary-
land in 1852, Orme moved to Missouri in 1866, attended Missouri
State University, and graduated in civil engineering in 1868. His first
job was resident engineer on the Texas and Pacific Railroad in southeastern Texas, but, after surviving a bout of malaria, he sought a
different climate. Orme worked in Colorado and California, yet
found neither to be helpful in maintaining good health; the hot des-
erts of Arizona, however, made him thrive. After short stays in Yuma
and Flagstaff, he finally settled in Phoenix in 1877, opening a corral
and settling 800 acres for a cattle ranch.

The need for water on his ranch prompted Orme to study irrigation, and he was one of the three who built the Maricopa Canal. When
his wife, Ella, died in 1898, Orme plunged into work and politics,
especially into the water-storage movement. He was elected to the
Association's Board of Governors in 1904, and was repeatedly
reelected until he became president of the Association in 1910. As his
son, Charles, said of him, "his hobby was work; he never stayed still
himself and he never let anybody else stay still."[47]

John Orme, a rancher and civil engineer, settled in the Phoenix area in 1877. The need for water on his ranch prompted him to study irrigation, and he became active in the Salt River Valley Water Users' Association, serving on its Board of Governors and as president in 1910. Much of the developing confidence within the Association was due to Orme's style of leadership. A consensus builder, he worked closely with the Association and other community leaders to educate, persuade and convince the water users of their ability to manage the Salt River Project during the transfer of operations to the Association in 1917.

In addition to his strong interest in irrigation, Orme was a political enthusiast. A Democrat, he was for nine years a member of the Maricopa County Board of Supervisors, was elected to the Arizona Constitutional Convention in 1911, and at the age of seventy-one became a member of the Arizona House of Representatives. Orme's gregariousness, knowledge of irrigation, rancher occupation, status as a valley pioneer, and political abilities made him popular locally.

Considered a harmonizer of competing valley interests, Orme essentially embraced the program of the Reclamation Service. Perhaps Frederick Newell's chief complaint against him, besides his challenge to Benjamin Fowler, was that Orme was a Democrat who did not also hold to the conservation philosophy of the Teddy Roosevelt men. Fowler and Orme came from different regions of the country, had different educational backgrounds and different politics. Yet what seemed to be the biggest difference between the two leaders was their approach to the Association. The issue of the power-plant assessment plan provides a useful example.

Although Fowler had originally proposed the assessment plan, whereby landowners would pay $2 per acre for two years in order to finance additional power facilities, he believed that, through his Washington connections, he could secure additional government funds for this project. Because of Fowler, then, the Association would pay for the power plant under more favorable terms. Clearly this was but another instance in which Fowler, through personal effort to influence decision-making in Washington, sought to secure advantages for the Association. But some water users were angry at their exclusion from the purchase negotiations of the northside canal system, and this time they decided to write the contract with the government to build the Crosscut Canal power facilities themselves, without personal diplomacy in Washington. They felt there was too much uncertainty in Fowler's gamble to wait for Congress, because the project might be completed, public notice issued, and repayment be necessary before the power facilities could be completed. The landowners under the project wanted both some part in the decision and more control over project affairs; they ratified the contract by agreeing to assess themselves for approximately $1 million.[48]

Salt River was not the only reclamation project in need of additional money from the reclamation fund to finish major construction. Nearly every project of the twenty-six sponsored by the government required more cash in 1910—some as much as $2 million. The reclamation fund, although it had taken in between $6 and $7 million each year since its creation in 1902, was nevertheless inadequate for the demands placed upon it. Too many projects had been authorized because of pressures to spend money in each public-lands state, and many remained incomplete as a result. As long as the projects were unfinished, repayment could not begin, and this situation further diminished the reclamation fund; as of June 30, 1910, $52,945,441 had been expended on federal projects, while only $902,822 had been repaid. To remedy this problem, President Taft recommended to Congress that it issue $20 million in certificates of indebtedness repayable with interest out of the reclamation fund; interest on the loan would be charged against the projects on the amount contributed for their completion. Legislation of June 25, 1910, made this appropriation, on the condition that the money be spent only on existing projects and their necessary extensions and that no part of it be spent until every project had been investigated and reported upon by a board of Army engineer officers.[49]

The Act of June 25, 1910, challenged both the U.S. Reclamation Service and the original repayment principle. President William Taft and Secretary of Interior Richard Ballinger had long been suspicious of the way the Reclamation Service administered the projects, and the mandatory examination of federal reclamation by its rival agency, the Army Corps of Engineers, further diversified project authorization procedures. The control that Frederick Newell once exercised over expenditures was diluted, because the Board of Army Engineers on Reclamation Projects now decided what funds would be allocated for each project for the four-year period 1911–1914. Taft, as a former Secretary of War, had great confidence in the Army Corps of Engineers, and intimated that its recommendations would have priority over the Service's.

Because the 1910 legislation authorizing a $20 million loan to the reclamation fund required repayment with interest, it created a disparity between those projects which had been largely completed with early, no-interest appropriations from the fund—like the Salt River Project—and later ones, which had to repay the greater part of their construction costs with 3 percent interest. The Salt River Project, thus, enjoyed a sizeable federal subsidy, as its water users had to repay only the principal.[50]

The Army board consisted of five engineer officers, plus retired General William L. Marshall (the consulting engineer to Secretary Ballinger) and Frederick Newell. The director of the Reclamation Service was pleased that Marshall was with the group, as "his wide experience and good common sense were invaluable."[51] For nearly four months the examining board of Army engineers visited each reclamation project authorized by the government, inspected the engineering performed, and held hearings in the local towns. They visited Salt River on October 8–10, 1910.[52]

By the time the Army Corps reached the Salt River Valley, changes had been made in the proposed power facilities which the landowners had voted to construct themselves in early July 1910. Instead of a 5,000-horsepower generating plant on the Crosscut Canal, new Reclamation-Service plans called for a 6,000-horsepower plant on the Crosscut, a 3,000-horsepower facility on the Consolidated Canal, and a 700-horsepower generating station at Arizona Falls on the Arizona Canal. The Salt River Valley Water Users' Association had already paid about $420,000 for these extensions to the project, and, in consideration of this work, the government had delayed issuing public notice for repayment. Now, in October 1910, the Army board recommended that $495,000 from the proposed $20 million loan to the reclamation fund be appropriated during 1911–1914 to finish this construction.[53]

The final report of this examining board was quite favorable to the Reclamation Service, which must have eliminated some of the bitterness the Service felt about being investigated by the Army Corps. In fact, director Frederick Newell wrote of the report that "I doubt whether I could have prepared as appreciative a statement of the achievements."[54] The Board of Army Engineers on Reclamation

Projects found nearly all the projects feasible, both economically and technically, and generally endorsed the program of the Reclamation Service.

On the Salt River Project, the Army engineers believed all had been constructed in a proper manner, and they made no reference to any expenditure which might be considered excessive. They praised the work at the cement mill and the power canal for reducing the overall costs of the project. The landowners of the Association, meanwhile, were pleased that they could finish the remaining construction with federal money, rather than their own.[55]

Despite the Army engineers' report, President Taft and Secretary Ballinger believed that modification of the Reclamation Act of 1902 was needed. Taft recommended legislation to permit disposition of surplus stored water available from reclamation projects to persons, associations, or corporations operating non-project water-delivery systems (Warren Act), thus bringing additional revenue to the reclamation fund. He also recommended that Congress authorize the Secretary of Interior to modify conditions of repayment for certain projects on which conditions did not yet allow the return of the cost of the project (Curtis Act). Both of these legislative suggestions were in line with Richard Ballinger's philosophy that private interests should have greater involvement with the federal projects, and both of them were passed by Congress. This official show of flexibility in reclamation policy encouraged demands for modification of repayment procedures on projects all across the arid West.[56]

Of the more than one million irrigable acres available for cultivation and ready to receive water from federal reclamation projects in 1911 (about 40 percent of the projects' estimated total irrigable acreage), just 20 percent were actually being irrigated. On Salt River the figures were considerably higher than the national average: 72 percent of the total project irrigable acreage was available in 1911, and 50 percent was irrigated. The increased costs on many federal projects, coupled with the small number of landowners actually irrigating their lands, meant that repaying the reclamation debt in ten years would be impossible for most and difficult for all the participating landowners. Nationally, prices for wheat and barley—staple crops on many of the projects—fell during this period. Because it cost more to farm the same crop on an irrigated acre than it did on a non-irrigated acre in more humid regions, arid-land farmers under the reclamation projects faced a double financial burden.[57]

After achieving some success—the $20 million loan from Congress to the reclamation fund and passage of the Curtis Act—the

Roosevelt Dam as it looked in February 1911. Work on the northern tower (center top) was nearly finished, and electric lamps on top of the dam and bridge were just being fitted with their globes. The northern spillway is visible at upper left. The completed dam was 284 feet high; built on the arc of a circle to give added stability, the upper face of the top has a radius of 410 feet.

water-users' associations on federal projects lobbied to extend their repayment schedules from ten to twenty years, if not to repudiate the reclamation debt fully. The Salt River Valley Water Users' Association remained outside the loose federation of dissident water-users' associations; but rising costs on the Salt River Project, completion of the Roosevelt Dam in 1911, and the rapidly nearing date for the issuance of public notice brought many of the landowners there into the extension movement.[58]

Some of the reason for the controversy over reclamation policy in the West was due to the turmoil within the Department of Interior. Richard Ballinger had been forced to resign in March 1911, as a result of the furor, led by Gifford Pinchot, over his handling of the department, and President Taft replaced him with Walter Fisher, a politically attractive and reputable reformer from Chicago. Fisher was hesitant in initiating changes because of the Ballinger-Pinchot controversy, and he tried to serve as the arbiter of conflicting interests in the arid region. Fisher disliked Frederick Newell's inordinate influence within the department and tried to have him replaced; Taft refused to do so for the same political reasons he had considered when Ballinger had sought Newell's resignation.[59] It is also probable that Newell's command of the technical information required to run the Reclamation Service dissuaded Taft from replacing him.

Newell did not dislike Walter Fisher as much as he had resented Richard Ballinger, but he considered the new Secretary of Interior to be a timid man:

> Fisher took hold of affairs in a rather cautious way . . . . At first [he] tried to look into details, but [he was] . . . overwhelmed with these because of the accumulation of troubles of the previous two years. He was naturally timid about taking any steps which might involve him in further criticism. The most that can be said is that he neither helped nor hindered, but permitted matters to go forward as best they might.[60]

Two Secretaries of Interior had attempted to replace Newell, yet somehow he had managed to emerge the victor in these contests of power. Such victories could only have fed his own view that he was the Reclamation Service. The work of the Service progressed, but the enthusiasm of earlier times was never quite restored.[61] What took its place were the "seeds of dissatisfaction everywhere sowed by Ballinger," which bore fruit in criticism of the Reclamation Service and demands for repudiation of debts to the government.[62] From Newell's perspective, settler complaints were thus illegitimate, generated for political reasons.

It was Benjamin Fowler, ironically, who first advocated extension policy on behalf of the National Irrigation Congress. As president of the national irrigation group, Fowler had taken great interest in the repayment question and, through his own experience with the Salt River Valley Water Users' Association and exposure to other projects, he understood what was required locally to come up with the money for the government. He shared his views with Assistant Secretary of Interior Samuel Adams and with Frederick Newell in October 1911:

> The [Salt River] valley has secured a project four times as good as originally planned, but that doesn't increase the productivity of the acres four times . . . . If the government would extend the

time at least to double what the law now demands the people would still be paying for construction twice as fast as they expected to when work was undertaken.[63]

Fowler did not need to point out what was well known in Washington and in the valley: the project now cost nearly four times the original estimated price. Again, in his speech before the Nineteenth National Irrigation Congress in Chicago, Fowler said that:

> The time limit of ten years in which to return to the government in annual payments the cost of construction of a project is now recognized as too short and the necessity of an extension is generally understood and admitted by everybody.[64]

Everyone understood and admitted the necessity, that is, but Newell; to him the extension movement was heretical. In February 1912, several months after his return to Washington from another trip through the arid West, Newell wrote Dwight Heard to request data concerning production per acre and other conditions which would illustrate the problem of repayment on Salt River:

> If, as is now being asserted, the lands of the Salt River Valley cannot pay the cost of reclamation in less than 20 or 30 years, we must be seriously misled or else there are conditions which are not yet well understood.[65]

There were many land transfers on the Salt River Project in the year ending April 30, 1911, and Heard told Newell that homemaking—the purpose of the Reclamation Service's irrigation of arid lands—had hidden costs. New settlers had to spend money to support their families, to build homes, to clear and improve their land, to pay interest on any unpaid balance for the land, and to contribute their share of community improvements. All of these expenses had to be met from the gross revenue of their farms or ranches. Added to these costs were assessments for the Association, and now, the proposed construction cost of $45 per acre. Although the average crop value of $1,699 per farm on Salt River was the highest of all the projects, there would be little left at the end of the year after paying the price of federal reclamation; clearly, something had to change.[66]

Newell and the Reclamation Service consistently underrated problems of economic development on the projects and gave little consideration to the income-producing capacity of the land. The engineers seemed to approach the problem of determining project financial feasibility from the perspective of the land's market value, although, as historian Peggy Heim had noted, "they were vague as to what was a sufficient margin over the costs."[67] Since Newell considered himself an expert on reclamation, he probably viewed his own knowledge as adequate to judge a project's success potential; this attitude—that he could solve any problem—may have stemmed from his earlier experiences with his father's business. There were other reasons for project failure, not the least of which was the settlers' own lack of experience with irrigated farming and capital, and the absence of economists' and agricultural specialists' contributions to studies of project economic feasibility was a serious oversight.[68]

Late in February 1912 John Orme and D. P. Jones, chairman of the Council, went to Washington to petition the Reclamation Service and the Congress for an extension of time for repayment on Salt River. After a few days in the nation's capital, Orme sent word to the valley that "Newell is unfavorable to extension of time and wants graduated payments . . . . Much interest is manifested in the question; senators and representatives are willing to help so far as they have been seen."[69] Leaders of the Association were not pleased with Newell's attitude and wired Orme the following:

> Say to Newell the graduated payments will not do; also that unless he gets busy and helps to procure extension of time the people will demand of congress an investigation of extravagance and useless expenditure of money on the project. Two agitated meetings have been held since you left and signatures to petition asking for investigation are being solicited.[70]

THE COST INVESTIGATION ISSUE

Dissident farmers under the Salt River Project formed an organization called the Farmers' Protective Association to push for an investigation into the expenditure of funds on Salt River; by February 27, 1912, they had over three hundred names on their petition. They directly challenged the Reclamation Service by calling for an investigation of the project, and, by forming an independent association, they indicated their lack of confidence in the Salt River Valley Water Users' Association. The days when landowners followed Benjamin Fowler and Frederick Newell's gentlemen's agreements and verbal commitments were over.

The Farmers' Protective Association believed that an extension of time before repayment began was desirable; they contended, however, that a great deal more money had been spent in construction work than was necessary. If Congress approved the Board of Governors' petition for an extension, and the landowners then accepted the extension, they would be approving the full indebtedness charged to the Association without any investigation as to the correctness of the charges. The chief complaint the rebellious landowners had against the fees outlined by the Reclamation Service was that an item by item accounting of the money—or, for that matter, a simple monthly report of expenditures on the project—had never been submitted or requested. From the time of the first estimate of $3,750,000 as project cost until March 4, 1912, the landowners "were kept in ignorance of the amount of expenditures, knowing only in a general way that it was much in excess of the original estimate."[71] What they discovered in March was that the revised estimated cost was $10.5 million, or $6.75 million more than had been thought in 1903. The Farmers' Protective Association, in calling for an investigation, simply wanted to know why the current estimate exceeded the original estimate by nearly 200 percent.[72]

If the spoken issue of the Farmers' Protective Association was an investigation of the costs of the project, the unspoken one was government paternalism. Integral to the conservation policy of the Progressives, and part of the engineering credo, was the concept of decision making by experts through centralization of authority. The Reclamation Service under Frederick Newell had carried this policy to an extreme by virtually eliminating any role for local water users in the decision-making process; if the farmer received promptly and regularly a sufficient water supply, why should he not be satisfied? Instead, as John Widstoe suggested in *Success on Irrigation Projects*, farmers increasingly misunderstood government decisions due to a lack of general information, and they became bitterly opposed to Reclamation Service management. Landowners resented the inference that they were incapable of understanding the details of their reclamation projects. Finding avenues of redress through the Interior Department's bureaucracy blocked to them, they went to their representatives in Congress.[73] Since Arizona had become a state on February 14, 1912, landowners in the valley had one representative and two senators, and for them, this meant an end to the "state of vassalage to the bureaus of Washington as of yore."[74]

The Association attempted to convince its members that the extension movement, not an investigation, was the solution to their problems at the present time. Dwight Heard, who had not always been the voice the water users listened to, was nonetheless singled out as the reasonable spokesman for valley interests; he was also a "farmer" with personal relationships in Washington. The cost of the project was "manifestly greater" than originally anticipated, and Heard told the water users that they themselves had solicited most of

the additions that contributed to the increased cost. Yet there had
been expended quite a large sum which Heard believed should prop-
erly be charged to an experimental account. Even if the landowners
in the Farmers' Protective Association were correct in assuming
that there had been excessive costs due to poor administration,
Heard advocated "vigorous team play on the part of all interests to
secure without delay the reasonable extension of time which has been
asked for."[75]

Extension was a policy "that would be expected in a business deal
between individuals," the *Republican* editorialized on March 6, 1912,
"and surely the government can hardly afford to proceed on a lower
level than that."[76] The Association's Board of Governors appointed a
special committee to decide whether the water users under the Salt
River Project should also request an investigation (perhaps in an
effort to halt any momentum of the Farmers' Protective Association);
it recommended that a congressional investigation into the conduct
of affairs of the U.S. Reclamation Service not be conducted "at
this time."[77]

The special committee, led by John Orme and D. P. Jones, presid-
ing officers of the Board and Council respectively, believed extension
should be the central issue before the Congress and the Department
of Interior; "nothing should be allowed to hinder passage of legislation granting extension of time for repayments." In addition to its
concern that nothing interfere with the extension question, the committee believed that any review of costs should wait until the Secretary
of Interior apportioned the charges per shareholder, as the 1904
contract between the Association and the government outlined; any
differences would be taken up then. Repudiation of the debt owed
the government was not what the Association sought; rather, it
wanted relief from the "onerous schedule of repayments."[78] Only if
the 1904 contract proved unworkable and the Secretary of Interior
unresponsive to local needs, the special committee's report to the
Board stated, should the Association go to Congress for an investigation. As it was, the threat of an investigation would only delay the
passage of an extension for repayment of construction costs.

These diverging views of the proper policy that landowners in the
valley should pursue shaped the 1912 elections to the Salt River Valley
Water Users' Association Board and Council. The Farmers' Protective
Association, now called the Landowners' Protective Association, nom-
inated its own slate of candidates, much as Heard had done in earlier
elections. C. B. Wood, a state senator, landowner, and water user was
this group's candidate for the Association presidency. His platform
included two main points: (1) water distribution based on the check-

ing system, according to which water flowed constantly and was drawn on demand, and (2) delay of repayment until the total acreage to be irrigated was determined and the total cost of the project ascertained.[79]

The Association's John Orme was running for re-election, but not with the same degree of support he enjoyed in 1910. The *Republican* reported that many landowners were anxious to have Benjamin Fowler run again for the presidency of the water-users' organization. Yet "despite the pressure that has been brought to bear upon him to enter the race for the presidency of the SRVWUA," Fowler's reply was that he would not be a candidate. The *Republican* was confident that if he did enter the race, Fowler would be elected, but all of his friends combined could not persuade the former president of the Association to enter the contest.[80]

Perhaps because he remained somewhat bitter over the events of two years past or because the issues of the 1912 election were complex and political in nature, the idea of returning to leadership in the Salt River Valley Water Users' Association was not appealing to Fowler. The valley was, indeed, divided over reclamation policy and the *Republican* must have hoped Fowler would be able to unite all the interests, much as he had done in the initial stages of organization. But the belief that Fowler could win was really unwarranted; the issues had changed, the sense of mission had dissolved, and Fowler's moral view of reclamation was out of place in 1912. Of significance, too, was the current dissatisfaction with both the U. S. Reclamation Service and the water-users' association, which, in many ways, implied an indictment of past policies and leadership. In the absence of a compromise candidate, John Orme and C. B. Wood tested each other's political strength in the valley.

Amid this internecine struggle, Arthur P. Davis, chief engineer of the Reclamation Service, appeared before the Association's Board of Governors to answer criticisms raised against the Service. The checking system of water delivery, which C. B. Wood of the Landowners' Protective Association and a considerable minority in the Salt River Valley Water Users' Association favored, was wasteful, Davis told the Board. Instead he advocated the rotation system, which the Service had introduced and which was currently in use. In it farmers took "turns" at water, thus regulating the flow; Davis thought this "the proper, economical, and satisfactory method." Questioned about extravagance and waste on the project, Davis reported that his investigations of complaints revealed that most of them were exaggerated and unfounded. Charges of government loafing on the job prompted Davis to tell the Board that if anyone were to witness such a thing, he should tell the foreman at once so that the man could be fired and his pay stopped. The Association had a responsibility for insuring productivity. "Don't treasure these things up in your mind[s] and tell me a year afterward," Davis requested of the group, "but help us by reporting it at once."[81]

When representatives of the Landowners' Protective Association asked Davis whether he objected to a congressional investigation, he replied that he did not but that he was uncertain what new information such an investigation would reveal:

> A senatorial investigation has already been made [1909]; an investigation by a board of army engineers especially appointed for that purpose was made [1910]; and it has been investigated by three separate secretaries of interior.[82]

Still, the national political climate favored an investigation of the Reclamation Service. Powerful Senator William E. Borah of Idaho, in particular, and most other western legislators advocated changing the reclamation concept, partly to ease the financial burdens on project settlers and partly in response to the growing political power of the water-users' lobby. Groups like the National Federation of Water Users and the local Landowners' Protective Association found their congressional delegations receptive to an investigation of the Service, and in April 1912 the House of Representatives Committee on Expenditures in the Interior Department began an investigation of the Reclamation Service and the Salt River Project.[83]

A subcommittee of the House Committee on Expenditures in the Interior Department traveled to Phoenix to hear testimony from the water users there from April 12 through May 2, 1912. Many members of the Association were included on the subcommittee's list of witnesses, including John Orme, Joseph Kibbey, Benjamin Fowler, Dwight Heard, and A. J. Chandler, but the chief instigators of the Landowners' Protective Association did not address the group of three congressmen, led by Walter Hensley of Missouri. Despite the absence of personal testimony from C. B. Wood, Freeman T. Powers, Sam Barrett, and Herman Bustrim, the report of the subcommittee overwhelmingly favored the position of the Landowners' Protective Association. Stating that the "business transactions of the Reclamation Service generally in Arizona have been conducted in the twilight zone," the Hensley group lashed out at the Service.[84] The subcommittee from Washington believed that the "'service' has become the master—harsh, cruel, unjust and accountable to no one for its conduct or its expenditures of the farmers' and the Government's money."[85]

Frederick Newell considered the report of the Hensley subcommittee a result of Walter Hensley's being on the "warpath"; the hearings were "so obviously unfair they were regarded almost as a joke."[86] When the final report was released, Newell wrote that it was under the caption, "Newell Says It's a Lie." "The official stenographer in those pre-prohibition days was not in any fit condition to take down the testimony," the director of the Service wrote in his defense, "so that the recorded testimony was largely faked-up."[87] The Hensley subcommittee hearings were rather like a political show, and their recommendations were not taken too seriously, even by the House Committee sponsoring them; Representative Frank Mondell of Wyoming objected so strenuously that he wrote a dissenting minority report. Although committee chairman James Graham of Illinois requested a status quo situation on Salt River, in which reclamation would be on "hold" pending a full investigation, Secretary of Interior Walter Fisher regretted that compliance with such a request would be impossible.[88]

Before the Hensley subcommittee completed its investigations, the elections for the Salt River Valley Water Users' Association took place, and the results were decisive. John Orme captured 75 percent of the votes cast, running strong in all districts; C. B. Wood had only 23 percent of the vote.[89] The particularly vicious report of the 1912 congressional investigation was perhaps taken lightly on Salt River for this reason. The issues that Wood and the Landowners' Protective Association had addressed, however, remained alive despite Orme's overwhelming victory; particularly vital issues were the method of water delivery and the attitude of the Reclamation Service toward the water users.

Farmers in the Salt River Valley had been used to getting their water upon demand. Those with old water rights had not considered the idea of imposing a higher duty of water on the land for more efficient crop production or of using a rotation method in getting their water in order to save on seepage and evaporation. Frederick Newell considered this attitude a selfish one:

> . . . Orme and his associates are very insistent that we shall not measure the water to them this year, but let the system go on, permitting them to have all the water they want at a flat rate. What Orme fears is that we will discover that they can and will get along with much less water than in the past and will extend the project to more lands. He and many of the other old-timers are not particularly desirous of having more people in the Valley, and he cannot understand why he should be called upon to economize water and to go to more expense and trouble in securing such economy simply to provide water for other people.[90]

Newell found it hard "to convince men of this type that there is something higher and more important than their own immediate personal gain."[91]

In this instance, as in others before it, the director of the Reclamation Service believed the question of water delivery to be clear-cut; those who did not follow the Reclamation Service line were "trying to find the drift of public opinion rather than adhere to some fixed principle."[92] John Orme and his followers did not represent the ideas of the majority to Newell, and he thought they had lost touch with the larger interests in the valley. How the director of the Service was able to justify this view, given Orme's great victory in the April elections, is difficult to know; Orme's failure to follow the Service in these matters may have been reason enough for Newell. The attempt continually to feel the pulse of the people rather than consider the big permanent interests, Newell wrote Samuel Adams at Interior, was a weakness; the director of the Service believed this weakness plagued all the water-users' associations.[93]

If leaders of the water-users' associations, like John Orme on Salt River, paid particular attention to local concerns, it was in many ways a response to their inability to influence Reclamation Service decisions. Farmers legitimately complained that the Reclamation Service left them out when policy was formulated; landowners under the projects were subject, ultimately, to Interior Department fiat. Samuel Adams, an Assistant Secretary of Interior, Frederick Newell, Louis Hill, and Howard Reed, the engineer in charge of operation and maintenance on Salt River, "have conducted themselves in a most exclusive way," wrote two members of the Salt River Valley Water Users' Association Board of Governors to the Secretary of Interior, "and have refused and still continue to refuse to hear any suggestions or consult with or in any way regard the judgment or the wishes of the users of the water."[94] This "lofty bearing and unapproachable attitude," the two men complained, was really "the burr under the saddle."[95]

Some of the leaders of the old Landowners' Protective Association, which had faded in importance as a political group after the 1912 election, petitioned Interior Secretary Walter Fisher in October 1912, claiming three serious objections to the Reclamation Service. First, the disgruntled petitioners, a minority in the valley, thought Newell, Hill, Reed, and Adams incompetent, basically because of the tremendous increase in project costs and because of their refusal to deliver water when it was needed, or on demand. Second, those signing the letter of complaint to Fisher believed there was pronounced "discrimination in favor of persons known to be supporters of Colonel Roosevelt in his campaign for the presidency." Dwight Heard, W. J. Murphy, R. S.

Goodrich, and A. J. Chandler all received "special privileges" because they were "Roosevelt shouters." Finally, this group of dissatisfied water users on the Salt River Project objected to the water contract which they would have to sign before being served water from the Roosevelt Reservoir. Not only did the contract violate traditional methods of irrigation and a decree of the court, which set the duty of water at a lower rate than the Reclamation Service used, but it also gave "so much additional discretion to Adams, Hill, Newell, and Reed that they will be enabled to discriminate still further against water users they wish to punish for political or other reasons."[96] While a majority of the water users did not agree that the Reclamation Service was incompetent, they were generally dissatisfied with having no role in managing the project.

Woodrow Wilson defeated William Taft and Theodore Roosevelt in the 1912 elections and became the first Democrat to hold the White House since 1892. His new Secretary of Interior, Franklin K. Lane, a widely respected lawyer from California and a former member of the Interstate Commerce Commission, was immediately confronted with the issues concerning federal reclamation. Frederick Newell was initially cheered by Lane's appointment, writing that "the people in the Reclamation Service welcomed him with great enthusiasm, as it was everywhere assumed that he would look into matters and give support to the efficient and economical work carried on."[97] Lane himself wrote that "ever since I came here Senators and Congressmen have been overwhelming me with curses upon the Reclamation Service, and I thought I ought to find out for myself what the facts were."[98] In order to dig out the facts, Lane gave all involved a chance to tell their story—landowners under the projects, businessmen in the nearby communities, and officials of the Reclamation Service.

In May 1913 in Washington, D.C., Lane called what he thought would be a short conference of water users under federal reclamation projects; it lasted more than two weeks. During this conference water users and the National Federation of Water Users' Associations had the opportunity to tell Lane directly of their troubles. As Newell viewed the situation, Lane "was induced to encourage complaints from the landowners of the Reclamation Projects and was soon flooded with vague statements, distorted and abusive."[99] The Secretary of Interior had decided to ease western discontent with the Reclamation Service, however much Newell disagreed with his methods. In the case of Salt River, he asked for a Reclamation Service investigation of its administrative procedures.

While the Reclamation Service was ordering its project engineer at Yuma, Frank Hanna, to conduct an inquiry into the Salt River

Project, Lane also requested reports on the Salt River Project from other persons in the Department of Interior familiar with the work there. Otis Goodall, a supervisor in the Office of Indian Affairs, told the Secretary after a visit to Phoenix that "at least 70 percent of the water users are dissatisfied."[100] The prevailing uncertainty about repayment for the completed project and the feeling that the Reclamation Service had ignored them had resulted in the landowners' growing discontent with federal reclamation.

Frank Hanna reported much the same to Frederick Newell. The Reclamation Service Inquiry Board on the Salt River Project found the administration of the project in disarray. Howard Reed, the engineer in charge of operation and maintenance, through long familiarity with the project and the landowners under it, had aggrandized his authority and had left the project engineer, C. H. Fitch, somewhat out in the cold. Some landowners did receive special privileges when it came to using water on excess lands or securing government construction on nearby laterals. Hanna recommended that the project be thoroughly reorganized, from the project engineer to the canal superintendents, with strict instructions to follow Reclamation Service regulations.[101]

Two weeks after the Reclamation Service Inquiry Board made its report on the administration at Salt River, Hanna submitted additional information on the status of farmers under the project. He wrote Newell the following:

> The farmers on the Salt River project are generally in the best financial condition of any of the projects of the Service that I have thus far inspected, [but] the wealth of the farmers is not evenly distributed and there are some people on the project who are in hard financial circumstances.[102]

In particular, Hanna noted that approximately 40 percent of the land being farmed under the project was in the hands of tenants; this situation was due to leased school lands, which the state refused to sell, and to the negligible amount of land transfers that had occurred because of high prices and unstable national economic conditions. Newell's investigator thought the project could pay for itself in fifteen years, with no charge made for construction for the first five years so that farmers could make their farms more productive and have time to invest in and develop stock industries. This viewpoint directly challenged Newell's own position that the Service should retain the ten-year period mandated by the Reclamation Act of 1902.

Hanna noted a lack of cooperation between the water users on Salt River and the Reclamation Service, mostly due to the feeling that the "Service is autocratic in its dealing with the farmers."[103] The engineer from the Yuma Project placed responsibility for this situation on Reed, and he noticed a number of inequities taking place, including the construction of new laterals to new lands under the project while old laterals under older lands were neglected, and government delivery of water to landowners holding in excess of 160 acres.

All of these investigations, beginning with the Hensley subcommittee and ending with the Reclamation Service's own inquiry, revealed the Reclamation Service's apparent administrative failure, in greater or lesser degrees. Landowners under the project were in various states of financial chaos, which contributed to a rising number of tenants and mortgages.[104] Much of this unsatisfactory state was attributable to poor administration locally, but another problem was the general unwillingness of Newell and the Service to modify earlier expectations of what reclamation could do on the arid lands.

"Colonization, social development, and all other present needs of the irrigated West, depend on a readjustment by which the farmer can meet the obligations from his land income and yet live as men should," John Widstoe wrote the American Society of Civil Engineers.[105] Yet the Reclamation Service under Newell remained rigidly fixed to the conservation ideals of the Roosevelt years, disregarding both changes in western politics and the depressed state of the national agricultural economy. By insisting that construction payments be made within the ten-year period fixed by law, Newell believed the reclamation fund would function as a revolving fund as originally intended; he refused to see that farmers heavily in debt simply could not make the payments. Instead, he attributed this failure to comply with the law's provisions to a moral failure on the part of the settlers. If a strict payment policy was maintained, the director of the Service thought the "unfit [would be] eliminated, the speculator annihilated" from the projects.[106] He romanticized the farmer of the arid West, seeing in him a pioneer tradition in which "all men are beginners and all are forced to work with a certain degree of equality, and where health, strength and ability count for more than previous social position."[107] This Jeffersonian ethic was resurgent in the Reclamation Service but out of place in the twentieth-century economic world. While the Salt River Valley Water Users' Association saw a little of this agrarian democratic philosophy in its early stages of organization, by 1914 it had disappeared.

Although Newell can be criticized for many of the disappointments on the federal reclamation projects, it would be unfair to judge his position on repayment too harshly. If repayment policy was not well thought out during Newell's tenure as director, it does not mean that Newell was essentially wrong in calling for complete repayment under the terms of the Reclamation Act. The very elements of excessive public subsidy and concentration of resources in the hands of a few, which the act was designed to prevent, became the legacy of the reclamation program through the 1950s and 1960s. In 1914, however, Newell's inflexibility and inability to persuade both western congressmen and water users of the benefits of repayment in ten years precluded any real compromise satisfactory to all parties. This failure to fit the political world in which they operated made Newell and the Service open targets for water-user complaints.

Ashley Schiff wrote of the U.S. Forest Service under Gifford Pinchot that aggressive militancy in its early years contributed to an institutional inflexibility usually seen in an organization of advanced years:

> While the conservation movement invoked the authority of science, it also resorted to highly emotional appeals in an attempt to enlist support for its policies. Unfortunately, the evangelistic approach introduced elements of parochialism and rigidity into analyses of problems, thereby contributing to erosion of the movement's scientific base.[108]

What Schiff called "bureaucratic introversion"—in which an emotional orientation helped conceal possible solutions from view at the same time that it discouraged cooperation with other groups advancing contrary interpretations—struck the Reclamation Service, just as it did the Forest Service.[109] Newell's self-righteous attitude filtered down through the organization and fostered Reclamation Service evangelism while shutting out complaints and suggestions. The Reclamation Service was out of step with the landowners it had earlier converted.

Secretary of Interior Franklin Lane moved quickly to improve the Service's administrative efficiency in order to placate the West. Legislation designed to alter the repayment schedule on the reclamation projects had been introduced nearly every year since 1909, but had been blocked in Congress by the disapproval of the Interior Department. Lane came out in support of the extension movement, and on August 13, 1914, Congress finally passed the Reclamation Extension Act. This act provided that repayment take place over a twenty-year period, instead of the ten-year period originally legislated in 1902, and it constrained the powers of the Secretary of Interior and the Reclamation Service in selecting new projects. From August 1914 on, the Congress would approve both project selection and expenditures.[110]

Franklin Lane praised the Roosevelt administration's construction work in reclamation, but he believed its efforts to consider the human problems had been inadequate. He moved quickly to curtail Newell's influence within the Interior Department and succeeded where other Secretaries had failed, largely due to Newell's lack of resistance and the public's failure to take note of the subtle changes made in the Service. In May 1913 Lane demoted Newell to the position of chief engineer, and, in place of the director position, he created a reclamation commission of five men: three political appointees, whom Lane selected, and two engineers from the Service—Newell and A. P. Davis. The commission resulted in "almost interminable talk," according to Newell, but when he complained to Lane about the inefficiency he saw, Lane suggested that "quite possibly [Newell] was the stumbling block."[111]

In December 1914 Lane removed Newell as chairman of the Reclamation Commission, appointing Davis to the position, and placed the former director in a per-diem job of consulting engineer, with no duties. Frederick Newell, at fifty-three years of age, was bitterly disappointed and discouraged. He left the Reclamation Service, which had been largely his creation, to take a teaching position at the University of Illinois. While continuing to be active in the engineering profession, particularly in his efforts to unite the professional engineering societies into one organization, Newell's role in federal reclamation became more that of elder statesman. He continued to write and lecture on the subject of irrigation, but played no further role in the government bureau organized to institutionalize it.[112]

By 1915 federal reclamation had undergone profound shifts in emphasis and policy. The Jeffersonian philosophy which had imbued the conservation ethic, the reliance on scientific experts to make all the decisions, and the almost religious nature of the reclamation crusade had fallen victim to a complex, twentieth-century economy, western politics, and the growing number of unbelievers within the water-user associations. On the Salt River Project, criticism of the Reclamation Service had largely focused on the extension of repayment issue, as the Salt River Valley Water Users' Association consolidated its power over water users under the project and defused attempts by insurgent landowners to bring other issues to the foreground. The change in local leadership, from Benjamin Fowler to John Orme, in many ways suggested what Frederick Newell's fate ultimately became; it took someone of Franklin Lane's political party and persuasion, as well as his forceful leadership, to effect nationally what local water users had done at Salt River.

Reclamation was now a business, not a crusade. Extension of time for repayment was but the first issue to suggest that the Reclamation Service must also view it as a business by recognizing the conditions which made projects successful. Secretary of Interior Lane opened the door for change in federal reclamation policy with his support of the extension issue; he did not anticipate the multitude of requests for reconsideration of other aspects of reclamation policy that would follow.

From Conflict
to Cooperation

Secretary of Interior Franklin K. Lane had not anticipated that the reclamation conference he called in May 1913 would last more than two weeks, nor had he expected federal project water users to express such bitter opposition to the U.S. Reclamation Service. Most delegates to the conference had two main goals: to discredit certain Reclamation Service personnel (primarily Frederick Newell), and to achieve Lane's support for changes in reclamation policy. These policy changes included not only extension of time for repayment, but also increased federal contribution to the cost of the projects, an investigation into the construction charges for the purpose of eliminating excessive expenditures, and transfer of project operations to the water users.[1]

The conference convinced the Secretary that the Service had made mistakes and that reclamation policy needed modification. Lane, who had committed himself to easing the tensions between the water users and the government, sought a means to implement many of the delegates' demands without infringing upon reasonable Reclamation Service policies. He fastened upon the idea of creating independent boards of review to examine key issues in federal reclamation; in this way, the Secretary of Interior would receive a balanced assessment of each group's views.[2]

Lane's willingness to place key issues, such as the amount to be charged water users for project construction, within independent boards did much to alleviate some of the bad feelings between water-users' associations and the Reclamation Service. Water users' de-

mands for changes in reclamation policy were not completely
accepted, but Secretary Lane set in motion a process to include project landowners in reclamation decision making; their increased participation seemed to satisfy all but the most disgruntled.

The reexamination of reclamation policy and practices which
Lane directed his department to carry out also included a review of
the government's relationship to the projects. The change in federal
reclamation in the post-Newell years was one of both substance and
style. The reclamation crusade with its "gospel of efficiency" tended
to look out of place next to cost overruns and expensive acreage costs
for project participants. The use of agricultural and economic experts
in planning the projects seemed more important by 1915 than it had
thirteen years earlier. The water-users' associations rejected the
engineers' earlier perceptions that reclamation projects were merely
technical undertakings requiring only technical expertise to make
them successful. Instead, the farmers and landowners paying the
reclamation charges asked the Reclamation Service to treat them as
full partners.

John Orme and the rest of the Salt River Valley Water Users'
Association welcomed the "new" reclamation policy of Franklin Lane
because it promised to give greater attention to farmers' actual problems. They were negotiators with the Reclamation Service now, not
their puppets. The Salt River Valley Water Users' Association fashioned the debate on what its relationship with the Service would be: it
focused on whether the government was a contractor or a benefactor.
Although this question seemed impossible to resolve to everyone's
satisfaction, both Secretary Lane and the Association indicated their
determination to maintain their newly found harmony.

THE KENT DECREE

On the Salt River Project, the completion of both the Roosevelt
Dam in 1911 and the power facilities in 1912 – 1913 meant that by the
time of the conference the project should officially open; the opening would signify the beginning of repayment. Before the project
could be opened and public notice issued, however, the government
had to resolve the nagging problem of the amount of acreage to be
included within the project and how much of the final costs the water
users would have to repay. In order to find answers to these questions, the Interior Department authorized the formation of two independent boards; the Board of Survey, to determine the politically
sensitive issue of which lands to include within the project boundaries,
and the Board of Cost Review, to examine the accounting books

of the Reclamation Service at Salt River and fix the final cost of the project.

When the Association's creators first developed their plans in 1902 – 1903, they intentionally left the designation of member lands to the Secretary of Interior. The Articles of Incorporation of the Salt River Valley Water Users' Association provided only for inclusion of sufficient acreage which could be irrigated from the estimated water supply; cultivation of land was the dominant criterion. The Association itself did not have the power to allot shares; this successfully removed from the group political responsibility for admitting or excluding lands within the valley. Any criticism from landowners for the exclusion of subscribed land from the final boundaries of the project would have to be directed at the Secretary, not the leaders of the Association. As Benjamin Fowler had written in 1909, "the whole risk of the chance was left to the subscriber as the Association obviously could neither guarantee that he would be allotted shares or object to allotment of shares to him."[3]

In 1905 the Board of Governors of the water-users' association began to believe that priority of water right should play an important role in allotting membership shares. The *Hurley v. Abbott* suit, initiated in 1904 – 1905 to adjudicate the rights to use the Salt River, might also apply to the lands in the valley. By date of earliest cultivation, the government could decide upon the member lands. The Association determined to press for the conclusion of the suit as its chief means of collecting the information necessary for the Secretary of Interior to decide membership priority.[4]

Not everyone in the valley supported the *Hurley v. Abbott* suit as the best means to determine either water rights or membership shares in the Association. Many landowners believed the friendly suit to settle the issue of water rights was too expensive, too time consuming, and ill considered. They thought the final result of the litigation would only resolve Patrick Hurley's claim, not all rights to the river.[5] In this view at least two prominent valley attorneys, Judge Webster Street and Judge C. F. Ainsworth, supported them.[6]

Benjamin Fowler, recognizing the "active and bitter opposition" to the suit, wrote Arthur Davis of the Reclamation Service that he sought to find "some other way, *if it is possible*, by which these rights can be adjudicated."[7] For this purpose, the Association's Board of Governors appointed a Committee of Ten "to ascertain the best means of adjusting the rights to the use of irrigating water . . . irrespective of the present action brought by *Hurley v. Abbott*."[8] The Committee of Ten recommended forming a Committee of Sixteen, to be appointed by the president of the Association and chairman of the

Council, which would thoroughly investigate the claims of water users within, or in the vicinity of, the project. With this information, the Committee of Sixteen would suggest stipulations to the court for the *Hurley v. Abbott* suit. Inclusion of the Committee's proposal as a stipulation in the court decision would give the authority of law and save a considerable expense.

The Committee's plan, in brief, based water rights on how much of the water received between 1890 and 1905 had actually been used. Using a "stepladder plan," the various canals would receive from the Association the amount of water due the lands irrigated from them; the landowners under each canal would have to adjust among themselves their "carriage rights" in the canal. The Pima Indians living on the north side of the river, whose reservation contained lands irrigated from the Arizona Canal, were entitled to and received under this plan 500 inches of water at all stages of the river.[9] They had taken this amount of water for cultivation of their land for more than forty years, and the Committee believed this prior right to be above all others.

Despite this attempt to achieve consensus, the Committee of Sixteen's plan received little support from individual water users because, among other reasons, it paid scant attention to individual claims to flood water, and landowners refused the required three-fourths approval.[10] The water users in the valley could not agree whether to press the friendly suit, defer to the government by having the Secretary of Interior determine all rights claimed (which the government did not want to do), or work out the various claims by individual contract with the Association.

The Reclamation Service was quite concerned with the apparent inability of the water users to stop their bickering; the government had to be protected against litigation if it was to continue developing the project. Both Arthur P. Davis and Morris Bien of the Service went to Phoenix in late July 1906 to discuss the situation with the Association's Board of Governors. Although both men thought an adjustment of the water rights by contracts was preferable to the lawsuit, both were also convinced it would be impossible to secure a binding adjustment of rights from them. The Reclamation Service thought the *Hurley v. Abbott* suit the only available means to safeguard the United States in its operations under the Reclamation Act; without it, the Service could not store any water behind the gates of Roosevelt Dam. "The matter is of extreme importance to the Reclamation Service," Davis wrote Benjamin Fowler, "as the progress in this case must guide its future policy."[11] In February 1907, the Board of Governors again endorsed the continuation of the *Hurley v. Abbott* suit.[12]

The *Hurley v. Abbott* suit was very difficult to bring to trial. Every one of the 4,800 defendants besides Charles Abbott had to file a statement with the court regarding the amount of land each had cultivated and the year in which each had first put water to a beneficial use upon the lands. Many had to hire attorneys, and for those who were nonresident landowners, the suit required a trip to Phoenix. It was no surprise to Judge Edward Kent, who was sitting as district judge of the Third Judicial District Court in Maricopa County, that he had received so few statements, while the number of disclaimers, which a defendant used to show that he was not obligated to answer, grew.

Kent was an outsider to the valley, and this may have contributed to the reluctance on the part of some to become involved in the case. President Roosevelt had selected Edward Kent, a successful lawyer (educated at Harvard and Columbia universities) and a leading Colorado Republican, to be Chief Justice of the Arizona Territory Supreme Court in 1902. Roosevelt had been unhappy with the political quarreling among Republicans in Arizona and had turned to Kent to restore order. Although nearly everyone in the valley grew to respect Judge Kent's decisions, he had faced much skepticism at the outset of the *Hurley v. Abbott* suit.[13]

While many in the valley believed the suit would only resolve Patrick Hurley's claim, Judge Kent believed he could determine the rights of all the parties who were defendants in the suit and enter a decree resolving these rights. A number of valley attorneys, however, advised their clients that a final adjudication could not be had in the *Hurley v. Abbott* case. Since a decree of the court would deprive the many who were not filing of their rights because they had acted in good faith upon the advice of their attorneys, Judge Kent suggested to Louis Hill and C. S. Witbeck of the Reclamation Service that the government file an interpleader in the case. This action by the United States would technically compel all the parties to assert their rights. Since the government had purchased the northside canal system on behalf of the Association for the Salt River Project, it was an interested party, although it claimed no right to water. Joseph Kibbey also urged the government to interplead. Hill and Kent called in for consultation J. L. B. Alexander, the U. S. Attorney for Arizona, and Alexander agreed with the two men that it was appropriate for the government to become involved. On June 10, 1907, Alexander filed with the court, on behalf of the United States, a motion to interplead; Kent granted the motion.

What Judge Kent, Louis Hill, and Joseph Kibbey had hoped for slowly began to take shape: more answers were filed, due to the government's involvement, and the case was brought to trial in 1907 –

1908. Judge Edward Kent handed down his decision in the *Hurley v. Abbott* case, known as the Kent Decree, on March 1, 1910. In what was to become the most important water-rights case in the Salt River Valley, Kent not only determined each acre's prior right to use the normal flow of Salt River, but also classified the land in the valley according to date of cultivation.[14]

Kent's method for classifying lands was simple. Those lands with old water rights, which had been continuously cultivated, were termed "Class A"; owners of these lands would have the first opportunity to become members of the Salt River Project. Kent placed those lands with some right to flood water, which had been cultivated prior to (but not after) 1903, next in line for inclusion within the project; these lands were termed "Class B." Those lands which had no right to the water and which had never been cultivated were termed "Class C"; these lands would be considered for inclusion last. Judge Kent's arrangement of the valley lands into three classes did not automatically give the Class A and B lands a project reservoir right, but, according to the Judge, it did allow them preference.[15]

THE BOARD OF SURVEY

The Kent Decree provided a framework for selecting project lands, but it did not completely settle the membership dispute. In August 1913 Assistant Secretary of Interior A. A. Jones wrote the Association that recent Reclamation Service maps showing the irrigable area of the valley as determined by the Kent Decree revealed a larger acreage than could be served water from the storage reservoir. "It is therefore necessary," noted Jones, "to somewhat arbitrarily select certain lands which will be watered and reject others."[16] Jones suggested creation of a small committee or board to review the situation and mark on the maps which lands would be included. The following principles, he suggested, should guide the board:

(1) Lands selected should be in as compact a body as possible;

(2) Preference should be given to lands of highest productivity;

(3) In the case of the small landowners, the man living upon his land and cultivating it should be given first consideration.[17]

The Association's Board of Governors agreed with Assistant Secretary Jones's suggestion in principle, and offered its own idea on how to compose the board: the Board of Governors should select one representative, the Reclamation Service another, and the third member, acting as chairman, would be a mutual selection from outside the state. Secretary of Interior Franklin Lane agreed to this proposal.

The Board selected Frank Parker, former secretary of the Association, as its representative.[18]

Although the chairman of the board was to be impartial in all matters pertaining to the project (hence the requirement that he be from another state), John Orme suggested to both Frederick Newell and Secretary of Interior Lane that Frank Hanna fill this position.[19] Hanna, previously the Reclamation Service's project engineer at Yuma and chairman of the 1913 Reclamation Service Inquiry Board investigating the administration of the Salt River Project, was now manager on the Boise, Idaho, project. While he fit the requirement of being a nonresident, the Association's solicitation somewhat thwarted the spirit of the provision. Lane, however, agreed to Orme's request and appointed Hanna as chairman of the Salt River Project Board of Survey.[20]

The Reclamation Service originally intended to appoint J. E. Sprague, an engineer on Salt River, as its representative to the Board. Further discussions with Charles Fitch, project manager at Phoenix, persuaded Arthur Davis and Frederick Newell to select William Farish instead.[21] What Fitch said is not known, but it is likely that the project manager was concerned that the representative be acceptable to the Association. Since the majority of the Board of Governors at that time was composed of "prior righters," whose main concern was limiting the acreage to a low figure, the selection of Farish, who supported the position of that group, was likely to be well regarded.[22]

Farish was indeed acceptable to the Board of Governors. "This appointment will meet with the hearty endorsement of the Board of Governors," Orme wrote Arthur Davis in late October 1913. The Board had considered "unofficially" asking the Service to appoint Farish, but "felt they would not be justified in formally naming any more members than they had done."[23] Although the water users technically had only one representative on the Board of Survey, in reality they approved of all three members. Secretary Lane's new spirit of cooperation between the water users and the Reclamation Service was evident at last.

Louis Hill, former project manager at Salt River and now supervising engineer of the Service's southern division, and Frederick Newell expressed some concern, however, over the Survey Board's bias in favor of prior righters. Hill strongly recommended to Newell that the first meeting of the Board of Survey be postponed until after the rainy season; otherwise, with the reservoir low, the landowners with old water rights might pressure the Survey Board into excluding from irrigation more acreage than necessary. "I hardly think that you could get the prior righters today to use good judgement in studying

the question," Hill wrote Newell; "they only realize that the amount
has been depleted [in the reservoir] and do not seem to have any idea
that this will ever be replenished."[24] While Newell seemed to agree
with Hill on the matter of postponing the meeting of the Survey
Board, the Reclamation Service acknowledged a scheduling conflict;
Hanna was already on his way to Phoenix. The Board of Survey
would meet at the end of November 1913, as planned, and Hill would
have to send all his material on the valley's water supply to Phoenix
by then.[25]

The Board of Survey held daily meetings from November 18
through December 9, 1913. Although it prepared a preliminary
report on its findings, Hanna believed the inquiry to be incomplete.
He believed the Board needed more information regarding the cultivated and occupied lands, the size of the individual holdings, and
their water rights classification before a final delimiting of the project
took place. The chairman of the Survey Board recommended
adjourning until this information became available.[26] At the same
time, several legal questions bothered Hanna, and he thought the
Board needed to anwer them before selecting or rejecting any lands.
Fundamentally, they all focused on the legal and moral strength of
the Kent Decree as the basis for choosing lands entitled to participate
in the project.[27]

The Reclamation Commission, which consisted of Frederick Newell and Arthur Davis as the engineers, I. D. O'Donnell as superinten-
dent of irrigation, Will R. King as chief counsel, and W. A. Ryan as
comptroller (the last three were Secretary Lane's appointees),
reviewed Hanna's report and questions, and formulated new selection guidelines to submit to the water users for comments. The Survey Board had initially favored limiting the total acreage to 170,000;
the Reclamation Commission raised the limit to 175,000 acres.[28]

The most controversial of all the Commission's recommendations, however, was its response to Hanna's questions regarding
whether it was appropriate for the Reclamation Service to implement
the Kent Decree. The Reclamation Commission created new guidelines, using Judge Kent's land classification system, a notion of fair
play, and the cultivation criterion of the Association's Articles of
Incorporation.[29] Basically, the Commission wanted to limit landowners of cultivated Class A and B lands to project membership for
160 acres. In this way the Reclamation Commissioners hoped to
defuse a potentially volatile situation by spreading the membership
lands among many landowners holding various classes of land. They
hoped this course would prevent landowners holding lands for speculative purposes from becoming project members before those who

were genuine farmers. Under no conditions would the Commission accept any uncultivated and unsubscribed land into the storage project.[30] Coincidentally, these new principles for selection were most favorable to the landowners who held lands with prior rights.

Delimiting the project was destined to be unpopular with some, but the Board of Survey and the Reclamation Commission were optimistic about their actions. While they eliminated from the project lands not fitting the government requirements, they also recommended that the Association develop new sources of supply. By building Horseshoe Dam on the Verde River and by constructing pumping plants, eventually there would be enough water to serve all the subscribed land in the valley.[31]

The Board of Survey published these guidelines for selecting lands under the Salt River Project on January 15, 1914, and distributed copies to landowners in the valley. Public meetings to discuss the limitation plan with I. D. O'Donnell and Arthur Davis of the Reclamation Commission as well as with the Board of Survey and officers of the Association were set for March 13 and 14, 1914. The only significant change that the Board of Survey made in the Reclamation Commission's recommendations was to increase the total estimated project acreage to about 180,000 acres including townsite and school lands; of the 211,000 acres of irrigable land subscribed to the Association and within the Board of Survey boundaries at that time, 31,000 would have to be excluded. The excluded lands included those not fitting the Reclamation Commission's guidelines, those not cultivated within the previous three years, and state school lands.[32]

Fewer landowners in the valley turned out for the meetings than either John Orme or Arthur Davis expected; they interpreted this lack of response to mean that there was little dissatisfaction with the arrangements of the Board of Survey. It was predictable that those holding uncultivated lands—largely for speculative purposes—would be unhappy with the preferences outlined by the Board, and a few, like Ralph Murphy, complained that the project should be held open until an adequate water supply was developed for all the lands. But in the main, valley landowners were satisfied that the best job possible had been done, given the nature of the task.[33]

It was the beginning of an era of collaboration between the water users and the Reclamation Service. No one expressed this new feeling better than Arthur P. Davis:

There has been too much disregard of the water users; we do not mean of their material interests, but of their personal interest in the project. They have been asked to take too much for granted and to trust blindly to the scientific skill and technical knowledge of the members of the service.

Many things have been done which they have not understood, though they have been done right. And some things have been done wrong which might have been avoided if the water users had been taken into the confidence of the reclamation officials. If a man is having a house built, though he may know nothing of architecture and little of construction, he has certain ideas, for reasons which the architect may not appreciate, he would like to have incorporated into the structure.[34]

Both Davis and I. D. O'Donnell of the Reclamation Commission enjoyed the water users' hearty welcomes, and farmers particularly appreciated O'Donnell's visit, as he provided them with advice on better farming and securing larger markets for their crops.[35]

If there was one person responsible for the changed relationship between the Reclamation Service and the Salt River Valley Water Users' Association, which had deteriorated in the last years of Newell's tenure as director, it was Secretary of Interior Franklin Lane. Lane was an ambitious man, determined to put his own imprint on the department. Two themes underlay Lane's conservation philosophy: greater development and greater democracy. While not fundamentally different from the beliefs of Walter Fisher or Gifford Pinchot, whom he continued to consult on matters of concern to them, Lane's ideas regarding the public domain were tested not by the rational, scientific method, but by their political acceptance in the West. For this reason, as well as for his personality, which was described as "magnetic," President Wilson's first Secretary of Interior was very popular with westerners in all walks of life and especially with the water users on the federal projects.[36] He "shaped the affairs of the reclamation service so as to give the fullest hearing to the expression of the wishes and desires of . . . the water users."[37] Work had been undertaken and policies decided upon without consultation between the officers of the government and those of the Association before Lane came to office; now, "by direct orders of the Secretary," the administrative bodies of the water-users' associations reviewed all of these matters.[38]

The local leadership of the Salt River Valley Water Users' Association delighted in the turn of events, as did most of the landowners under the project. Even C. B. Wood, the former candidate for president of the water users on the Landowners' Protective Association ticket, approved the Board of Survey report and the new cooperative efforts of the Service.[39] The Board of Governors enthusiastically endorsed the government recommendations to construct a storage reservoir on the Verde River and to install pumping plants to increase the developed water supply, and agreed to put them to an immediate vote by the water users.[40]

The Secretary of Interior reviewed the final report of the Board of Survey, which essentially followed the same form as the preliminary one except for small modifications of the boundary line, in August 1914, and approved it on November 14, 1914.[41] From this date to the early 1920s, those owners of uncultivated land within the reservoir district boundaries that were not included in the project petitioned the Association and the Secretary of Interior for admittance. When the reservoir was full, the owners of these lands rented water for irrigation of their crops, but this supply was only temporary water; rental contracts were subject to renewal or cancellation each year. Owners of fragmentary Class A lands—small, odd-shaped parcels adjacent to member lands, but not included in the final report because of their erroneous classification as uncultivated lands—were successful in having a second Board of Survey include them permanently within the project in 1916.[42]

In addition to the fragmentary Class A lands, there were about 23,000 acres of land that were not included within the project, although they were located within the reservoir district boundaries. The owners of these so-called "dry lands" also appealed to the Association and the Secretary of Interior for admittance to the project, but were not accepted until an additional water supply was developed in the early 1920s.[43]

Fixing 180,000 acres as the amount of land to be served reservoir water on a continuing basis finally resolved the conflict over membership priorities that had been raised in 1903 by Dwight Heard and the minority report. Although it had been a bitter issue between those with old water rights and new landowners in the early years of the Association, by 1914 it ceased to have the same emotional appeal. This change was due in large part to Secretary Lane's board of review procedure. By bringing the water users into the decision-making process through representation on the board and through public hearings, the landowners directly participated in the delimiting of the project. The final decision, of course, was the Secretary's, but in this instance, Lane successfully eliminated the water users' complaints of Reclamation Service tyranny.

THE BOARD OF COST REVIEW

In the same spirit of cooperation which imbued the proceedings of the Board of Survey, Secretary of Interior Lane decided to review the costs of constructing the projects; this process would satisfy the

one outstanding grievance among the water users. Lane planned to
review the charges to the water users under the federal projects and
to examine the justice of the repayment assessment. He told the water
users that this review was dependent, however, on their agreement
that they would pay in full the resulting final costs.[44] The selection
process for the Board of Cost Review was similar to that for the Board
of Survey: one member to be selected by the Association, one by the
Reclamation Service, and the chairman to be an independent
engineer, agreed upon by both parties.

The Association, hoping to avoid friction with the Service and to
facilitate the work of the Board, decided to employ an independent
engineer, rather than to appoint one of its own members. As John
Orme said of the water-users' position in the matter, "We desire to see
the United States Reclamation Service efficiency increased, but not
the Service destroyed."[45] Moreover, reevaluation of the project costs
required some expertise in both technical and administrative aspects
of large construction work. Although the Association had usually
relied on the engineering judgment of the Reclamation Service for its
technical information, in this review procedure it seemed best to hire
an Association advocate. The water users selected Fred A. Jones of
Texas, a civil and electrical engineer with construction experience in
both power stations and reservoirs.[46]

The Reclamation Service appointed Frank Hanna, the Salt River
Project's perennial investigating engineer, as its representative.
Hanna, who had replaced Louis Hill as supervising engineer of the
southern division in February 1914, viewed the project as the biggest
and most important of all those under his purview.[47] Hanna, furthermore, understood the local conditions and local leaders, and was well
regarded in the valley.

The independent engineer was Thomas U. Taylor, dean of
engineering at the University of Texas and a former engineer for the
U.S. Geological Survey's Hydrographic Branch. Although Taylor was
chosen as the third man and, thus, would serve as chairman, he had
also applied to the Association to serve as its representative on the
Board of Cost Review.[48] The chosen representatives of the Board of
Cost Review were all, therefore, more than acceptable to the Association.

Secretary of Interior Lane instructed the local Board of Cost
Review to ascertain the proper construction cost to be collected under
the terms of the Reclamation Act, to fix the proper charges on projects where they had not been announced and where it was practicable
to do so, and to determine whether any expenditure had been
unnecessary.[49]

Jones, the representative of the Association, interpreted this last task to mean that the local Board of Review should determine the *proper value* of the works. He wanted to create on paper a "substitute system" as a measure of comparison, in which a theoretical project would serve as a base by which mistakes and errors in the actual project might be judged.[50] The Association took the position that the construction work on the Salt River Project should be analyzed as thoroughly as any business or construction contract. While the water users appreciated that mistakes were bound to occur on the Salt River Project, one of the first projects constructed, they also were of the opinion that the primary reason behind the cost overruns was that the construction work performed by the Service had been done without any contract or fixed percentages of overhead.[51]

The local Board of Cost Review held public hearings throughout June 1915, although the technical nature of the work kept attendance down. The three engineers examined at least fourteen categories of construction under the project, ranging from the building of the storage works, power system, diversion works, and canal systems to telephone lines and irrigation wells; operation and maintenance were also included.[52]

Jones and Hanna, who basically provided the differing analyses of the charges, while Taylor served as arbiter of evidence, agreed on several points. Some items were more expensively constructed than necessary, especially the power canal and the hydraulic sluice gates. They did not agree, however, on Jones's method of creating an imaginary substitute system as the basis for comparison. To Hanna, this ignored the difficult problems of terrain, location, transportation, climate, and maintaining an adequate labor force at the remote reservoir site that the Reclamation Service had encountered. Even the heavy railroad work of the transcontinental period of U.S. history provided too poor an analog on which to create a substitute system on paper. The Reclamation Service engineer was also of the opinion that Jones performed his calculations a bit hastily.[53]

Because of this fundamental difference, the Board of Cost Review could not submit a unanimous report; Jones and Taylor signed the majority report and Hanna a minority report. Of course, the most serious point of disagreement was over the amount to be repaid to the United States for building the Salt River Project. Jones and Taylor figured the cost of the project (as of June 1, 1915) at about $13 million. They found that the books and records of the work showed $3.5 million worth of defective construction, excessive expenses, and bad management, which should be deducted from the total cost. After subtracting the revenues and credits from water rentals and power sales, Jones and Taylor estimated that the water users owed the government $7.2 million.[54]

Hanna figured the total cost of the project to be nearly the same as Jones and Taylor—about $13 million. However, he found only about $640,000 worth of defective construction and excessive costs. After subtracting the revenues and credits, which Hanna calculated a little higher than the other two engineers, his minority report suggested the landowners on the Salt River Project had to repay the government $9.5 million.[55]

The difference between the majority and minority figures essentially focused on the notion of value. While Jones and Taylor evaluated items like the power canal on the basis of how it *could* have been built, Hanna looked at its actual cost and benefits. No matter what the canal cost, Frank Hanna believed that the expense was not excessive if the water users derived substantial benefit from it. Rather than measure it against a *possible* power canal, the representative of the Reclamation Service viewed its expense within the total context of the alternative power systems available when construction occurred: high-priced oil and higher freighting costs. As the power canal's benefits outweighed this latter estimated charge, Hanna decided it to be a legitimate charge against the water users.

The process of cost review that Franklin Lane had envisioned included local Boards of Review and a Central Board, which would examine the findings of the local reports and adjust any differences. The local Board of Review on the Salt River Project mailed its reports to Elwood Mead, an expert on land reclamation and settlement and now chairman of the Central Board of Cost Review, in the summer of 1915. Mead, as a member of the Department of Agriculture's Irrigation Investigations at the turn of the century, had investigated and reviewed reclamation possibilities on Salt River and, since then, had been highly critical of the Reclamation Service; this criticism had as much to do with bureaucratic in-fighting as it did with differing points of view.[56] The Cental Board of Cost Review had two other members besides Mead: William Marshall, the retired general from the Army Corps of Engineers who had also served on the Board of Army Engineers that had investigated reclamation projects in 1911, and I. D. O'Donnell of the Reclamation Commission. All three men had extensive knowledge of conditions on Salt River.

Despite the emphasis on dollars, the central question involved in adjusting the final cost of the Salt River Project was the relationship between the Association and the government. The water users—perhaps under the tutelage of Fred Jones, who focused on an idealistic, "proper" value of the project—defined that relationship as one of owner to contractor.[57] The Association's obligation to the government was, under this interpretation, to pay only the *"proper"* cost, rather than the actual cost. Elwood Mead and the other members of the Central Board disagreed completely. "The Government was regarded as a benefactor rather than a contractor," Mead wrote in their report to Secretary of Interior Lane, "and it maintained this role throughout the whole of the construction period."[58]

If there had been poor administration, defective construction, or excessive costs, Mead did not think the government was responsible. Reclamation of the arid lands was, after all, an experiment. The Reclamation Service was *not*, Mead emphasized, an ordinary contractor working for profit. Such a profit-oriented contractor would assume risks, guarantee the cheapest possible work and the infallibility of its engineers. A contractor working for monetary gain would also be punished by not receiving full payment if it failed to meet its obligations.[59] The Reclamation Service was only the conduit through which the federal government assisted the Salt River Valley farmers in building their project.

If the results of the completed reclamation project at Salt River were worth the final cost, no matter what errors had occurred or what experiment had failed, the Central Board of Cost Review believed that the landowners under the project should pay the price, not the public.[60] Still, the Central Board thought $382,408 should be deducted from the total cost "due to works of an experimental nature which failed and were abandoned [chiefly the hydraulic sluice gates], for material purchased for use elsewhere [by O'Rourke's construction company], and for administrative expenses of the Washington office."[61]

Unlike Fred Jones and Thomas Taylor, who had compared costs on Salt River to some imaginary project, the Central Board of Cost Review sided with Frank Hanna's interpretation. Furthermore, it viewed the construction charges within the larger perspective of agricultural profits and enhanced land values in the Salt River Valley. Homebuilding in the arid West could not be achieved under the normal process of doing business, contrary to earlier beliefs by Frederick Newell and the Congress. The critical problem on Salt River, according to Elwood Mead, was not unfair construction costs as much as it was inflated land prices.[62]

In November 1915 the Reclamation Commission received the Salt River Project report of the Central Board of Cost Review (which included the local board's report) for its examination and opinion. The Commission surprised nearly everyone by rejecting both reports. In deciding not to follow the recommendation of either board of review, but to adhere to the Reclamation Service book cost of the project, Arthur P. Davis had this to say:

I cannot conceive that any official connected with the Reclamation Service could have the hardihood to recommend elimination of a dollar of the cost of the project as it appeared in the books.[63]

To disallow any of the charges would be nothing less than admission by the Service of its technical and administrative errors. Since Reclamation Service officials viewed their own uniqueness as stemming from technical and scientific expertise, such an admission would be nearly impossible for them to countenance. In addition, Will King, the Service's chief counsel, was convinced that eliminating any charges for the project would be against the law.

Rather than accept the figure of the Central Board of Cost Review, the Reclamation Commission chose to raise the total cost to about $11 million, with charges of $64 per acre. Commission members justified this increase because of continuing construction work on the Granite Reef and Roosevelt dams; apparently, they did not trust the Association to repay more than the final cost which would be determined at the issuing of public notice. The Reclamation Commission decided therefore, to issue public notice with the new charges as soon as possible.[64]

The Association was outraged over the actions of the Reclamation Commission. Irritated initially by the Central Board's failure to allow it a hearing on the Local Board of Review's report, and then faced with rejection of both revaluation reports, the Association Board of Governors determined to send representatives to Washington. They would present the Association's case before the Reclamation Commission, the Secretary of Interior, and, if necessary, the Congress. The Board of Governors had never officially been notified that the Salt River Project was completed or that public notice was to be issued, yet the government circulated a carbon draft of the public notice in the Phoenix office of the Reclamation Service's district counsel as early as November 1915. Joseph Kibbey, who, after renewed and repeated requests by the Board of Governors, was again the Association's legal counsel, and John Orme felt betrayed; the fragile rebuilding of cooperative relations by Secretary Lane was endangered.[65]

Since the Reclamation Commission would not budge from its stance on repayment costs, Orme and Kibbey appealed to Lane. After a thorough examination of both reports, during which the Secretary of Interior seemed to rely greatly upon the opinion of Elwood Mead, Lane overruled the Commission. He accepted the report of the Central Board of Cost Review and fixed the final amount to be repaid at $10,279,191; the charge per acre would be $60. He also indicated that the Salt River Project should now be turned over to the water users of the valley, perhaps revealing both his own frustration with reclamation problems and preoccupation with international events.[66]

TRANSFER OF PROJECT OPERATIONS
TO THE WATER USERS

When Franklin Lane had become Secretary of Interior, he had sought to remove federal reclamation from the grips of government paternalism and Reclamation Service politics. He wanted to return control of the projects to the landowners wherever possible. The Secretary realized that it was the landowner on the project who would have to work diligently and through difficult times to repay his share of the costs of federal reclamation, not the engineers of the Service. Lane had kept his word to the water users when he had promised a thorough review of project costs; he expected the landowners to uphold their agreement to pay.

The members of the Association's Board of Governors, who had earlier been dissatisfied with the report of the Central Board of Review, reluctantly accepted the Secretary's decision; compared to the Reclamation Commission's intentions, the Central Board's small reduction in costs was still relief. Yet the belief that the Service had swindled the water users on final costs to be repaid persisted in the valley. *The Chandler Arizonan* editorialized that:

> At no time has the government conceded a single point to the men who are trying to wrest a living from the irrigable farms of the valley. Time and again has the Reclamation Service been used by youthful engineers with little actual experience as the experimental grounds for good jobs with corporations who demand ability . . . .[67]

Although the Service was absolutely justified in holding to its view of the government as benefactor rather than contractor, the more than $3 million difference between the reports of the two Boards of Cost Review continued to be a source of local agitation.

The Salt River Valley Water Users' Association had not advocated taking over management of the project before 1917, when Secretary Lane insisted the project be turned over to the water users. The Reclamation Commission, however, had begun to create irrigation districts to replace water-users' associations. This impetus, along with the excellent agricultural profits resulting from World War I and the superb state of the reservoir, changed the minds of many local residents.[68] A reinterpretation of reclamation policy—which allowed profits from the sale of power to be used in any way the water users

wanted, including application of these profits against the general
project debt—also helped persuade the Board of Governors to consider Lane's timely offer.[69]

Secretary Lane, who was quite anxious to "get rid of the project,"
offered to turn it over to the Association, which could then use the
power receipts in "any way [it] saw fit," if it would pay for all future
expenditures and repay the project cost according to the Central
Board of Review's figure in the twenty-year period allowed. Lane had
written in 1913 that he "was not going to be a party to gold-bricking
the poor devil of a farmer," but Elwood Mead had assured him the
final cost of $10.2 million could be repaid in twenty years. Lane's offer
was directly contrary to Arthur Davis's recommendations; however,
Joseph Kibbey and John Orme thought the water users would
approve such a contract.[70]

Arthur Davis and Will King, the Reclamation Service's chief legal
counsel, were not at all pleased with the decision by the Secretary of
Interior to turn over the project to the Salt River Valley Water Users'
Association. The Secretary's plan would give away the "only security
we have for the repayment of a debt which their attorney has publicly
denounced as unjust and oppressive."[71] Both Davis and King found
Lane's proposal "so destructive of the spirit and purpose of the Reclamation laws that we cannot accede thereto."[72] Lane, who was
unhappy with the Reclamation Commission's rejection of the Central
Board of Cost Review's report and the resulting distrust that it caused
within the Association's Board of Governors, ignored these cries of
alarm from the Reclamation Service and proceeded with his proposal
to the water users.

The Salt River Valley Water Users' Association and the government tentatively agreed to a contract in which the Salt River Project
would be turned over to the Association and be operated, maintained,
and managed by the water users. The water users would repay the
government according to the terms of the Reclamation Extension Act
(1914), which included provisions both for a twenty-year repayment
period under graduated terms and for the Secretary of Interior's
retaining authority to approve substantial changes in the works.[73]

After all the earlier debate and discussion about the water users'
control of the project, the actual process by which they gained control
received little attention in the Salt River Valley. World War I, the
draft, and local, sometimes violent, labor disputes dominated the
news.[74] Since "practically all the water users [were] in favor of the
Association taking over [the project]," the limited attention the issue
received in the press may also have been due to the lack of controversy.[75] Economic conditions on Salt River had never been as good as

they were during 1916 – 1917; farmers conservatively estimated agricultural revenue for 1917 at over $21 million, and "Alfalfa was King, Cotton was Queen, and every Dairy Cow was a Princess."[76] John Orme, president of the water-users' association, estimated his net profit on seventy acres planted with wheat at $100 per acre.[77] The reservoir had filled to capacity and spilled surplus water in 1916 and, although the level of water stored behind the dam was not quite as high in 1917, the capacity of the Roosevelt Dam insured a good supply for several years. It was no wonder the water users were somewhat complacent about transfer of the project to their control.

Charles Van der Veer, secretary of the Association, wanted the 3,632 individual voters on the project to make their desire to manage it known to Washington, since a small voter turnout would give the "element in the Service opposing the surrender of the project to the water users . . . an argument in their favor because of the apparent lack of interest here."[78] Despite Van der Veer's request that as many as possible of the 167,068 acres subscribed to the Association go on record in support of the project transfer, a small vote took place: 48,883 "acre-votes" were in favor of the contract, while 3,100 were against the transfer.[79]

The Reclamation Service immediately raised a question on whether the election to transfer the project management was a valid one, since a majority of the acreage signed up under the Association had not voted in favor of the proposal.[80] Although legal opinions within the Service varied on this issue, there was consensus on this crucial point:

> It has, of course, been understood that this whole matter has been conducted in the Department directly by the Secretary and it may well be assumed, we take it, that the matters referred to have all had proper consideration.[81]

Despite protests from Arthur Davis, Will King, and others that the contract would have injurious legal ramifications and set dangerous precedents for other projects, Secretary Lane ordered it ratified September 6, 1917.[82]

The Reclamation Service did not want to lose control over the project for a variety of reasons, although the stated one was the risk of the Association's default on the repayment of the building charges. Behind this posture, however, was the Reclamation Service's firm belief that no group could administer and control the storage, the distribution works, or the power facilities as well as its own engineers. The Reclamation Service had invested years in order to build the Salt

River Project, which was unquestionably the government's most successful reclamation project, but the Service resisted its final obligation: relinquishing authority over the project to its users. At the same time, the water users had not made any plans to hire a permanent general manager for the project or to recruit engineers to supervise operations and maintenance of the irrigation and power systems. There was nothing in the behavior of the Association's management that suggested it was ready to assume responsibility for the physical plant. If Arthur Davis and others in the Reclamation Service were reluctant to release the Salt River Project from their control, there was some support for their position.

On the Salt River Project, the profits from crops and power sales seemed to insure that the Association would remain a thriving one. Water users under the project, while not eagerly anticipating the repayment of more than $10 million in construction charges, did believe that power revenues would materially aid their financial situation; some estimated power profits at $25,000 per month.[83] The Board of Governors, after tackling the controversial and complex problems of extension, water rights, project limitation, and repayment, were content in the belief that they could manage the project themselves quite well; no longer would a president of the Association say, as Benjamin Fowler had in 1906, "I was not an engineer and therefore not an expert."[84] They had learned that engineers make mistakes and they had learned a great deal about negotiating with the federal government.

Much of this developing confidence within the Association was due to John Orme's style of leadership. Unlike Fowler, who generally worked alone in promoting the water-storage movement and the implementation of federal reclamation, Orme was a consensus-builder. He worked closely with D. P. Jones of the Association Council, with Joseph Kibbey, and with other community leaders to educate and persuade the water users to accept unpopular policies, such as acreage limitation and the higher final repayment figure. John Orme listened to the complaints and needs of the landowners of the Association and—also unlike Fowler—had no personal ties to Washington. While Fowler's relationship with Frederick Newell had been a great asset to the project in its formative years, by 1909 it was more a liability. Orme was a good president to lead the Association through the sometimes tumultuous years of project completion and transfer of control because of these differences. It was fortunate for him that the problem years were also generally profitable ones.

The government retained title to the Roosevelt Dam and the other facilities it had built or purchased for the Salt River Project. The

Secretary of Interior also retained the right to review and approve any changes the Association might make in the project. The Secretary reserved this authority over the project to protect the government's investment and to insure that the Association would operate the project in a manner consistent with reclamation law. But for all intents and purposes, in 1917 the Salt River Project belonged to the water users. Although the transfer period provided opportunities for the water users and the Reclamation Service to separate on less than amicable terms, John Orme, Joseph Kibbey, and Arthur Davis provided the continuity necessary to keep the project running smoothly. Orme retained the presidency of the Association through April 1918. In 1916 Kibbey unsuccessfully challenged Henry Ashurst for one of Arizona's seats in the U.S. Senate, and, although his political dreams were never realized, his law firm of Kibbey, Bennett, and Gust continued to serve the Association as legal counsel. Arthur Davis, who had succeeded Frederick Newell as director of the Reclamation Service, maintained a thoroughly professional relationship with the water users near Phoenix. Despite his own personal misgivings regarding the transfer of project management to Orme and the water users, Davis directed the Service to assist the Association in its selection of managing engineers, if asked, and to aid generally in their training by showing the individuals selected how the project worked.

Franklin Lane's promise to cooperate with the water users muted considerably the sometimes sharp disagreements between the engineers of the Reclamation Service and the landowners in the Association over the best way to do things on the project. The Reclamation Service under Arthur Davis seemed to shift quite easily to serving in an advisory, rather than a supervisory, capacity to the landowners under the project. Davis seemed better attuned to Secretary Lane's political concerns than Newell had been; perhaps his understanding was a result of his extensive international work as a consulting engineer on the Panama Canal, on the Huai River Conservancy Project in China, and in the Kara Kum Desert in Turkestan, all projects which required both patience and flexibility.[85] If he disagreed with the Secretary over policy, Davis was practical enough to realize that confrontation was not the best method to persuade Lane to take a different stand.

In 1917 Americans were distracted by the European war—some more by its profits than its horrors. America's entry into the battle in April 1917 directed resources, manpower, and energy away from national reform movements like federal reclamation. Questions of water rights, repayment, and economic viability on the projects received less attention than did matters related to increasing the

nation's food and fiber supply. Few outside of the Reclamation Service and the Salt River Valley noticed when John Orme and the Salt
River Valley Water Users' Association quietly took control of what the
New York Times later called the "one outstanding successful example"
of federal reclamation.[86] Both groups were determined that it should
remain so.

The Magnificent Experiment
in Perspective

The history of the Salt River Project through 1917 provides a micro-cosm of the implementation of national irrigation policy. The national government provided the opportunity for Salt River Valley citizens to build their water-storage project. Farmers and landowners there, through the Salt River Valley Water Users' Association, attempted to reconcile federal reclamation principles with local irriga-tion practices. Neither the Association nor the project ever really fit the reclamation ideal of triggering pioneer home-building, however, chiefly because of the lack of public lands on Salt River to reclaim and settle. On the other hand, the preponderance of private lands may have been the project's greatest asset. Farmers in the Salt River Valley were generally experienced irrigators; if they were new to the region, there were adequate models to follow. Additionally, because the val-ley had been settled for at least thirty years prior to the entrance of federal reclamation on the local scene, a vibrant town and business life complemented the established, diversified agriculture. A commu-nity with strong leaders and organizations, therefore, existed to take advantage of the reclamation program. Other national projects, plagued by insufficient numbers of homesteaders or inadequately prepared settlers, had neither the resourcefulness nor stability of the Salt River Valley Water Users' Association.

One measure of the significance of the accomplishments at Salt River is to compare its status in 1917 with three of the other reclama-tion projects selected by the Secretary of Interior at the same time

[147]

(1903): the Truckee-Carson, or Newlands, Project located in Churchill County, Nevada; the North Platte Project, situated in eastern Wyoming and western Nebraska along the North Platte River; and the Milk River Project, containing (originally) the lower Milk River Valley lands adjacent to the Milk River in Valley and Chocteau counties, Montana.[1]

MEASUREMENT OF SUCCESS AND FAILURE ON FEDERAL IRRIGATION PROJECTS

Key elements of success or failure on water-reclamation projects were engineering difficulties, the amount of acreage irrigated, the number of settlers, and the ability of the land to repay the construction debt to the government. Construction on Salt River Project consisted primarily of one gravity arch masonry storage dam (the Roosevelt Dam), a low diversion dam (Granite Reef Dam), and ancillary power-producing facilities to accompany these main irrigation features. Most of the canals and laterals carrying water to the farmlands were already in place and, since all the lands were held in private ownership (with the exception of about 10,000 acres of state school lands), most of the acreage was prepared for immediate irrigation. The large number of landowners and the quality of the irrigated soil ensured that repayment, although rescheduled and revised, was accomplished. In addition, all the water supply was developed from the Salt River watershed, and the river itself was entirely within Arizona. All of these favorable conditions helped to produce successful completion of the project; in contrast to the Salt River Project, construction designs which varied widely, and legal questions involving water were labyrinthine on the Newlands, North Platte, and Milk River projects.

For the Newlands Project, the Reclamation Service initially envisioned irrigating about 200,000 acres in western Nevada in the Carson Sink Valley. Because the Carson River was inadequate to irrigate that much land, the Service proposed to divert the Truckee River (flowing out of California and Lake Tahoe into the Sierra Nevada) into the Carson River channel at a place called Derby. A canal thirty-one miles long would carry water from the Truckee to the Carson River.

Reclamation Service engineers mapped complex plans for an earth-filled diversion dam with concrete sluiceways at Derby, water distribution canals within the project area, and a main concrete-lined canal; they did not include water storage.[2] The Service assumed it

would be able to use Lake Tahoe for a storage reservoir, although this
assumption considered neither the legal status of the lake, located in
both California and Nevada, nor the protests of property owners
along its shoreline. Lawsuits filed by lakeside residents delayed a decision on the use of Tahoe until 1915, and the final result was that the
lake had little value as a storage reservoir under the operating conditions imposed by the court.[3]

Because there was no water storage, the total amount of available
water severely limited the acreage which could be irrigated on the
Newlands Project. The distribution canals and the diversion dam that
the Service initially thought were more important than a water-storage plan were relatively useless without it. Reclamation Service
engineers finally began construction of a storage dam on the lower
Carson River in 1911 (the 124-foot-high, earth and gravel fill Lahon-
tan Dam), but, by this time, the discovery of large, spreading areas of
alkali in the soil and the generally unsuccessful farming ventures by
homesteaders had given the Newlands Project an unhappy reputation.

In addition, the Newlands Project had been overbuilt. The area
the optimistic engineers thought could be irrigated was too vast for
the water supply, and the construction plans were too ambitious for
the few settlers taking up the lands. By 1907, when the first unit of the
project opened for settlement, only 31,000 acres were in cultivation,
and these mainly in pasture lands.[4] This figure changed little over the
next ten years: in 1910 the Service was prepared to irrigate 85,000
acres, but only 35,000 acres were irrigated; by 1916, the Service was
prepared to irrigate 69,100 acres, but only 47,000 acres were actually
irrigated. Without the use of Lake Tahoe for storage, the project's
acreage was reduced dramatically, from 200,000 to 73,000 acres.[5]

Despite the minimal irrigation results in Nevada and despite the
fact that a separate drainage project would now be necessary, due to
the alkali, the Service still portrayed this project as a potentially successful one. The 1910 investigation by the Army Board of Engineers
on Reclamation Projects found the Newlands Project "feasible in an
engineering and economic sense."[6] The Board estimated the final
cost of the project at $7 million, with acreage charges of $35 to $45;
this estimate was based upon the assumption that all 200,000 acres
would be cultivated.[7]

Part of the Reclamation Service commitment to the Newlands
Project lay in the fact that 60 percent of its lands were public and open
to settlement. Although settling public lands embodied the spirit of
the Reclamation Act, such lands proved more expensive to reclaim,
because a total irrigation system had to be created for them. By 1916

only 2,000 people on 575 farms would attempt to repay the $7 million they owed the government.[8] A second factor in the government's determination to push through completion of the Newlands Project was political. Francis Newlands, author of the National Reclamation Act and a powerful force in natural-resource matters, had hand-picked the project. This relationship placed pressure on the Service to continue with the project no matter what the economics might be.

By 1917, when the government officially opened the Salt River Project, the Newlands Project was only 63 percent completed. Construction charges for the project had risen since the Service's first estimates. On the three units opened, landowners were to repay the government $22, $30 and $60 per acre. In 1917 farmers on this project averaged a wartime-inflated $51 per acre cropped—primarily in alfalfa, small grain, and dairy products. Landowners with vested rights under the first unit might profit from reclamation, but few homesteaders on the third unit could.[9]

Another problem on the Newlands Project was that the Reclamation Service had built the project before there were adequate numbers of people prepared to settle and farm the land. This error resulted in excessive costs to the government: because less than half of the projected area of 200,000 acres had been taken up, the Department of Interior had to write off nearly two-thirds of the construction charges in 1926.

Failure of the Newlands Project to materialize as planned divided the landowners and homesteaders into several factions, and the absence of a single, advocatory organization of water users hampered any progress which might have been made on the project. The Truckee-Carson Association at Fallon, Nevada, was one of the founder associations of the National Federation of Water Users' Associations, the maverick group which demanded reorganizaton of the Reclamation Service and readjustment of the construction charges. The Fernley Water Users' Association consisted of "quite a wide-awake band of settlers who are off to themselves in what is virtually a separate project, taking water from the main Truckee Canal."[10] Two other groups—the Southside Water Users' Association and the West Side Water Users' Association, located south and west, respectively, of Fallon—organized in 1915–1916, with their main focus on project costs and repayment.[11]

Negotiating with the Reclamation Service was difficult enough for a well-organized and adequately funded association like Salt River's. To have as many as four independent groups of landowners trying to accomplish in differing ways the problematic goals of securing both extension and additional features to the project only could have added to the general frustration.

The Newlands Project had been publicized as a veritable Garden of Eden, but the Reclamation Service and project homesteaders realized too late the enormous amounts of personal capital and hard work required to make desert land productive. They also learned that no amount of water would make bad soil into good. Everyone underestimated the difficulties that settlers faced on this Nevada project, and the Newlands Project was not successful.

The North Platte reclamation project was located in eastern Wyoming and western Nebraska along both sides of the North Platte River. In his initial examinations of the project area, John J. Field of the Reclamation Service thought one of the main problems for the project might be a legal one: the water originated in Colorado, was to be stored and diverted in Wyoming, and possibly would find its ultimate use in Nebraska.[12] Although adjudication of the water rights on the North Platte Project was complicated due to the interstate nature of the river, it did not seem to hinder the pace of the work.

The centerpiece of the North Platte Project was the Pathfinder Dam, a 218-foot-high, masonry-arch structure located in a deep canyon on the North Platte River, about thirty miles below its confluence with the Sweetwater River in eastern Wyoming. Complementing the Pathfinder was the Whalen Diversion Dam, a low, concrete, weir structure on the river 150 miles below the main storage dam. The Whalen Dam diverted the water into the 95-mile-long Interstate Canal, which carried it into Nebraska.[13] While the Pathfinder Dam was unique at that time, representing a major advance in arch-dam design, the Reclamation Service modeled portions of the North Platte Project after the Roosevelt Dam. The engineering plans for this project were well thought out generally, and the major structures for storage and diversion rose quickly; most were completed by 1909.[14]

Like those under the Newlands Project, the majority of the lands under the North Platte Project were open for public settlement. The remaining lands were private, state school, and Carey Act lands. The 129,270 acres under the Interstate Unit, the first and largest of three units planned on the North Platte, divided roughly into 69 percent public lands, 17 percent private, 2.5 percent state school and the remaining 1.5 percent into Carey Act lands farmed by the North Platte Canal and Colonization Company. The total acreage served under the Interstate Canal system increased slightly between 1910 and 1917 to 129,891 acres.[15]

The estimated cost for constructing the Interstate Unit of the North Platte Project was about $6.8 million; this meant acreage charges of about $55.[16] The Board of Army Engineers thought, in 1910, that a $60 per acre charge would be the maximum which the land could bear. With repayment costs so high, the army engineers believed "the public lands will probably be slowly taken up for settlement."[17] This prediction by the Board of Army Engineers proved to be the case. Reclamation Service engineers thought the North Platte Project would be able to irrigate the total project irrigable acreage in 1916, and they estimated water-right applications and contracts for 112,698 acres. The 1915 statistics indicated, however, that for this estimate to be realized, nearly half as much new land would have had to contract for water as was irrigated in that year.[18] Even with the war-time inflation in agricultural prices, the average crop value on the North Platte Project was only $42.[19] Clearly, those on the Interstate Unit would lose money if the profitable war years showed an acreage return more than ten dollars short of the acreage charge.

Despite the financial problems on the North Platte Project, it enjoyed a greater success than it would have otherwise, due to the great capacity of the Pathfinder Reservoir. Because the number of acres irrigated never reached the maximum which could be served from the reservoir, the Reclamation Service used the principles of the Warren Act (1911) to sell surplus water to off-project irrigation districts and private canal companies. Because at least ten irrigation districts in Nebraska used the Warren Act to secure stored-water contracts, the landowners on the government project were relieved of payment of approximately 50 percent of the construction cost.[20]

In 1910 the Board of Army Engineers recommended completion of the North Platte Interstate and Fort Laramie units, but not the proposed third unit at Goshen Park; the repayment charge of $80 to $90 per acre was more than those lands could afford.[21] By 1917, with the Interstate Unit nearly 100 percent completed, results on the North Platte Project suggested that profitable irrigation there depended upon the sizeable number of Warren Act contracts between the government and landowners farming off-project. While those off-project irrigation districts helped the North Platte Project landowners financially, they, nevertheless, diminished the responsibility of project landowners for insuring the project's success. North Platte Valley farmers were "up to date and progressive,"[22] and they modeled their association after the Salt River Valley Water Users' Association.[23] But as early as 1909, the North Platte Valley Water Users' Association demanded that the government pay for everything on the project except their ditches and diversion facilities.[24] Rather than view the North Platte Project as their own, project landowners seemed to look at it as a government project for which they had no obligation. Although the project was essentially completed in 1917, the North Platte Valley Water Users' Association resisted taking over its management. The government did not force local water users to assume responsibility for the North Platte Project until the late 1920s.

The Milk River Project in Montana was conceptually complex. The initial plans called for the diversion of the St. Mary River into the Milk River, and for using the waters stored on the St. Mary Unit and behind two earth-fill storage dams on Milk River to irrigate approximately 250,000 acres. Although Reclamation Service engineers did not think transporting the waters of the St. Mary River across the Continental Divide into the lower Milk River Valley a difficult task, negotiation of the rights to the rivers was a major problem: the headwaters of the St. Mary River were in Canada, and the Milk River, which meandered back and forth across the Canadian border, was used by Canadian farmers before it reached the lower Milk River Valley.[25] In addition to the international water-rights issue, the rights to the waters of the Milk River for 31,000 acres of Indian lands on the Fort Belknap Reservation needed to be determined.[26]

Unlike Reclamation Service policy on the Newlands and North Platte projects, which allowed for building the irrigation structures while negotiation for water and storage rights was going on, policy on the Milk River Project allowed no major construction until 1910, after similar questions had been resolved. Great Britain signed a treaty in 1909 adjudicating the international rights to the two rivers. The U.S. Supreme Court settled the Indian claims in 1908 with *Winters v. United States*. Although the Dodson Diversion Dam and the Dodson South Canal were completed by the time the Board of Army Engineers surveyed the Milk River Project in 1910, the Reclamation Service had only tentatively designed other major structures.[27]

Despite the uncertain nature of the construction plans, the Board of Army Engineers believed that "in view of the probable returns from the lands when under full irrigation, the land will bear any reasonable building charge."[28] A very rough estimate based upon a few "ifs" predicted a construction charge of approximately $40 per acre, determined from a total project cost of about $7 million.[29]

The lands included among the 196,000 acres of the project were almost equally private and public, in contrast to both the Newlands and North Platte projects, with their preponderance of public lands. On the Milk River Project 41 percent of the land was privately held, 39 percent was public land, 15 percent belonged to the Indians, and the remaining 5 percent was state school land.[30] By 1916 the amount of land held in private ownership under the project increased to 50 percent, as the total project acreage grew to 200,000. Although the Reclamation Service was prepared to irrigate 64,000 acres in 1917, only a little less than 4,500 acres contracted for water the year before; it was unlikely an additional 60,000 acres would come under the project within a few months.[31]

The fact that reclamation was expensive and not always worth the great cost was apparent on the Milk River Project in 1917. The increase in crop returns per irrigated acre was a mere $3 over the returns from a similar acre dry-farmed within the project boundaries. The war-time profits of 1917 did not increase the farmer's return much, allowing about $19 per acre.

To make matters worse, only 400 people on 190 farms would have been liable for the construction debt estimated at $6 million if the government had issued public notice in 1917. Although the Board of Army Engineers seemed confident that the project lands could reasonably return the acreage charge of reclamation, the fact that more than 60 percent of the agricultural production was in forage crops, like hay, with the remainder in grains, was evidence that the Army Board was a bit optimistic. Farms on the Milk River Project lacked the crop diversity and lengthy growing season necessary to insure a profitable return from the irrigated land.[32]

By 1917 the Milk River Project was more than 60 percent completed, yet the prospects for its success were dim. The Reclamation Service changed the engineering plans and reduced the size of the project after indications that the acreage to be included within the project would not reach the estimated 250,000. When the Fact-Finder's Commission appointed by the Secretary of Interior made its report in 1924, the special advisers on reclamation noted that a material loss to the government would result from this project. It seemed, in the final analysis, that the most beneficial result of federal reclamation on the Milk River Project was the settlement of vexing water-rights problems.[33]

The Reclamation Service thought two water-users' associations would be best on the Milk River Project because of the great distances encompassed within the Milk River Valley. The Lower Milk River Valley Water Users' Association was formed in Malta, Montana, and the Upper Milk River Valley Water Users' Association was headquartered near Chinook and Harlem, Montana.

Water users on the project faced several problems: the delay in construction discouraged landowners from subscribing to the project;[34] the Secretary of Interior had yet to reopen public land for reclamation previously withdrawn for coal deposits;[35] and the two water-user associations were unable to work together harmoniously.[36] Continued delays in construction, the increased costs of building the project, and the disappointing financial returns from irrigated farming aggravated the tendency for water users to be at odds with the Reclamation Service. Secretary of Interior Franklin Lane wrote disappointedly to William M. Boyle of the *Great Falls [Montana] Tribune* that "there really was a very bad showing made by the Montana projects . . ., [and] the government was looked upon as a bunko sharp."[37] By 1917, the situation on the Milk River Project had deteriorated to such a level that federal reclamation was apparently a contributor to agricultural stagnation and decline, not salvation.

"A fundamental error was made in believing that the construction of irrigation works would of itself create irrigated agriculture," wrote the Secretary of Interior's Commission of Special Advisers on Reclamation in 1924.[38] An overemphasis had been placed on the engineering side of reclamation to the detriment of the human side. Settlers were accepted on the projects without capital or experience. They were not organized to work together, but were left to struggle without sufficient aid or direction to complete what the government had only begun.[39] This problem with the reclamation program in its first years was never more apparent than in Churchill County, Nevada; Scotts Bluff, Nebraska; and Malta, Chinook, and Harlem, Montana.

GOALS AND RESULTS OF THE SALT RIVER PROJECT

The early proponents of a government reclamation program—the Frederick Newells and the George Maxwells—viewed national irrigation as a means of social reform; it would put otherwise barren lands to use for the greatest good for the greatest number of people over the longest period of time. Federal reclamation was, thus, a clarion call for those who believed that government scientists and engineers could manage the nation's streams and public lands more democratically than politicians. Promoters publicized the national irrigation program as the solution to American social and economic problems, and it soon took on the dimensions of a crusade.

The history of the Salt River Project reinforces some of reclamation's important themes: the concept of efficiency, rational use of resources, and application of expertise to broad national problems; an interpretation of progressive reformers' motivation as one guided primarily by self-interest; and the importance of a new engineering ideology, emerging during the Progressive Era, which cast the engineer in the role of a missionary to society.

The emphasis of reclamation under Frederick Newell and Theodore Roosevelt was on scientific planning for decision-making, and on centralized, or executive authority. With federal reclamation, engineering science was prepared to conquer the second frontier—

the lands of the West which settlers had neglected due to problems of aridity. In its place, the Reclamation Service engineers would build a new frontier for twentieth-century pioneers. Science and technology would not only enable these new settlers "to enjoy the fruits of the great sources of power in Nature,"[40] but, through the elimination of partisan non-experts from natural-resources decision-making, would also make the new frontier more democratic.[41]

Federal reclamation was viewed as both a physical and a human engineering problem. The structures needed for water storage and distribution were generally well designed and built, and they served the purposes for which they had been constructed. The human problem was not as successfully resolved. "The application of the engineering method to human affairs implied treating men as material," wrote Edwin Layton. This philosophy was clearly embraced by Frederick Newell: human groups, Newell argued, should be viewed as machines, in which "the wheels and bearings are men and not metals."[42] This approach called for replacement of bad parts or failures with new ones. In reclamation, Newell was said to believe that only the third crop of settlers could be expected to succeed.[43] Engineering the irrigation works created few unanswered questions for the Reclamation Service; the puzzle was the human element.

On the Salt River Project, the great Roosevelt Dam was evidence of the satisfactory resolution of physical engineering problems; the controversies over repayment and control gave testimony to the unsatisfactory solution of the social-engineering end of things. Yet the Salt River Project's story modifies some of these themes in important ways. When the scientific, "centralized authority" expert collided with local interests in the Salt River Valley, compromise was born in the form of a bureaucratic process which was subject to local influence. Those who witnessed the problems of financing, repayment, and control over decision-making on the Salt River Project realized that the reclamation program envisioned by Progressive reformers was unrealistic. Secretary of Interior Franklin Lane seemed to understand the inherent contradiction between the Jeffersonian democracy that was the goal of the early Reclamation Service and the centralized authority through which Frederick Newell tried to implement it. Compromise between the water-users' notion of individual rights and the Progressives' reclamation crusade required flexibility and a commitment to cooperate. Lane persuaded the water users to accept compromise and repressed Reclamation Service attempts to resist it; reclamation as Progressive reform became reclamation as bureaucracy. This acceptance of give-and-take meant that local interests in the valley helped transform nationally stated goals into something more acceptable to Salt River Project landowners.

Solving the water-storage problem through the construction of the Salt River Project was probably the most important turning point in the rise of Phoenix as a major southwestern city. Throughout the years during which valley farmers first planned to build the dam themselves, and then lobbied the government to build it for them, farm and town united in the effort to store water for the future. City of Phoenix businessmen like Aaron Goldberg, of the Old Settlers' Protective Association, and Charles Goldman, of the Maricopa County Water Storage Commission, were intimately involved in early water-storage proposals. The City of Phoenix itself launched a subscription effort to help pay for construction of the road to Roosevelt. Most Phoenix businessmen would have seconded Harry Welch, secretary of the Phoenix Chamber of Commerce, when he said, "You cannot dream your town into a city; you must build and boost it into one."[44]

The key to "boosting" Phoenix was water; with it, land was valuable and a worthwhile investment. The Phoenix Board of Trade advertised heavily, focusing on the size of the Salt River Project and the abundant water it made available for land cultivation. The Board of Trade directed its effort primarily to midwestern farmers, and the great success of the Salt River Project secured for Phoenix a good deal of free advertising. Government statisticians, like Clarence J. Blanchard, compiled crop statistics, weather, and land conditions in the Salt River Valley, as well as the social and cultural advantages offered by valley cities and towns. The government published these facts and figures in advertising folders about the possibilities on the Salt River Project and generously distributed them to agricultural areas of the nation.[45] Unlike other reclamation projects, the Salt River Project surrounded the capital of the state, with its attendant political, social, and economic infrastructure.

Completion of Roosevelt Dam and improvements in water distribution and power facilities contributed to an expansion of the size and importance of Salt River Valley agriculture. Farmers placed thousands of acres of new land in cultivation—both within the project boundaries and in outside, peripheral areas where project electricity powered pumps to raise groundwater for surface irrigation.[46] New farmers and those already there, who decided to take advantage of increasing prices for raw commodities like cotton, needed tools, equipment, and building supplies. Agricultural implement firms, sugar beet refineries, meat processing plants, and building- and materials-supply companies, therefore, grew and developed within Phoenix and other valley towns. Investment companies sprouted to lend money and develop land. Corporate agribusiness interests, like Goodyear Rubber and Southwest Cotton Company, became involved in loan and investment transactions, agricultural expansion, and new town development. In 1916 cotton showed a net return of $125 per acre, citrus made big returns, and "the valley [was] certainly prosperous."[47]

Success often begets success. The Salt River Project proved to be the foundation upon which the future of both town and farm was built. The project represented the stable, assured water supply necessary for Phoenix's growth. With the security which Roosevelt Dam provided by capturing flood waters and storing them for use in dry years, the agricultural sector of the local economy grew far beyond what it would have without the project. This growth, in turn, created other opportunities.

Benjamin Fowler left Phoenix for California in 1916 a bitter man, believing his work for reclamation in the Salt River Valley unappreciated. Frederick Newell was forced out of the Reclamation Service a year later, feeling much the same about his role in creating the organization designed to oversee the national irrigation program. Both men had fallen out of step with the changing perceptions and needs of the reclamation farmer, and their exits from the forefront of policy-making reflected grass-roots demands for a new direction. They had, however, been essential to the movement's beginnings; their imagination and faith in what was possible shaped the fundamental institutions of national reclamation.

Reclamation of the arid West had begun as a magnificent experiment. Neither Newell nor Fowler knew in 1903 whether the national irrigation program they planned and implemented at Salt River would succeed. It was clear by 1917, however, that the Salt River Project was the most successful of the government's reclamation efforts. National policy to reclaim arid lands and generally improve western lands effectively eliminated the irrigation heritage of individual rights and responsibilities in the Salt River Valley. In its place the Salt River Valley Water Users' Association created the conditions for community management of the valley's water resources. For better or worse, federal reclamation changed water institutions throughout the West in significant ways, just as it changed those in central Arizona; indeed, the national irrigation program was rapidly becoming an institution by 1917.

Although the heady goals of the early reclamation movement had been swept aside as the daily problems of construction costs and repayment obligations preoccupied water user and engineer alike, reclamation's legacy on Salt River was not an illusion. Despite the sometimes uneasy alliance between the Reclamation Service and the Salt River Valley Water Users' Association, their joining together in

1903 to master Salt River made possible both agricultural prosperity and the rise of an urban regional center in Phoenix. The Salt River Project had its share of conflict and compromise and of engineering miracles and mistakes; landowners in the area were both community-minded and self-interested. Although the project had several important advantages in its damsite and rich farmland, there was no magic formula for its favorable outcome; there was only a common vision among Salt River Valley residents of what their valley could become if it had the water.

Notes

THE CAMPAIGN FOR WATER STORAGE

1. Leahmae Brown, "The Development of National Policy with Respect to Water Resources," (Ph.D. dissertation: University of Illinois, 1937), p. 88.
2. John T. Ganoe, "The Origin of a National Reclamation Policy," *Mississippi Valley Historical Review* 18 (June 1931): 34 – 52.
3. Gifford Pinchot, cited in Otis L. Graham, Jr., *The Great Campaigns: Reform and War in America, 1900 – 1928* (Englewood Cliffs, N. J.: Prentice-Hall, Inc., 1977), p. 249.
4. Ibid., p. 251.
5. Discussion on "Irrigation," *Transactions of the American Society of Civil Engineers*, 62 (1909): 10.
6. Address of President Theodore Roosevelt to the 57th Congress, cited in the Institute for Government Research, *The U.S. Reclamation Service*, (New York: D. Appleton & Co., 1919), p. 19.
7. For the early history of Phoenix and the Salt River Valley, see Karen L. Smith, "From Town to City: A History of Phoenix, Arizona, 1870 – 1912," (M.A. thesis, University of California at Santa Barbara, 1978), and Geoffrey P. Mawn, "Phoenix, Arizona: Central City of the Southwest, 1870 – 1920," (Ph.D. dissertation: Arizona State University, 1979). For information on canals in the Salt River Valley before 1900, see E. F. Young, compiler for the United States Bureau of Reclamation, *Early History of the Salt River Project*, unpublished typescript, 1917, Salt River Project Archives, and Earl Zarbin, "Salt River Valley Canals: 1867 – 1875," unpublished typescript, 1980, Salt River Project Archives.
8. George Strebel, "Irrigation as a Factor in Western History, 1847 – 1890," (Ph.D. dissertation, University of California at Berkeley, 1965); *Campbell v. Shivers* 1 Ariz. Rep. 161 S.C. 25 Pac. Rep. 540, (1874).
9. Young, *Early History*; Strebel, "Irrigation as a Factor."
10. Mawn, "Phoenix, Arizona," pp. 114, 240; Maricopa County Immigration Union, "What the Salt River Valley Offers to the Immigrant, Capitalist, and Invalid: A Land for Homes, for Health, for Investments," 1887, Arizona Department of Library and Archives; *Phoenix Herald*, 4 October 1890.

11. Mawn, "Phoenix, Arizona," p. 114; W. H. Code, "Irrigation in the Salt River Valley," U.S. Department of Agriculture Bulletin No. 104, Washington, D. C., 1902.

12. S. M. McCowan, Chairman, Phoenix and Maricopa County Board of Trade, April 10, 1900, Salt River Project Archives. Examples of litigation regarding the canals and water rights during this period are *Biggs v. Utah Canal Company*, 64 Pac. 494 (1899), and *Slosser v. Salt River Valley Canal Company*, 65 Pac. 332 (1899).

13. John W. Caughey, "The Insignificance of Frontier in American History," *Western Historical Quarterly* V (1974): 13 – 14.

14. Ralph Murphy, "W. J.," unpublished typescript, no date, Phoenix History Project, Phoenix, Arizona; Arizona Agricultural Experiment Station Bulletin Number 3, "Irrigation in Arizona," 1891; Mawn, "Phoenix, Arizona," chapter five.

15. Benjamin Hibbard, *A History of the Public Land Policies*, (Madison: University of Wisconsin Press, 1965), p. 439.

16. Institute for Government Research, *The United States Reclamation Service*, (New York: D. Appleton & Co., 1919), pp. 9 – 10; Stanley R. Davison, "The Leadership of the Reclamation Movement, 1875 – 1902," (Ph.D. dissertation: University of California at Berkeley, 1951), pp. 96 – 97; James McClintock, *Arizona—The Youngest State*, vol. 3 (Chicago: S. J. Clarke Publishing Co., 1916), p. 431.

17. Davison, "Leadership," p. 100; McClintock, *Arizona*, p. 431.

18. McClintock, *Arizona*, p. 431.

19. Davison, "Leadership," p. 100.

20. Samuel P. Hays, "Conservation and the Structure of American Politics: The Progressive Era," in Allan G. Bogue, Thomas D. Phillips, and James E. Wright, eds., *The West of the American People*, (Itasca, Illinois: Peacock Publishers, 1970), pp. 612 – 621; Hibbard, *History of Public Land Policies*, p. 439; John T. Ganoe, "The Origin of a National Reclamation Policy," *Mississippi Valley Historical Review* 18 (June 1931): 34 – 52.

21. Institute for Government Research, *The United States Reclamation Service*, pp. 10 – 12.

22. Alfred Golze, *Reclamation in the United States* (New York: McGraw-Hill, 1952), p. 18; McClintock, *Arizona*, p. 432; Henry H. Man to Binger Hermann, September 16, 1899, Railroad and Reservoir Right of Way Files, Records Relating to Administration, Records of the Bureau of Land Management, Record Group 49, National Archives, Washington, D. C.; U.S. Congress, House, Committee on Indian Affairs, *Compilation of Laws Relating to Indian Irrigation Projects*, Hearings before the House Committee on Indian Affairs, 2 vols., (Washington, D.C.: Government Printing Office, 1919), vol. II, p. 303; Arthur P. Davis, *Irrigation Near Phoenix, Arizona*, Water Supply and Irrigation Paper of the U.S. Geological Survey, No. 2, House of Representatives Document No. 342, 54th Congress, 2d session, 1897.

23. *Arizona (Phoenix) Republican*, 20 April 1893, 16 December 1894, 13 January 1895; Mawn, "Phoenix, Arizona," pp. 223 – 224; *Arizona (Phoenix) Gazette*, 21 December 1898.

24. *Gazette*, 29 December 1898.

25. *Republican*, 4 July 1896.

26. Ibid.

27. George Rogers Taylor, *The Transportation Revolution, 1815 – 1860*, (New York: Rinehart & Co., Inc., 1958), particularly Chapters 2, 3, 5 and 16; see also Carter Goodrich, "American Development Policy: The Case of Internal Improvements," *Journal of Economic History* 16 (December, 1956): 449 – 460, and "The Revulsion Against Internal Improvements," *Journal of Economic History* 10 (November, 1950): 145 – 169; Stuart Bruchey, *The Roots of American Economic Growth, 1607 – 1861*, (New York: Harper and Row, 1965); and *Republican*, 16 December 1896.

28. *Republican*, December 1896, pp. 15 – 18. Newell later wrote that the Fifth National Irrigation Congress favored the construction of storage reservoirs by the federal government where necessary to furnish water for the reclamation of public lands, yet the local reaction immediately following the irrigation congress seems to sug-

gest that there was less enthusiasm than Newell remembers; see Frederick H. Newell, "The History of the Irrigation Movement," from the *First Annual Report of the United States Reclamation Service, June 17, 1902*, to December 1, 1902, House of Representatives Document No. 79, 57th Congress, 2d session, Washington, D.C., 1903, p. 7.

29. Mawn, "Phoenix, Arizona," pp. 230 − 231.
30. *Gazette*, 29 December 1898.
31. Newell, "History of the Irrigation Movement," p. 5.
32. Samuel P. Hays, in *Conservation and the Gospel of Efficiency: The Progressive Conservation Movement, 1890 − 1920* (New York: Atheneum, 1975) discusses the rivalry between the various government water agencies; see particularly chapter six. This concern with bureaucratic turf was also evident on the Salt River Project, as the Department of Agriculture's Division of Irrigation Investigations challenged the authority of the U. S. Reclamation Service to conduct irrigation investigations and experiments. See, for example, Charles Walcott to James Wilson, May 13, 1903, Records of the Bureau of Reclamation, Record Group 115, Salt River, 1902 − 1919, series 305, National Archives, Washington, D.C.
33. Frederick H. Newell, *Autobiography*, unpublished typescript, no date (c. 1927), American Heritage Center, University of Wyoming, Laramie, Wyoming, p. 23.
34. Ibid., pp. 27 − 33.
35. Ibid., pp. 26.
36. Ibid., pp. 32 − 33.
37. Ibid., pp. 34 − 38; Hays, *Conservation and the Gospel of Efficiency*, p. 7; William E. Smythe, *Conquering the Arid West* (Seattle: University of Washington Press, 1969) p. 297.
38. Davis, *Irrigation Near Phoenix*, p. 66; Newell, "History of Irrigation Movement," p. 4.
39. *Republican*, 2 February 1900.
40. McCowan, *Report to the Phoenix and Maricopa County Board of Trade.*
41. Ibid.
42. *Republican*, 20 March 1901.
43. Ibid.
44. G. Wesley Johnson, Jr., "Dwight Heard in Phoenix: The Early Years," *The Journal of Arizona History* 18 (Autumn, 1977): 267; *Arizona (Phoenix) Republic*, 9 May 1950.
45. Jo Conners, *Who's Who in Arizona* vol. I (Tucson: by the author, 1913), pp. 796 − 797, Arizona Collection, Arizona State University; James McClintock, *Arizona's Twenty-first Legislature, Phoenix, Arizona, 1901*, (Phoenix: by the author, 1901), p. 39, Arizona Collection, Arizona State University; *Reclamation Record*, June 1921, p. 267 clipping in Salt River Project Central Records, Box 218 − 48.
46. Hays, *Conservation and the Gospel of Efficiency*, pp. 9 − 10.
47. George H. Maxwell, "Memorandum of Suggestions for Salt River Valley Water Storage Committee at the Request of B. A. Fowler, Chairman of the Committee," no date (c. 1900), Salt River Project Archives.
48. Maxwell, "Memorandum."
49. Ibid.; B. A. Fowler to Ethan A. Hitchcock, November 20, 1900, and Charles Walcott to Ethan Hitchcock, January 14, 1901, Records of the Bureau of Land Management, Record Group 49, Old Canal and Reservoir Files, National Archives, Washington, D.C.
50. Frederick H. Newell Papers, pocket diaries, November 24, and 26 − 29, December 20, 1900, Library of Congress, Washington, D.C.; *Republican*, 24 December 1900 and 3 January 1901.
51. *Republican*, 1 and 3 January 1901; Johnson, "Dwight Heard."
52. *Republican*, 3, 11, and 18 January 1901.
53. Ibid.

54. Ibid., 20 March 1901.

55. Ibid.

56. Ibid., 19 April 1901; J. T. Priest to Binger Hermann, January 25, 1902, Records of the Bureau of Land Management, Record Group 49, Division "F," Railroad and Reservoir Right-of-Way files, Hudson Reservoir and Canal Company, National Archives, Washington, D.C.

57. U. S. Congress, House, *Reclamation of Arid Lands*, House of Representatives Report No. 2927, 56th Congress, 2d session (1901).

58. *Republican*, 25 January 1901.

59. Hays, preface to the Atheneum edition of *Conservation and the Gospel of Efficiency*; William Lilley and Lewis Gould, "The Western Irrigation Movement, 1878 – 1902: A Reappraisal," in Gene M. Gressley, ed., *The American West: A Reorientation* (Laramie: University of Wyoming Press, 1968), pp. 72 – 73; see also Samuel P. Hays, *The Response to Industrialism: 1885 – 1914* (Chicago: University of Chicago Press, 1957), and Otis L. Graham, Jr., *The Great Campaigns: Reform and War in America, 1900 – 1928* (Englewood Cliffs, N.J.: Prentice-Hall, Inc., 1971); Leahmae Brown, "The Development of National Policy With Respect to Water Resources," (Ph.D. dissertation: University of Illinois, 1937).

60. The attitudes of McKinley and Hitchcock toward natural-resource policies are discussed in M. Nelson McGreary, *Gifford Pinchot: Forester-Politician*, (Princeton: Princeton University Press, 1960) (see particularly chapter three); see also Newell Papers, pocket diaries, 1901; and Lilley and Gould, "The Western Irrigation Movement," p. 73.

61. Newell Papers, pocket diaries, June 7, 1901; McGreary, *Gifford Pinchot*.

62. President Theodore Roosevelt, Message to the 57th Congress, December 1901, *in* the Institute for Government Research, *The United States Reclamation Service*, pp. 19 – 21; Davison, "Leadership," p. 150.

63. Newell Papers, pocket diaries, January, February, March, and April, 1902; Johnson, "Dwight Heard"; *Reclamation Record* (June 1921), p. 267.

64. Davison, "Leadership," p. 160; Institute for Government Research, *The United States Reclamation Service*, p. 27; George H. Maxwell, "Tombstone Luck," unpublished typescript, 1938, Arizona Department of Library and Archives, Phoenix, Arizona; Newell, *Autobiography*.

65. Peggy Heim, "Financing the Reclamation Program, 1902 – 1919: The Development of Repayment Policy," (Ph.D. dissertation: Columbia University, 1953), pp. 28 – 29.

66. Newell Papers, pocket diaries, June, July and August, 1902; Heim, "Financing the Reclamation Program," p. 14.

FORMING THE SALT RIVER VALLEY
WATER USERS' ASSOCIATION

1. *Arizona (Phoenix) Weekly Republican*, 31 July 1902.

2. Ibid.; G. Wesley Johnson, Jr., "Dwight Heard in Phoenix," *The Journal of Arizona History* 18 (Autumn, 1979): 275. Most of the information on Heard is from Johnson, "Dwight Heard," but see also F. H. Newell to Dwight Heard, 22 March 1922, Charles Walcott to Dwight Heard, 27 May 1903, Charles D. Walcott Papers, Smithsonian Institution Archives, Record Unit 7004/Box 1, Smithsonian Institution, Washington, D.C.; *Arizona (Phoenix) Democrat*, 29 May 1903.

3. Johnson, "Dwight Heard," p. 275.

4. *Arizona (Phoenix) Weekly Republican*, 31 July 1902.

5. Ibid.

6. *Arizona (Phoenix) Republican*, 3 August 1902.

7. Ibid.; *Republican*, 4 August 1902. Some canals only provided one representative. The water-storage conference group consisted of the following members: City of Phoenix: Frank T. Alkire and J. C. Adams; Maricopa Canal: John Orme and M. A. Sanford; Grand Canal: Sam F. Webb and S. S. Greene; Arizona Canal: B. A. Fowler and M. W. Messinger; Salt River Valley Canal: F. H. Parker and H. G. VanFossen; Grand Canal Company: William Christy; Maricopa Canal Company: Lin Orme; Salt River Valley Canal Company: T. W. Pemberton; Arizona Canal Company: A. P. Walbridge; Tempe Canal: J. W. Woolf, C. G. Jones and J. B. Stewart; Mesa Canal: Joseph Stewart, J. D. Loper and E. W. Wilbur; Utah Canal: James F. Johnson; Highland Canal: W. H. Wallace; Consolidated Canal: A. J. Chandler; San Francisco Canal: Ward Hughes. See also *Republican*, 10 August 1902.

8. U.S. Congress, House, *Second Annual Report of the U.S. Reclamation Service, 1903 – 1904*, House of Representatives Document No. 44, 58th Congress, 2d session, (Washington: Government Printing Office, 1904), p. 22.

9. *Republican*, 10 August 1902; *Arizona (Phoenix) Gazette*, 10 August 1902.

10. Ibid.

11. Ibid.

12. *Republican*, 3 October 1902. The executive committee consisted of: Joseph Kibbey, Patrick T. Hurley, William Christy, H. Simkins, W. Wallace, B. A. Fowler, A. J. Chandler, Frank Parker, Lin Orme, Dwight Heard, and Frank Alkire.

13. Ibid. The Water Storage Conference Committee's plan was largely developed by Kibbey; see U.S., Geological Survey, *Proceedings of the First Conference of Engineers of the Reclamation Service*, Water Supply and Irrigation Paper No. 93, 1904, pp. 133 – 140.

14. *Second Annual Report of the U.S. Reclamation Service*, p. 23.

15. *Republican*, 19 October 1902.

16. *Proceedings*, p. 132.

17. Ibid., p. 141.

18. George H. Maxwell to Frank Parker, November 17, 1902, Copies of Letters between Salt River Valley Water Users' Association and U.S. Reclamation Service, 1902 – 1909, Corporate Secretary's Office, Salt River Project.

19. Ibid.

20. *Gazette*, 9 August 1902.

21. *Arizona (Phoenix) Weekly Republican*, 19 November 1902.

22. U.S. Congress, House, *First Annual Report of the U.S. Reclamation Service, June 17 to December 1, 1902*, House of Representatives Document No. 79, 57th Congress, 2d session, (Washington: Government Printing Office, 1903), p. 95.

23. *Republican*, 26 November 1902.

24. Ibid., 6 January 1903.

25. Joseph H. Kibbey, Brief on Articles of Incorporation of the Salt River Valley Water Users' Association, May 25, 1903, Salt River Project Archives, Salt River Project, pp. 40 – 42; *Gazette*, 3 August 1902.

26. *Republican*, 3 January 1903.

27. Kibbey, Brief on Articles, p. 51.

28. F. H. Newell to Secretary of Interior Hitchcock, February 20, 1904, Records of the Bureau of Reclamation, Record Group 115, Salt River 1902 – 1919, series 261, National Archives, Washington, D.C.

29. "Minority Report," *Phoenix Enterprise*, 3 June 1903. The capital stock of the association was set at $3,750,000 and divided into 250,000 shares with a par value of $15 per share. U.S., Department of Agriculture, "Irrigation in the Salt River Valley," by W. H. Code, Bulletin No. 104, (1902).

30. Ibid.

31. *Proceedings*, pp. 141 – 142.

32. *Republican*, 18 January 1903; see also George Maxwell to Charles Walcott, June 5 and 7, 1903, Charles D. Walcott Papers, Smithsonian Institution Archives, Record Unit 7004/Box 1, Smithsonian Institution, Washington, D.C.

33. *Republican*, 19 January 1903.

34. Ibid.

35. Ibid., 21 January 1903.

36. Ibid., 28 January, 1 and 4 February 1903.

37. Ibid., 10 February 1903; Maxwell to Walcott, June 5, 1903.

38. Frederick Newell Papers, pocket diaries, January 4 – 6 and 8, February 17 and 21, 1903.

39. Charles D. Walcott to Secretary of Interior Hitchcock, March 7, 1903, Records of the Secretary of Interior, Record Group 48, Lands and Railroads Division: Reclamation, National Archives, Washington, D.C.; Newell Papers, pocket diaries, March 6, 1903.

40. Walcott to Hitchcock, March 7, 1903; Newell, *Autobiography*, p. 65; Newell Papers, pocket diaries, March 10, 1903. Secretary Hitchcock penned his approval of the projects on Walcott's submitted list.

41. *Phoenix Enterprise*, 3 June 1903.

42. Charles D. Reppy to E. A. Hitchcock, June 6, 1903, Records of the Secretary of Interior, Record Group 48, Lands and Railroads: Reclamation, National Archives, Washington, D.C.; *Minutes* of the Board of Governors of the Salt River Valley Water Users' Association, April 6, 1903, Corporate Secretary's Office, Salt River Project.

43. Charles D. Walcott to E. A. Hitchcock, March 29, 1903, Records of the Secretary of Interior, Record Group 48, Lands and Railroads: Reclamation, National Archives, Washington, D.C.; *Minutes* of the Board of Governors of the Salt River Valley Water Users' Association, April 6, 1903, Corporate Secretary's Office, Salt River Project.

44. Charles D. Walcott to Dwight B. Heard, May 27, 1903; *Second Annual Report of the Reclamation Service*, p. 47.

45. *Arizona (Phoenix) Democrat*, 24 May 1903.

46. Maxwell to Walcott, June 5 and 7, 1903.

47. *Phoenix Enterprise*, 3 June 1903.

48. Charles D. Walcott to George H. Maxwell, June 19, 1903, Charles D. Walcott Papers, Smithsonian Institution Archives, Record Unit 7004/Box 1, Smithsonian Institution, Washington, D.C.

49. Newell to Heard, March 22, 1922.

50. Dwight B. Heard to Members of the Salt River Valley Water Users' Association, April 2, 1906, pamphlet in 1906 newsclip file, Corporate Secretary's Office, Salt River Project.

51. *First Annual Report of the Reclamation Service*, p. 15; *Second Annual Report of the Reclamation Service*, p. 72. For details on the San Carlos – Salt River rivalry, see Karen L. Smith, "The Campaign for Water in Central Arizona, 1890 – 1903," *Arizona and the West* 23 (Summer, 1981): 127 – 148.

52. Joseph Kibbey to Benjamin Fowler, September 19, 1905, Copies of Letters between the Salt River Valley Water Users' Association and U. S. Reclamation Service, 1902 – 1909, Corporate Secretary's Office, Salt River Project; Kibbey, Brief on Articles, p. 48.

53. Ibid.

54. Kibbey to Fowler, September 19, 1905.

55. *Minutes* of the Board of Governors of the Salt River Valley Water Users' Association, February 18, April 21, and May 11, 1903. Others on the subscription committee besides Fowler were: George D. Christy, M. A. Stanford, A. J. Chandler and W. H. Wallace.

56. Ibid., June 22, 1903; Stock Subscription Book to the Salt River Valley Water Users' Association, 1903, Corporate Secretary's Office, Salt River Project.

57. Subscription Book, 1903.

58. The primary information base for this study is the Stock Subscription Book for the Salt River Valley Water Users' Association from February through June, 1903 (the initial period in which land could be subscribed). It is available in the Archives of the Salt River Project. A systematic random sample of 344 cases was constructed from the list of 1,033 individual subscribers. They were traced through three sources: the Federal Manuscript Census of 1900, the *Portrait and Biographical Record of Arizona*, 1901, and the Phoenix City and Maricopa County Directory, 1905 – 1906.

59. Crosstab tables were run on the following variables: subscription date by birthyear, birthplace, property status, property subscribed, and acres; acres by birthyear, birthplace, property status and property subscribed. Data with less than .05 significance were: subscription date by property subscribed (.01), acres by property status (.01) and acres by property subscribed (.001).

60. F. H. Newell, "National Efforts at Homemaking," *Annual Report of the Smithsonian Institution, 1922* (Washington, D.C.: Government Printing Office, 1924), p. 517.

INSTITUTIONAL FRAMEWORK FOR FEDERAL RECLAMATION

1. *Phoenix Enterprise*, 15 July 1903.

2. *Minutes* of the Board of Governors of the Salt River Valley Water Users' Association, July 13, 1903, Corporate Secretary's Office, Salt River Project; Salt River Valley Water Users' Association to Secretary of Interior E. A. Hitchcock, July 18, 1905, Copies of Letters between Salt River Valley Water Users' Association and U.S. Reclamation Service, 1902 – 1909, Corporate Secretary's Office, Salt River Project.

3. Frederick H. Newell to B. A. Fowler, December 1, 1903; B. A. Fowler to E. A. Hitchcock, July 18, 1905, Copies of Letters between Salt River Valley Water Users' Association and U.S. Reclamation Service, 1902 – 1909, Corporate Secretary's Office, Salt River Project.

4. Dwight B. Heard to Charles D. Walcott, April 11, 1904, Records of the Bureau of Reclamation, Record Group 115, Salt River 1902 – 1919, series 261, National Archives, Washington, D.C.

5. B. A. Fowler to Secretary of Interior Hitchcock, July 18, 1905; Joseph Kibbey to B. A. Fowler, September 19, 1905; A. P. Davis to B. A. Fowler, February 23, 1905; Charles D. Walcott to B. A. Fowler, November 11, 1905, Copies of Letters between Salt River Valley Water Users' Association and U.S. Reclamation Service, 1902 – 1909, Corporate Secretary's Office, Salt River Project.

6. E. A. Hitchcock to Charles D. Walcott, October 25, 1905, Copies of Letters between Salt River Valley Water Users' Association and U.S. Reclamation Service, 1902 – 1909, Corporate Secretary's Office, Salt River Project.

7. Ibid.; Kibbey to Fowler, September 19, 1905.

8. Kibbey to Fowler, September 19, 1905.

9. Ibid.; Joseph Kibbey to B. A. Fowler, November 9, 1907, Copies of Letters between Salt River Valley Water Users' Association and U.S. Reclamation Service, 1902 – 1909, Corporate Secretary's Office, Salt River Project; Samuel P. Hays, *Conservation and the Gospel of Efficiency*, pp. 242 – 243.

10. Heard to Walcott, April 11, 1904. Other members of this committee included Dr. E. W. Wilbur, Dr. A. J. Chandler, George Christy, John Orme and Frank Parker.

11. *Minutes* of the Board, April 11, 1904. Out of a total vote of 28,613 (each vote representing an acre, not a person), Fowler received 27,671 and Wilbur, 27,366.

12. Heard to Walcott, April 11, 1904.

13. B. A. Fowler to Morris Bien, May 4, 1904, Records of the Bureau of Reclamation, Record Group 115, Salt River 1902 – 1919, series 261, National Archives, Washington D.C.

14. Ibid.

15. *Minutes* of the Board, June 10, 1904.

16. Frederick H. Newell to Secretary of Interior Hitchcock, February 20, 1904, Records of the Bureau of Reclamation, Record Group 115, Salt River 1902 – 1919, series 261, National Archives, Washington, D.C.

17. Agreement between the United States of America and the Salt River Valley Water Users' Association, June 25, 1904, copy in Salt River Project Archives, Salt River Project.

18. *Minutes* of the Board, May 16, 1904.

19. "Benjamin A. Fowler, 1843 – 1921," *Reclamation Record* (June, 1921), p. 267, copy in Central Records Box 218 – 48, Salt River Project.

20. "Since Sims Went to Washington," clipping from the *Phoenix Daily Enterprise*, 20 February 1904, Central Records Box E-2-24 (1904 – 1906), Salt River Project. The "Phoenix assistant" was Sims Ely, managing editor of the *Arizona (Phoenix) Republican* and secretary of the Hudson Reservoir and Canal Company.

21. Deed Book 66, Maricopa County Recorder's Office, Phoenix, Arizona, pp. 350 – 354.

22. U.S., Department of Interior, Reclamation Service, *Fourth Annual Report of the U.S. Reclamation Service, 1904 – 1905*, p. 64.

23. *Minutes* of the Board, May 4, 1903.

24. B. A. Fowler to E. A. Hitchcock, June 26, 1905, Copies of Letters between Salt River Valley Water Users' Association and U.S. Reclamation Service, 1902 – 1909, Corporate Secretary's Office, Salt River Project. Fowler's letter as president of the Association contained its legal position, which Joseph Kibbey authored.

25. Circular letter from B. A. Fowler to the Members of the Salt River Valley Water Users' Association, March 31, 1906, 1906 Newsclip file, Corporate Secretary's Office, Salt River Project.

26. B. A. Fowler to Frederick Newell, in *Minutes* of the Board, May 6, 1905.

27. F. H. Newell to B. A. Fowler, in *Minutes* of the Board, May 8, 1905.

28. Charles Walcott to B. A. Fowler, May 22, 1905, Copies of Letters between Salt River Valley Water Users' Association and U.S. Reclamation Service, 1902 – 1909, Corporate Secretary's Office, Salt River Project.

29. B. A. Fowler and Hiram Steele to Secretary of Interior Hitchcock, June 7, 1905, and Secretary of Interior Hitchcock to B. A. Fowler, June 10, 1905, Copies of Letters between Salt River Valley Water Users' Association and U.S. Reclamation Service, 1902 – 1909, Corporate Secretary's Office, Salt River Project.

30. Secretary of Interior Hitchcock to Charles Walcott, June 14, 1905, Copies of Letters between Salt River Valley Water Users' Association and U.S. Reclamation Service, 1902 – 1909, Corporate Secretary's Office, Salt River Project; Fowler to Hitchcock, June 26, 1905.

31. Fowler to Hitchcock, June 26, 1905.

32. "The People and the Senatorship," October 30, 1916, prepared by the Committee to Elect Joseph Kibbey to the U.S. Senate, Salt River Project file, Arizona Department of Library and Archives.

33. B. A. Fowler to Joseph Kibbey, October 14, 1905, Copies of Letters between Salt River Valley Water Users' Association and U.S. Reclamation Service, 1902 – 1909, Corporate Secretary's Office, Salt River Project.

34. B. A. Fowler to Joseph Kibbey, September 24, 1905, and September 25, 1905, Copies of Letters between Salt River Valley Water Users' Association and U.S. Reclamation Service, 1902 – 1909, Corporate Secretary's Office, Salt River Project.

35. Joseph Kibbey to B. A. Fowler, October 19, 1905, Copies of Letters between Salt River Valley Water Users' Association and U.S. Reclamation Service, 1902 – 1909, Corporate Secretary's Office, Salt River Project.

36. Ibid.

37. B. A. Fowler to Joseph Kibbey, October 23, 1905, Copies of Letters between Salt River Valley Water Users' Association and U.S. Reclamation Service, 1902 – 1909, Corporate Secretary's Office, Salt River Project; Fowler circular to the Association, March 31, 1906.

38. Joseph Kibbey to B. A. Fowler, October 28, 1905, Copies of Letters between Salt River Valley Water Users' Association and U.S. Reclamation Service, 1902 – 1909, Corporate Secretary's Office, Salt River Project.

39. C. J. Hall to the Board of Governors, November 6, 1905; B. A. Fowler to Frank Parker, November 10, 1905, Copies of Letters between Salt River Valley Water Users' Association and U.S. Reclamation Service, 1902 – 1909, Corporate Secretary's Office, Salt River Project.

40. Commission of Engineers to Charles Walcott, December 8, 1905, Copies of Letters between Salt River Valley Water Users' Association and U.S. Reclamation Service, 1902 – 1909, Corporate Secretary's Office, Salt River Project.

41. B. A. Fowler to the Board of Governors, December 16, 1905, Copies of Letters between Salt River Valley Water Users' Association and U.S. Reclamation Service, 1902 – 1909, Corporate Secretary's Office, Salt River Project.

42. Ibid.

43. B. A. Fowler to the Board of Governors, January 6, 1906, and January 20, 1906, Copies of Letters between Salt River Valley Water Users' Association and U.S. Reclamation Service, 1902 – 1909, Corporate Secretary's Office, Salt River Project; Fowler circular to the Association, March 31, 1906.

44. B. A. Fowler to the Board of Governors, February 19, 1906, Copies of Letters between Salt River Valley Water Users' Association and U.S. Reclamation Service, 1902 – 1909, Corporate Secretary's Office, Salt River Project; *Minutes* of the Board, March 20, 1906.

45. Ibid.

46. B. A. Fowler to the Board of Governors, January 9, 1906, March 8, 1906, Copies of Letters between Salt River Valley Water Users' Association and U.S. Reclamation Service, 1902 – 1909, Corporate Secretary's Office, Salt River Project; *Minutes* of the Board, March 20, 1906.

47. Dwight B. Heard to the members of the Salt River Valley Water Users' Association, April 2, 1906, pamphlet in S.R.P. 1906 Newsclip file, Corporate Secretary's Office, Salt River Project.

48. Dwight B. Heard to Charles Walcott, March 28, 1906, Records of the Bureau of Reclamation, Record Group 115, Salt River 1902 – 1919, series 261, National Archives, Washington, D.C.

49. B. A. Fowler to Morris Bien, March 27, 1906, Records of the Bureau of Reclamation, Record Group 115, Salt River 1902 – 1919, series 261, National Archives, Washington D.C.

50. Ibid.

51. "An Earlier Water Users' Election," *Republican*, 3 April 1926, clipping in the Arizona Collection, Arizona State University.

52. F. H. Newell to Dr. E. W. Wilbur, March 29, 1906, Records of the Bureau of Reclamation, Record Group 115, Salt River 1902 – 1919, series 261, National Archives, Washington, D.C.

BUILDING THE ROOSEVELT DAM

1. U.S., Department of Interior, Reclamation Service, *Third Annual Report of the United States Reclamation Service, 1903 – 1904* (Washington, D.C.: Government Printing Office, 1905), p. 44.

2. U.S., Department of Interior, Reclamation Service, *First Annual Report of the United States Reclamation Service, June 17 to December 1, 1902* (Washington, D.C.: Government Printing Office, 1903), pp. 95 – 99. In 1986 the dam stood at 280 feet.

3. Chester Smith, "The Construction of the Roosevelt Dam," *Engineering Record* 62 (December 31, 1910): 756 – 762; "History of the Salt River Project," author unknown, no date (probably the U.S. Reclamation Service, c. 1911), pp. 65 – 66, 80 – 82, unpublished typescript, Salt River Project Archives; Chester Smith, "Progress on the Roosevelt Dam, Salt River Project," *Engineering News* 60 (September 10, 1908): 265 – 268; *Third Annual Report of the U.S. Reclamation Service*, p. 140. The "History of the Salt River Project" is primarily a technical report which describes the construction plans and specifications.

4. "History of the Salt River Project," pp. 59 – 74; *Third Annual Report of the U.S. Reclamation Service*, p. 140.

5. "History of the Salt River Project," pp. 65 – 67.

6. Ibid., p. 68.

7. Ibid., pp. 68 – 69.

8. Ibid., pp. 69 – 70.

9. Ibid., pp. 70 – 71.

10. Ibid., p. 71.

11. Ibid., p. 72; Salt River Valley Water Users' Association, "Data for the Committee of Special Advisers on Reclamation of the Department of Interior," December 24, 1923, pp. 3 – 4, Central Records Box S-7-21, Salt River Project.

12. "History of the Salt River Project," p. 73. Chester W. Smith, Diary No. 1, December 22, 1904, Salt River Project History Center, illustrates the use of Apache Indians on the Salt River Project. See also Clarence J. Blanchard, "A Great Work of Irrigation in the West," *Travel* 12 (August, 1907): 483.

13. *Third Annual Report of the U.S. Reclamation Service*, p. 141.

14. "History of the Salt River Project," p. 74.

15. Ibid., pp. 60 – 61. Chester W. Smith continually refers to engineers moving into new cottages throughout his diaries, and occasionally notes the workers in the tents.

16. Ibid.

17. *Who's Who in America, 1897 – 1942* (Chicago: The Marquis Company, 1943), p. 564; William E. Curtis, "Roosevelt Dam Gigantic Piece of Engineering," clipping April 19, 1911, McClintock Scraps: Arizona – Reclamation – Salt River Valley, Arizona Room, Phoenix Public Library, Phoenix, Arizona.

18. Chester W. Smith left four diaries of his work on the Salt River Project with the project upon its completion, and my general impressions of Smith are formed from these as well as his published pieces.

19. Chester Smith Diary No. 1, January – March, 1905.

20. Ibid.

21. "History of the Salt River Project," pp. 76 – 82.

22. Oscar C. S. Carter, "The Government Irrigation Project at Roosevelt Dam, Salt River, Arizona," *Journal of the Franklin Institute* 163 (April, 1907): 297 – 298; George H. Maxwell to Frederick H. Newell, April 23, 1903, and F. H. Newell to George Maxwell, May 1, 1903, Records of the Bureau of Reclamation, Record Group 115, Salt River, 1902 – 1919, series 305, National Archives, Washington, D.C.; Arthur P. Davis, *Irrigation Works Constructed by the United States Government*, (New York: John Wiley & Sons, Inc., 1917), pp. 17 – 18. A horsepower unit equals 746 watts.

23. Chester Smith Diary No. 1, June 7, 1905.

24. *Third Annual Report of the U.S. Reclamation Service*, p. 137; F. Teichman, "Rotating Screen of Power Canal, Salt River Project," *Transactions of the A.S.C.E.* 60 (1908): 337 – 338; "History of the Salt River Project," p. 118.

25. Chester Smith, "Reinforced Concrete Pipe for Carrying Water Under Pressure," *Transactions of the A.S.C.E.* 60 (1908), pp. 142 – 159.

26. Chester Smith, "Reinforced Concrete Pipe," pp. 124 – 141; "History of the Salt River Project," pp. 126 – 127.

27. Smith, "Reinforced Concrete Pipe," pp. 132 – 133.

28. Ibid., p. 133.

29. Ibid.
30. Ibid., p. 159.
31. Ibid., p. 156.
32. "History of the Salt River Project," pp. 88 – 89, 107 – 112; Chester W. Smith, "Progress on the Roosevelt Dam," pp. 265 – 268; Chester Smith Diary No. 2, March 15, 1906, and Diary No. 3, September 25, 26, and 28, 1906, Corporate Secretary's Office, Salt River Project; Teichman, "Rotating Screen," p. 337; Salt River Valley Water Users' Association to Secretary of Interior Franklin K. Lane, no date, (c. 1916), Central Records Box S-7-20, *Board of Review*, Salt River Project.
33. Davis, *Irrigation Works*, pp. 17 – 18; Chester Smith Diary No. 4, May 16, 20, and 25 – 27, and June 1, 1907, Corporate Secretary's Office, Salt River Project; Interview with A. E. McQueen, Manager of Civil Engineering, Salt River Project, November 17, 1981; "History of the Salt River Project," pp. 132 – 142.
34. "History of the Salt River Project," pp. 85 – 86.
35. Arthur P. Davis, "The Salt River Project," *Engineering Record* 57 (June 20, 1908): 769.
36. Ibid.
37. "History of the Salt River Project," pp. 132 – 165.
38. Ibid., pp. 167 – 168; Smith, "Progress on the Roosevelt Dam," p. 266; Davis, *Irrigation Works*, pp. 9 – 10.
39. Ibid.; Chester Smith Diary No. 2, February 27, 1906.
40. Chester Smith Diary No. 2, February 27 and June 4, 1906, and Diary No. 3, September 22 and November 11, 1906.
41. Chester Smith Diary No. 2, June 14 – 15, 1906.
42. Ibid., June 14 and 18, August 21, 1906.
43. Ibid., July 26 and August 3, 1906; Chester Smith Diary No. 3, September 20, 1906.
44. "The Salt River Project, U.S.R.S.," *Engineering Record* 52 (October 14, 1905): 422 – 423; Smith, "The Construction of Roosevelt Dam," pp. 756 – 762.
45. Smith, "The Construction of Roosevelt Dam," p. 761.
46. Chester Smith Diary No. 3, September 21 and October 10, 1906.
47. Ibid., October 13 and 15, November 11 and 18, 1906.
48. Ibid.
49. Chester Smith Diary No. 4, May 8, 1907, Corporate Secretary's Office, Salt River Project (see also entries for April 21 and 25, May 1, 4, and 6, 1907; interview with A. E. McQueen, November 17, 1981.
50. Chester Smith Diary No. 4, May 9, 1907.
51. Ibid., May 20 and 30 – 31, June 1, 3, and 13, 1907.
52. Ibid., May 12, June 17 and 19 – 20, 1907; interview with A. E. McQueen, November 17, 1981.
53. Chester Smith Diary No. 4, August 9 and 12, 1907; C. R. Weitze, U.S. Reclamation Service, Diary No. 2, February 5, 1911, Salt River Project History Center.
54. "History of the Salt River Project," pp. 168 – 171.
55. Dorothy Lampen, "Economic and Social Aspects of Federal Reclamation," *Johns Hopkins University Studies in Historical and Political Science*, 48 (1930): 54 – 55.

THE BUSINESS OF IRRIGATION

1. Arthur P. Davis, *Irrigation Works Constructed by the United States Government*, (New York: John Wiley & Sons, Inc., 1917), p. 7; *Arizona Republican*, 26 March 1912; U. S. Congress, House, Board of Army Engineers on Reclamation Projects, *Fund for Reclamation of Arid Lands*, House of Representatives Document No. 1262, 61st Congress, 3d session, (Washington, D.C., 1911), p. 27.

2. Peggy Heim, "Financing the Federal Reclamation Program, 1902 – 1919: The Development of Repayment Policy," (Ph.D. dissertation: Columbia University, 1953), pp. xii, 43 – 44.

3. F. H. Newell, "Irrigation: An Informal Discussion," *Transactions of the American Society of Civil Engineers* (March, 1909), p. 13.

4. Heim, "Financing Reclamation," p. 44; Gene M. Gressley, "Arthur Powell Davis, Reclamation and the West," *Agricultural History* 42 (July, 1968): 241 – 257; Ray P. Teele, *The Economics of Land Reclamation in the United States*, (Chicago: A. W. Shaw Co., 1927), pp. 204 – 205. From 1900 to 1910, the capital invested per acre was $20.05; from 1910 to 1920, it was $65.60 per acre.

5. Mrs. J. W. Stewart to President Roosevelt, October 16, 1908, Records of the Bureau of Reclamation, Record Group 115, Salt River Project Files 1902 – 1919, series 305, National Archives, Washington, D.C.

6. Ibid. (see also Heim, "Financing Reclamation," p. xii); Leahmae Brown, "The Development of National Policy with Respect to Water Resources," (Ph.D. dissertation: University of Illinois, 1937), pp. 104 – 105; Katherine A. Coman, "Some Unsettled Problems of Irrigation," *American Economic Review* 1 (March, 1911): 14.

7. U.S. Reclamation Service, compiler, "Salt River Irrigation Project," October, 1909, Arizona Collection, Arizona State University, p. 15.

8. Clarence J. Blanchard to B. A. Fowler, February 4, 1909, Copies of Letters between the Salt River Valley Water Users' Association and U.S. Reclamation Service, 1902 – 1909, Corporate Secretary's Office, Salt River Project.

9. Frederick H. Newell to B. A. Fowler, March 15, 1906, Records of the Bureau of Reclamation, Record Group 115, General Files 1902 – 1919, series 914 – 4, National Archives, Washington, D.C.

10. Frederick H. Newell to Louis C. Hill, March 15, 1906, Records of the Bureau of Reclamation, Record Group 115, General Files 1902 – 1919, series 914 – 4, National Archives, Washington, D.C.

11. Heim, "Financing Reclamation," pp. 130 – 132.

12. George H. Maxwell to Charles D. Walcott, March 4, 1909, Charles D. Walcott Papers, Record Unit 7004/Box 1, Smithsonian Institution Archives, Washington, D.C.

13. Ibid.

14. George H. Maxwell to Charles D. Walcott, April 9, 1909, Charles D. Walcott Papers, Record Unit 7004/Box 1, Smithsonian Institution Archives, Washington, D.C.; E. E. Roddis to Will R. King, October 2, 1916, Carl Hayden Papers 628/2, Arizona Collection, Arizona State University; Arthur J. Halton, Annual Report on Operation and Maintenance for Agricultural Year 1914 – 1915, Salt River Project, Salt River Project Archives, p. 110. The Act of April 16, 1906 (34 Stat., 116) provided for the leasing of power on reclamation projects.

15. *Arizona (Phoenix) Republican*, 22 April 1909.

16. Ibid.

17. Frederick H. Newell, *Autobiography*, unpublished typescript, (American Heritage Center: University of Wyoming, Laramie, Wyoming), p. 83.

18. Ibid., p. 76.

19. Ibid.

20. Martin Nelson McGreary, *Gifford Pinchot: Forester-Politician*, (Princeton, New Jersey: Princeton University Press, 1960), pp. 123 – 124.

21. Samuel P. Hays, *Conservation and the Gospel of Efficiency: The Progressive Conservation Movement, 1890 – 1920* (New York: Atheneum Press, 1975), pp. 154 – 155.

22. B. A. Fowler to F. H. Newell, December 26, 1909, Records of the Bureau of Reclamation, Record Group 115, San Carlos Project Files, series 429A, National Archives, Washington, D.C.

23. Ibid.

24. McGreary, *Gifford Pinchot*, p. 124; Elmo R. Richardson, *The Politics of Conservation: Crusades and Controversies, 1897 – 1913*, (Berkeley: University of California Press, 1962), p. 63.

25. Heim, "Financing Reclamation," pp. 130 – 131.

26. *Republican*, 20 October 1909.

27. Ibid.

28. Ibid.

29. Ibid., 28 October 1909.

30. Ibid.

31. Ibid.

32. Ibid., 14 August 1909.

33. Ibid., 25 November 1909.

34. Ibid.

35. Heim, "Financing Reclamation," pp. 230 – 233; "Secretary Ballinger and the U.S. Reclamation Service," *Engineering News* 63 (January 13, 1910): 46 – 48.

36. Newell, *Autobiography*, p. 78.

37. *Republican*, 11 March 1910.

38. Ibid.

39. Ibid., 23 July 1910, 17 March 1910.

40. Ibid., 4 – 5, 17, and 23 March, 1910. Fowler and Kibbey each received $2000 annually for their service to the Association until this Council action.

41. Ibid., 18 and 23 – 24 March, 1910; *The Taming of the Salt*, Salt River Project Communications and Public Affairs Department, 1979, Salt River Project, pp. 66 – 70. For Fowler's subscription to the Association, see the Stock Subscription Book, 1903, Corporate Secretary's Office, Salt River Project.

42. *Arizona (Phoenix) Republic*, 18 May 1969.

43. B. A. Fowler to F. H. Newell, March 25, 1910, Records of the Bureau of Reclamation, Record Group 115, Salt River Project Files 1902 – 1919, series 262, National Archives, Washington, D.C.

44. F. H. Newell to B. A. Fowler, March 30, 1910, Records of the Bureau of Reclamation, Record Group 115, Salt River Project Files 1902 – 1919, series 261, National Archives, Washington, D.C.

45. The idea of a self-righteous conservation movement is illustrated in Hays, *Conservation and the Gospel*, Richardson, *The Politics of Conservation*, McGreary, *Gifford Pinchot*, and Ashley Schiff, *Fire and Water: Scientific Heresy in the Forest Service* (Cambridge, Mass.: Harvard University Press, 1962).

46. Newell to Fowler, March 30, 1910.

47. *Taming of the Salt*, pp. 115 – 118; Jo Conners, *Who's Who in Arizona*, vol. 1, (Tucson: by the author, 1913), p. 794.

48. *Republican*, 27 March and 23 July, 1910.

49. Board of Army Engineers on Reclamation Projects, *Fund for Reclamation*, pp. 9 – 12.

50. Heim, "Financing Reclamation," pp. 250 – 251; Robert Daniel Thomas, "Policy-Making in the American Federal System: Intergovernmental Responses to Water Problems in Arizona," (Ph.D. dissertation: University of Arizona, 1970), p. 111; Board of Army Engineers, *Fund for Reclamation*, p. 11; Newell, *Autobiography*, p. 78.

51. Newell, *Autobiography*, p. 78.

52. Ibid.; Board of Army Engineers, *Fund for Reclamation*, p. 22.

53. *Republican*, 23 July 1910; Board of Army Engineers, *Fund for Reclamation*, p. 27.

54. Newell, *Autobiography*, p. 80.

55. Board of Army Engineers, *Fund for Reclamation*, pp. 22 – 29.

56. Ibid., p. 12. Modification of repayment found its legislative home in the Curtis Act (1911) which allowed the withdrawal of public notice already issued if repayment conditions were difficult, and the disposition of surplus water stored on reclamation projects (Warren Act) in general reclamation legislation passed the same year (Act of February 21, 1911, 36 Stat., 925).

57. Heim, "Financing Reclamation," Tables 30 – 32; Teele, *The Economics of Land Reclamation*, pp. 185 – 187; U.S. Bureau of the Census, *Historical Statistics of the United States, Colonial Times to 1970, Bicentennial Edition*, Part 1 (Washington, D.C.: Government Printing Office, 1975), pp. 511, 516 – 517. Heim's statistics are significantly higher than Teele's, but she acknowledges inclusion of Indian lands and lands served supplemental water in her figures, which would account for the difference. Irrigable acreage consists of lands for which the government was prepared to supply water.

58. Teele, *The Economics of Land Reclamation*, p. 205; Davis, *Irrigation Works*, pp. 2 – 3; F. H. Newell and Daniel Murphy, *Principles of Irrigation Engineering* (New York: McGraw-Hill Book Co., 1913), p. 281; Heim, "Financing Reclamation," p. 87.

59. Richardson, *The Politics of Conservation*, pp. 135 – 137.

60. Newell, *Autobiography*, p. 81.

61. Ibid., p. 82.

62. Ibid.

63. *Republican*, 28 October 1911.

64. Ibid., 6 December 1911.

65. F. H. Newell to Dwight B. Heard, February 2, 1912, Records of the Bureau of Reclamation, Record Group 115, Salt River Project Files 1902 – 1919, series 544 – B, National Archives, Washington, D.C.

66. Halton, *Annual Report*, 1914 – 1915, p. 110; Dwight B. Heard to F. H. Newell, February 12, 1912, Records of the Bureau of Reclamation, Record Group 115, Salt River Project Files 1902 – 1909, series 544 – B, National Archives, Washington, D.C.; Heim, "Financing Reclamation," Table 30: There were 1,020 transfers of land on Salt River; these transfers increased the number of names on the register by 500. See also Garth Cate to Dwight Heard, February 7, 1912, Records of the Bureau of Reclamation, Record Group 115, Salt River Project Files 1902 – 1919, series 544 – B, National Archives, Washington, D.C.

67. Heim, "Financing Reclamation," p. 32.

68. Ibid., pp. 30 – 33; Brown, "Development of National Policy," pp. 104 – 105.

69. *Republican*, 27 February 1912.

70. Ibid.

71. Ibid., 22 March 1912.

72. Ibid.

73. Hays, *Conservation and the Gospel*, pp. 241 – 260; John A. Widtsoe, *Success on Irrigation Projects*, (New York: John Wiley & Sons, Inc., 1928), p. 108; *Republican*, 28 February 1912.

74. *Republican*, 12 and 22 March 1912.

75. Ibid., 5 March 1912.

76. Ibid., 6 March 1912.

77. Ibid., 21 March 1912.

78. Ibid.

79. Ibid., 13 March 1912.

80. Ibid., 21 and 30 March 1912.

81. Ibid., 30 March 1912.

82. Ibid., 24 March 1912.

83. F. T. Powers, Chairman, Landowners' Protective Association, to Attorney General G. W. Wickersham, April 11, 1912, Records of the Bureau of Reclamation, Record

Group 115, Salt River Project Files 1902 – 1919, series 305, National Archives, Washington, D.C.; U.S. Congress, House, Committee on Expenditures in the Interior Department, *Report in the Matter of the Investigation of the Salt and Gila Rivers—Reservations and Reclamation Service*, House of Representatives Report No. 1506, 62nd Congress, 3d session (1913).

84. *Report in the Matter of the Investigation of the Salt and Gila Rivers*, p. 17.

85. Ibid.

86. Newell, *Autobiography*, p. 85.

87. Ibid.

88. James M. Graham to Walter Fisher, June 3, 1912; Walter Fisher to James Graham, June 11, 1912, Central Records Box 219 – 30, LEG 8 – 1, Salt River Project; Heim, "Financing Reclamation," pp. 122 – 123.

89. *Minutes* of the Board of Governors of the Salt River Valley Water Users' Association, April 8, 1912, Corporate Secretary's Office, Salt River Project. Out of 61,497 votes cast, Orme received 45,909 and Wood, 14,044.

90. F. H. Newell to Samuel Adams, September 28, 1912, Records of the Secretary of Interior, Record Group 48, Central Classified Files, Salt River Project 8 – 3, National Archives, Washington, D.C.

91. Ibid.

92. Ibid.

93. F. H. Newell to Samuel Adams, October 3, 1912, Records of the Secretary of Interior, Record Group 48, Central Classified Files, Salt River Project 8 – 3, National Archives, Washington, D.C.

94. E. A. Brown and Joseph Chafe to Secretary of Interior, October 11, 1912, Records of the Secretary of Interior, Record Group 48, Central Classified Files, Salt River Project 8 – 3, National Archives, Washington, D.C.

95. Ibid.

96. Petition to Secretary of Interior Fisher, October 9, 1912, Records of the Secretary of Interior, Record Group 48, Central Classified Files, Salt River Project 8 – 3, National Archives, Washington, D.C.

97. Newell, *Autobiography*, p. 85.

98. Anne Wintermute Lane and Louise Herrick Wall, eds., *The Letters of Franklin K. Lane*, (Boston: Houghton-Mifflin Co., 1922), p. 136.

99. Newell, *Autobiography*, p. 85.

100. Otis B. Goodall to Secretary of Interior Lane, April 22, 1913, Records of the Secretary of Interior, Record Group 48, Central Classified Files, Salt River Project 8 – 3, National Archives, Washington, D.C.

101. F. W. Hanna, Chairman, Inquiry Board, Salt River Project, to Director, U.S. Reclamation Service, August 8, 1913, Records of the Bureau of Reclamation, Record Group 115, General Files 1902 – 1919; series 314—Salt River, National Archives, Washington, D.C.

102. F. W. Hanna to F. H. Newell, August 20, 1913, Records of the Bureau of Reclamation, Record Group 115, General Files 1902 – 1919, series 314—Salt River, National Archives, Washington, D.C.

103. Ibid.

104. Heim, "Financing Reclamation," pp. 193 – 194, discusses the increase of mortgages and personal debt on Salt River. By 1915, mortgages covered about 85 percent of the project lands.

105. John A. Widstoe, "History and Problems of Irrigation Development in the West," *Transactions of the American Society of Civil Engineers* 90 (1927): 683.

106. F. H. Newell to supervising and project engineers, August 19, 1913, Central Records Box S-7-221/25-106, Salt River Project.

107. F H. Newell, "National Efforts at Homemaking," *Annual Report of the Smithsonian Institution, 1922*, (Washington, D.C.: Government Printing Office, 1924), p. 520.

108. Schiff, *Fire and Water*, p. 165.
109. Ibid., p. 166.
110. Institute for Government Research, *The U.S. Reclamation Service: Its History, Activities and Organization*, (New York: D. Appleton & Co., 1919), pp. 31 – 32; Act of August 13, 1914 (38 Stat., 686).
111. Newell, *Autobiography*, p. 89.
112. Ibid., pp. 88 – 91; Hays, *Conservation and the Gospel of Efficiency*, p. 248; Edwin T. Layton, Jr., "Frederick Haynes Newell and the Revolt of the Engineers," *Midcontinent American Studies Journal* 3 (Fall, 1962): 17 – 26.

FROM CONFLICT TO COOPERATION

1. Peggy Heim, "Financing the Federal Reclamation Program: The Development of Repayment Policy, 1902 – 1919," (Ph.D. dissertation: Columbia University, 1953), pp. 155 – 161.
2. Franklin K. Lane, Circular Letter to the Reclamation Projects, January 2, 1914, *Proceedings of the Board of Cost Review*, volume 1 of exhibits, Corporate Secretary's Office, Salt River Project; Keith Olson, *Biography of a Progressive: Franklin K. Lane, 1864 – 1921*, (Westport, CT: Greenwood Press, 1979), p. 77.
3. B. A. Fowler to Judge Hiram Steele, April 28, 1909, Records of the Bureau of Reclamation, Record Group 115, Salt River Project Files 1902 – 1919, series 261, National Archives, Washington, D.C.; see also Joseph H. Kibbey to B. A. Fowler, September 19, 1905, Copies of Letters between the Salt River Valley Water Users' Association and the U.S. Reclamation Service, 1902 – 1909, Corporate Secretary's Office, Salt River Project.
4. The history of the Kent Decree, the decision of the United States to intervene in 1907, and the implications for water users both in 1910 and in the 1980s are complex and worthy of more attention than I am able to give here. However, for the Association leadership's position, see B. A. Fowler to A. P. Davis, April 11, 1905, Records of the Bureau of Reclamation, Record Group 115, Salt River Project Files 1902 – 1919, series 261, National Archives, Washington, D.C.; Resolution of the Board of Governors, Council and Shareholders, April 13, 1905, Box A-4, Corporate Secretary's Office, Salt River Project; for the government view, see Louis C. Hill to F. H. Newell, June 11, 1907, Records of the Bureau of Reclamation, Record Group 115, Salt River Project Files 1902 – 1919, series 118, National Archives, Washington, D.C.
5. S. Baker to E. A. Hitchcock, May 18, 1905, Records of the Secretary of Interior, Record Group 48, Lands and Railroads: Reclamation, National Archives, Washington, D.C.; A. P. Davis and Morris Bien to F. H. Newell, August 13, 1906, Records of the Bureau of Reclamation, Record Group 115, Salt River Project Files 1902 – 1919, series 118, National Archives, Washington, D.C.
6. Joseph H. Kibbey to B. A. Fowler, March 28, 1905, Records of the Bureau of Reclamation, Record Group 115, Salt River Project Files 1902 – 1919, series 261, National Archives, Washington, D.C.
7. Fowler to Davis, April 11, 1905.
8. Gerard H. Matthes to L. C. Hill, April 20, 1905, Box A-4, Corporate Secretary's Office, Salt River Project.
9. Report of the Committee of Sixteen to the Salt River Valley Water Users' Association, C. T. Hirst, Chairman, November, 1905, Salt River Project Archives, Salt River Project.
10. A. P. Davis and Morris Bien to F. H. Newell, August 13, 1906.
11. Ibid.; Morris Bien to E. A. Hitchcock, October 5, 1906; A. P. Davis to B. A. Fowler, February 28, 1907, Copies of Letters between the Salt River Valley Water

Users' Association and the U.S. Reclamation Service, Corporate Secretary's Office, Salt River Project.

12. *Minutes* of the Board of Governors of the Salt River Valley Water Users' Association, February 4, 1907, Corporate Secretary's Office, Salt River Project.

13. John S. Goff, *Arizona Territorial Officials I: The Supreme Court Justices, 1863 – 1912*, (Cave Creek, Arizona: Black Mountain Press, 1975), pp. 170 – 174.

14. L. C. Hill to F. H. Newell, June 11, 1907; J. L. B. Alexander to the Attorney General, June 17, 1907, Records of U.S. Attorneys and Marshalls, Record Group 118, Arizona: Letters Sent 1899 – 1907, Federal Archives and Records Center, Laguna Niguel, California; W. H. Code to Secretary of Interior, June 11, 1907; Louis C. Hill to F. H. Newell, August 9, 1907, Records of the Bureau of Reclamation, Record Group 115, Salt River Project Files 1902 – 1919, series 118, National Archives, Washington, D.C.; In the District Court, Maricopa County, Arizona, *Patrick T. Hurley v. Charles F. Abbott, et al.*, No. 4564, Copy of Answer and Cross Complaint, by Joseph L. B. Alexander, U.S. Attorney, August 31, 1907, Salt River Project Archives, Salt River Project. The United States Department of Justice instructed Alexander to intervene in the *Hurley v. Abbott* suit rather than to interplead, so that the Indian water rights would be considered. The decision to intervene was also based upon the great increase in costs of a new suit, which Alexander's motion to interplead would have caused.

15. In the District Court of the Third Judicial District of the Territory of Arizona, In and For the County of Maricopa, *Patrick T. Hurley, Plaintiff, the United States of America, Intervenor, v. Charles F. Abbott and 4,800 others, Defendants*, No. 4564, Salt River Project Archives, Salt River Project.

16. Abstract of letter from A. A. Jones to the Salt River Valley Water Users' Association, August 21, 1913, Salt River Project Archives, Salt River Project.

17. Ibid.

18. Charles Van der Veer, secretary of Salt River Valley Water Users' Association, to A. A. Jones, September 3, 1913; John P. Orme to A. P. Davis, October 8, 1913, Records of the Bureau of Reclamation, Record Group 115, Salt River Project Files 1902 – 1919, series 544 – D, National Archives, Washington, D.C.

19. John P. Orme to F. H. Newell, September 4, 1913, Salt River Project Archives, Salt River Project.

20. A. P. Davis to John P. Orme, September 17, 1913, Records of the Bureau of Reclamation, Record Group 115, Salt River Project Files 1902 – 1919, series 544 – D, National Archives, Washington, D.C.

21. A. P. Davis to F. H. Newell, October 17, 1913, Records of the Bureau of Reclamation, Record Group 115, Salt River Project Files 1902 – 1919, series 544 – D, National Archives, Washington, D.C.

22. L. C. Hill, supervising engineer, to Director, U.S. Reclamation Service, October 1, 1913, Records of the Bureau of Reclamation, Record Group 115, Salt River Project Files 1902 – 1919, series 544 – D, National Archives, Washington, D.C.

23. John P. Orme to A. P. Davis, October 22, 1913, Records of the Bureau of Reclamation, Record Group 115, Salt River Project Files 1902 – 1919, series 544 – D, National Archives, Washington, D.C.

24. L. C. Hill to Director, U.S. Reclamation Service, October 1, 1913.

25. Morris Bien to Louis C. Hill, November 6, 1913, Records of the Bureau of Reclamation, Record Group 115, Salt River Project Files 1902 – 1919, series 544 – D, National Archives, Washington, D.C. Newell wrote a "yes" in the margin of Hill's letter to him dated October 1, 1913, suggesting postponement of the Survey Board meeting until after the rainy season.

26. Survey Board to Director, U.S. Reclamation Service, December 9, 1913, Records of the Bureau of Reclamation, Record Group 115, Salt River Project Files 1902 – 1919, series 544 – D, National Archives, Washington, D.C.

27. F. W. Hanna to Director, U.S. Reclamation Service, December 19, 1913, Records

of the Bureau of Reclamation, Record Group 115, Salt River Project Files 1902 – 1919, series 544 – D, National Archives, Washington, D.C.

28. Reclamation Commission to F. W. Hanna, January 9, 1914, cited in Department of the Interior, U.S. Reclamation Service, *Salt River Project, Arizona: Limiting Irrigable Area of Land,* January 15, 1914, Salt River Project Archives, Salt River Project. The Reclamation Commission also added a fourth principle of guidance, giving the small landowner preference over the larger one.

29. Ibid. (For the view of the legal division of the U.S. Reclamation Service on the binding nature of the Kent Decree, see also E. B. Hoffman to Morris Bien, December 23, 1913, and Morris Bien to the Director, U.S. Reclamation Service, December 29, 1913, Record of the Bureau of Reclamation, Record Group 115, Salt River Project Files 1902 – 1919, series 544 – D, National Archives, Washington, D.C.)

30. Ibid. The Commission issued the following guidelines: Select Class A holdings of 160 acres or less first; then cultivated Class B lands of 160 acres or less; then cultivated Class C lands of 40 acres or less, giving preference to those who did not have Class B lands. If this did not provide enough land to fill the project area, uncultivated and subscribed Class B and C lands of 40 acres or less would be accepted according to their date of subscription.

31. Ibid. See also *Arizona (Phoenix) Republican,* 14 March 1914.

32. Board of Survey to the Board of Governors, Salt River Valley Water Users' Association, February 26, 1914, Records of the Bureau of Reclamation, Record Group 115, Salt River Project Files 1902 – 1919, series 544 – D, National Archives, Washington, D.C.; *Republican,* 2 and 8 March 1914.

33. *Republican,* 11, 12, and 14 March 1914. The Survey Board determined that there were 176,337 acres of land cultivated within the reservoir district boundaries and 8,336 acres of townsite lands for a total reservoir area of 184,673 acres. Since townsite lands required less water than farm lands, the Board assumed the cultivated acreage equivalent to 180,000 acres of farm land. Of this area, 10,000 acres were school lands, which could not be awarded a reservoir right until Arizona changed its law preventing their sale; when this was done, the Board assumed the Association would develop an additional water supply to meet their needs through installing pumping plants or lining the project canals with cement to conserve water normally lost through seepage. The acreage to receive water from the reservoir would thus initially be about 170,000. See also Minutes of the Mass Meetings held in Phoenix and Mesa, 13 and 14 March 1914, on the limiting of the project, Report File 2/15b, Board of Survey, Corporate Secretary's Office, Salt River Project.

34. *Republican,* 15 March 1914.

35. Ibid., 18 March 1914; also 14 and 15 March 1914.

36. Olson, *Biography of a Progressive,* pp. 10, 13; Anne Wintermute Lane and Louise Herrick Wall, eds., *The Letters of Franklin K. Lane* (Boston: Houghton Mifflin Company, 1922).

37. *Republican,* 26 March 1914.

38. Ibid.

39. Ibid., 14 March 1914.

40. Ibid., 26 March 1914. The pumping program was approved before 1920, but legal challenges to the Association's right to build Horseshoe Dam prevented its construction until the 1940s.

41. Board of Survey to the Reclamation Commission, Final Report of the Board of Survey—Salt River Project, Arizona, August 19, 1914; A. P. Davis to Secretary of Interior, November 11, 1914, Records of the Bureau of Reclamation, Record Group 115, Salt River Project Files 1902 – 1919, series 544 – D, National Archives, Washington, D.C.

42. Report of the Second Board of Survey, May 25, 1916, Report File 2/15b, Boards of Survey, Corporate Secretary's Office, Salt River Project. Arizona passed legisla-

tion in 1915 – 1916 providing for the sale of school lands, and the Second Board of Survey was obliged to take in all these lands (11,030 acres) irrespective of the water supply. The area of fragmentary Class A lands was 996.32 acres. The total project area was now increased to 191,647.60 acres, inclusive of townsites, or about 12,000 acres over that earlier recommended. To cope with this excess, the Survey Board advocated increasing the duty of water to 4.2 acre-feet (2.86 acre-feet at the land when canal losses were subtracted). This change meant that less water would be available on a per-acre basis than under prior irrigation practices.

43. On the "dry lands" problem, see George L. Christy to the U.S. Reclamation Commission, April 25, 1916, and the Reclamation Commission to the Secretary of Interior, June 26, 1916, Records of the Bureau of Reclamation, Record Group 115, Salt River Project Files 1902 – 1919, series 544 – D1, National Archives, Washington, D.C. The Association built three more dams on Salt River in the 1920s—at Mormon Flat, Horse Mesa, and Stewart Mountain.

44. Franklin K. Lane, Circular Letter, January 2, 1914, p. 486.

45. *Proceedings of the Board of Cost Review*, Salt River Project, May – June, 1915, Corporate Secretary's Office, Salt River Project, p. 4.

46. Fred A. Jones to John P. Orme, December 31, 1914, Salt River Project documents, Arizona Department of Library and Archives, Phoenix, Arizona.

47. *Republican*, 10 March 1914; Elwood Mead, Chairman, Central Board of Review, to Franklin K. Lane, November 19, 1915, Records of the Bureau of Reclamation, Record Group 115, Salt River Project Files 1902 – 1919, series 261, National Archives, Washington, D.C., p. 2.

48. Thomas U. Taylor to John P. Orme, November 30, 1914, Salt River Project documents, Arizona Department of Library and Archives; Heim, "Financing Reclamation," pp. 215 – 216. Taylor also served as the chairman of the other Boards of Cost Review in the U.S. Reclamation Service southern division, and Heim found him to be partial to the water users over the Service; the Reclamation Service apparently felt the same.

49. *Proceedings of the Board of Cost Review*, May – June, 1915, pp. 14 – 15.

50. Ibid.

51. Ibid., p. 4.

52. Ibid., p. 7. The items the Board considered in its discussions were, in order: storage works, power system, diversion works, northside canal system, southside canal system, irrigation wells, plant account, real estate—rights and property, irrigable lands, telephone lines, roads, drainage, examination of the project, and operation and maintenance.

53. *Proceedings of the Board of Cost Review*, May – June, 1915.

54. Mead to Lane, November 19, 1915, p. 2.

55. Ibid. The exact figures of the majority report were: project's total cost $13,100,500; revenues and credits $2,309,450; defective construction, excessive costs $3,537,809; total amount to be repaid $7,253,241. The minority report: project's total cost $13,108,862; revenues and credits $2,941,127; defective construction, excessive costs 641,220; total to be repaid $9,527,515.

56. For information on Mead and his point of view on reclamation see Michael C. Robinson, *Water for the West: The Bureau of Reclamation, 1902 – 1977*, (Chicago: Public Works Historical Society, 1979); "Irrigation Works: An Informal Discussion," *Transactions of the American Society of Civil Engineers* 49 (December, 1902): 24 – 44; Elwood Mead, "Irrigation in the United States," *Transactions of the American Society of Civil Engineers* 54 (Part C, 1905): 83 – 110; and a series of letters between Secretary of Agriculture James Wilson and U.S. Geological Survey director Charles Walcott, May, 1903, Records of the Bureau of Reclamation, Record Group 115, Salt River Project Files 1902 – 1919, series 305, National Archives, Washington, D.C.

57. Mead to Lane, November 19, 1915, p. 5.

58. Ibid., p. 16.

59. Ibid., p. 15.

60. Ibid., p. 7.

61. Ibid., p. 25.

62. Ibid., pp. 9—10. Mead suggested instituting a low-interest federal loan program strictly for farmers to help many under the reclamation projects through the difficulties of 9—12 percent mortgages and loans. This program was realized in the Federal Farm Loan Act of July 17, 1916, and was more extensively amplified in the plethora of New Deal legislation aimed toward assisting the agricultural sector.

63. *Republican*, 8 February 1916.

64. Ibid.

65. Ibid.; John P. Orme to Franklin Lane, November 15, 1915, Central Records Box 218-27/890, Salt River Project.

66. Carl Hayden to John P. Orme, January 31, 1917, Hayden Papers 628/2, Arizona State University, Tempe, Arizona; *Republican*, 15 March 1917; Memorandum of Conference between Secretary Lane, John Orme, Carl Hayden, Joseph Kibbey and A. P. Davis, February 20, 1917, Records of the Bureau of Reclamation, Record Group 115, Salt River Project Files 1902—1919, series 261, National Archives, Washington, D.C.; Arthur S. Link, *Woodrow Wilson and the Progressive Era, 1910—1917*, (New York: Harper and Row, 1954); Olson, *Biography of a Progressive*.

67. *The Chandler Arizonan*, newsclipping, n.d. (c. November 1917), Hayden Papers 628/2, Arizona State University, Tempe, Arizona.

68. See "The People and the Senatorship," prepared by the Committee to Elect Joseph Kibbey to the U.S. Senate, October 30, 1916, Arizona Department of Library and Archives, and Ray P. Teele, *The Economics of Land Reclamation in the United States*, (Chicago: A. W. Shaw Co., 1927), p. 128, on the threat of replacing the water-users associations with irrigation districts; and *Republican*, 18 January 1916, for examples of both good agricultural prices and a full reservoir. E. E. Roddis to Will R. King, October 2, 1916, Hayden Papers 628/2, Arizona State University, Tempe, Arizona, more fully describes the good economic situation in which the water users in the Salt River Valley found themselves due to the high prices for cotton during the war.

69. *Republican*, 1 March 1917; *Sixteenth Annual Report of the Reclamation Service, 1916—1917*, Washington, D.C.: 1917, p. 8; Roddis to King, October 2, 1916. Previous to this change, the Reclamation Service interpreted the law in such a way that the power profits would automatically be used against the construction debt on Salt River until the sixteenth year of repayment when the Association could decide on its own authority how it would utilize the power profits; this allowed the Service to divert the power receipts into the general reclamation fund for fifteen years. Since this policy was a clear violation of earlier promises made to the Association, Secretary Lane again overruled the Reclamation Commission and supported the Association's position. The continued effort to change the Service's power policy was led in Congress by Carl Hayden. See Hayden to Orme, January 31, 1917.

70. Lane and Wall, eds., *The Letters of Franklin K. Lane*, p. 137; Memorandum of Conference, February 20, 1917, p. 8.

71. Arthur P. Davis and Will R. King to Secretary of Interior Lane, February 24, 1917, Records of the Bureau of Reclamation, Record Group 115, Salt River Project Files 1902—1919, series 261, National Archives, Washington, D.C.

72. Ibid.

73. Memorandum of Agreement between the United States and the Salt River Valley Water Users' Association, September 6, 1917, Records of the Secretary of Interior, Record Group 48, Central Classified Files, 1907—1936, National Archives, Washington, D.C.

74. The *Arizona Republican* stressed these events throughout August and September, 1917, to the exclusion, really, of local events. The draft issue—requirements for exemption and the large number of draft evaders or "slackers"—especially dominated the news. Notice of the Salt River Valley Water Users' Association special election received little space in the paper—usually a small column on a back page—and no editorial comments at all.

75. *Republican*, 17 August 1917; see also 14 August 1917.

76. Ibid., 19 August 1917.

77. Ibid., 10 September 1917.

78. Ibid., 14 August 1917.

79. William Cone to Reclamation Commission, August 22, 1917, Records of the Bureau of Reclamation, Record Group 115, Salt River Project Files 1902 – 1919, series 782 – A, National Archives, Washington, D.C.

80. J. Beadle to Judge Will King, August 23, 1917; Oliver P. Morton to Chief Counsel, August 29, 1917, Records of the Bureau of Reclamation, Record Group 115, Salt River Project Files 1902 – 1919, series 782 – A, National Archives, Washington, D.C.

81. Morton to Chief Counsel, August 29, 1917.

82. Agreement between the United States and the Salt River Valley Water Users' Association, September 6, 1917.

83. *Republican*, 1 March 1917.

84. Circular Letter from B. A. Fowler to the Members of the Salt River Valley Water Users' Association, March 31, 1906, 1906 Newsclip File, Corporate Secretary's Office, Salt River Project.

85. *Transactions of the American Society of Civil Engineers* 100 (1935): 1582 – 1591.

86. *New York Times*, 16 November 1924.

THE MAGNIFICENT EXPERIMENT IN PERSPECTIVE

1. These three projects were selected from Dorothy Lampen's list of initial projects considered by the Reclamation Service. See her "Economic and Social Aspects of Federal Reclamation," *Johns Hopkins University Studies in Historical and Political Science* 48, No. 1 (Baltimore: 1930), p. 53. As of the mid-1980s little had been written about reclamation generally, and far less on individual projects. The best documented of the projects is the Newlands Project. Mary Ellen Glass, in particular, has performed excellent research on its history and development. See her "The Newlands Reclamation Project: Years of Innocence, 1903 – 1907," *Journal of the West* 7 (1968): 55 – 63 and "The First Nationally Sponsored Arid Land Reclamation Project: The Newlands Act in Churchill County," *The Nevada Historical Society Quarterly* (Spring, 1971): 2 – 12. Also contributing to the understanding of reclamation in Nevada have been Donald J. Pisani ("Conflict Over Conservation: The Reclamation Service and the Tahoe Contract," *Western Historical Society Quarterly* 10 [April, 1979]: 167 – 190) and John M. Townley (*Turn This Water into Gold: The Story of the Newlands Project*, [Reno, Nevada: Nevada Historical Society, 1977]). For all the projects, the best sources are the Annual Reports of the Reclamation Service. Also useful for the early years is the report of the Board of Army Engineers Investigating Reclamation Projects, U.S., House, "Fund for Reclamation," House Document No. 1262, 61st Congress, 3d session (1911).

2. Glass, "The Newlands Reclamation Project," pp. 56 – 57.

3. Pisani, "Conflict Over Conservation."

4. Glass, "The Newlands Reclamation Project," p. 61.

5. U.S., Department of Interior, Reclamation Service, *Ninth Annual Report of the U.S. Reclamation Service, 1909 – 1910*, p. 191, and *Fifteenth Annual Report of the U.S. Reclamation Service, 1915 – 1916*, p. 281; see also U.S., Senate, "Federal Reclamation by Irrigation," by the Committee of Special Advisers on Reclamation, Senate Document No. 92, 68th Congress, 1st session, p. 17.

6. Board of Army Engineers, "Fund for Reclamation," House Document No. 1262, 61st Congress, 3d session, p. 91.

7. Ibid.

8. *Fifteenth Annual Report of the U.S. Reclamation Service*, p. 293.

9. Ibid., pp. 281 – 283; Peggy Heim, "Financing the Federal Reclamation Program: The Development of Repayment Policy, 1902 – 1919," (Ph.D. dissertation: Columbia University, 1953), Tables 28 – 29. In 1924 the Fact Finders Commission on Reclamation reported to Secretary of Interior Hubert Work that nearly $45 million should be charged off the Newlands Project because settlers would not be able to pay the final costs.

10. D. W. Cole, project manager, to A. P. Davis, January 8, 1916; see also D. W. Cole to West Side Water Users' Association, March 12, 1915, Records of the Bureau of Reclamation, Record Group 115, Newlands Project Files 1902 – 1919, National Archives, Washington, D.C.

11. John E. Field to Morris Bien, May 17, 1905, Records of the Bureau of Reclamation, Record Group 115, North Platte Project Files 1902 – 1919, National Archives, Washington, D.C.

12. *Second Annual Report of the U.S. Reclamation Service*, 1903 – 1904, p. 499.

13. *Fifteenth Annual Report of the U.S. Reclamation Service*, pp. 258 – 262.

14. Norman Smith, *A History of Dams*, (Secaucus, N. J.: Citadel Press, 1972), p. 222; "Fund for Reclamation," pp. 81 – 86; *Fifteenth Annual Report of the U.S. Reclamation Service*, pp. 258 – 263.

15. "Fund for Reclamation," p. 84; *Fifteenth Annual Report of the U.S. Reclamation Service*, p. 255.

16. *Fifteenth Annual Report of the U.S. Reclamation Service*, p. 257.

17. "Fund for Reclamation," p. 84.

18. *Fifteenth Annual Report of the U.S. Reclamation Service*, pp. 255 – 256. During the 1915 season 78,057 acres were irrigated, including 8,050 acres of the North Platte Canal and Colonization Company. The small amount of acreage irrigated on the North Platte Project persisted into 1918, when only 85,000 acres were served water. See Newell, *Water Resources*, pp. 157 – 158.

19. Heim, "Financing Federal Reclamation," Table 29.

20. *Reclamation Record* (March, 1923), p. 110.

21. "Fund for Reclamation," pp. 85 – 86.

22. Charles A. Morrill to Department of Interior, Geological Survey, October 19, 1904, Records of the Bureau of Reclamation, Record Group 115, North Platte Project Files 1902 – 1919, National Archives, Washington, D.C.; *Fourth Annual Report of the U.S. Reclamation Service, 1905 – 1906*, p. 28.

23. F. H. Newell to William Morrow, June 24, 1907, Records of the Bureau of Reclamation, Record Group 115, North Platte Project Files 1902 – 1919, National Archives, Washington, D.C.

24. Heim, "Financing Reclamation," p. 143.

25. Newell, *Water Resources*, pp. 171 – 174; *Ninth Annual Report of the U.S. Reclamation Service*, pp. 155 – 156.

26. B. W. Brockway to Cyrus C. Babb, July 17, 1906, Records of the Bureau of Reclamation, Record Group 115, Milk River Project Files 1902 – 1919, National Archives, Washington, D. C. The adjudication of these Indian water rights resulted in the famous Winters Doctrine (1908) which reserved to the federal reservation all the water the irrigable lands there can beneficially use. Despite this

broad and far-reaching proclamation, the Reclamation Service believed that the minimum flow of the river through the reservation was the maximum amount of water the Indians could take. See Norris Hundley, "The 'Winters Decision' and Indian Water Rights: a Mystery Reexamined," *Western Historical Quarterly* (January, 1982): 17 – 42, for an excellent discussion of the *Winters* case and the Milk River Project.

27. "Fund for Reclamation," pp. 65 – 71.

28. Ibid., p. 70.

29. Ibid., p. 71.

30. Ibid., p. 70.

31. *Fifteenth Annual Report of the U.S. Reclamation Service*, p. 212.

32. Ibid., p. 221. The growing season was approximately five months in duration. Principal crops on the other projects discussed here were divided between alfalfa, grain crops, sugar beets, corn, garden vegetables, and dairy products.

33. Ibid., p. 211; "Federal Reclamation by Irrigation," p. 173; Heim, "Financing Reclamation," Table 28. The Department of Interior in 1926 charged off nearly $2 million for the Milk River Project.

34. George Vennum to F. H. Newell, December 15, 1906, Records of the Bureau of Reclamation, Record Group 115, Milk River Project Files 1902 – 1919, National Archives, Washington, D.C.

35. H. H. Nelson to A. P. Davis, May 11, 1909, Records of the Bureau of Reclamation, Record Group 115, Milk River Project Files 1902 – 1919, National Archives, Washington, D.C.

36. B. W. Brockway to Cyrus Babb, July 17, 1906, Records of the Bureau of Reclamation, Record Group 115, Milk River Project Files 1902 – 1919, National Archives, Washington, D.C.

37. "Federal Reclamation by Irrigation," p. xii.

38. Ibid.

39. Samuel P. Hays, *American Political History as Social Analysis* (Knoxville: University of Tennessee Press, 1980), p. 7.

40. George Morrison, President of the American Society of Civil Engineers in 1895, also called the engineers, "priests of material development." See Edwin T. Layton, Jr., *The Revolt of the Engineers: Social Responsibility and the American Engineering Profession* (Cleveland: Case Western Reserve University Press, 1971), pp. 58 – 59.

41. Lampen, "Economic and Social Aspects," p. 38.

42. Layton, "Frederick Haynes Newell," p. 18.

43. Glass, "The First Nationally Sponsored Arid Lands Reclamation Project," p. 9.

44. Mawn, "Phoenix, Arizona," p. 507.

45. Ibid. pp. 288 – 289.

46. Ibid., pp. 497 – 498.

47. E. E. Roddis to Will R. King, October 2, 1916, Hayden Papers 628/2, Arizona State University.

Selected Bibliography

MANUSCRIPT AND ARCHIVAL COLLECTIONS

Arizona, Phoenix. Arizona Department of Library and Archives.
———. Arizona Room, Phoenix Public Library.
———. Phoenix History Project.
Arizona, Tempe. Arizona Collection, Arizona State University.
　　Carl Hayden Papers.
———. Salt River Project Archives, Salt River Project.
Arizona, Tucson. Arizona Historical Society Library and Archives.
———. Special Collections, University of Arizona.
California, Laguna Niguel. Federal Archives and Records Center.
　　Record Group 118. Records of U.S. Attorneys and Marshalls.
　　　　Arizona: Letters Received 1903 – 1910.
　　　　Arizona: Letters Sent 1899 – 1908.
California, San Marino, The Huntington Library.
Washington, D. C. Library of Congress.
　　Frederick Haynes Newell Papers.
———. National Archives.
　　Record Group 48. Records of the Secretary of Interior.
　　　　Central Classified Files, 1907 – 1936.
　　　　Lands and Railroads Division: Reclamation Projects—
　　　　Salt River.
　　　　Miscellaneous Hearings, Franklin Lane: Project Complaints,
　　　　1913.
　　　　Miscellaneous Reports, James Garfield: Reclamation Project
　　　　Studies, 1907 – 1909.
　　Record Group 57. Records of the Geological Survey.

Classified Expenditures, Hydrographic Branch, 1895 – 1899.
Water Resources Division: Irrigation Branch Report File,
1890 – 1898.
Record Group 60. Records of the Department of Justice.
U. S. Attorneys: Correspondence, 1908 – 1919. Straight
numerical files.
Record Group 75. Records of the Bureau of Indian Affairs.
Irrigation Service—Arizona.
Record Group 115. Records of the Bureau of Reclamation.
General Files, 1902 – 1919.
Milk River Project Files, 1902 – 1919: Water-Users' Associations.
Newlands (Truckee-Carson) Project Files, 1902 – 1919: Water-
Users' Associations.
North Platte Project Files, 1902 – 1919: Water-Users' Associations.
Salt River Project Files, 1902 – 1919.

GOVERNMENT DOCUMENTS

United States Congress, House. Board of Army Engineers on Recla-
mation Projects. *Fund for Reclamation of Arid Lands*. 61st Congress,
3d Session, 1911. H. R. Doc. No. 1261.
———. Committee on Expenditures in the Interior Department.
*Report in the Matter of the Investigations of the Salt and Gila Rivers—
Reservations and Reclamation Service*. 62nd Congress, 3d Session,
1913. H. R. Report No. 1506.
———. Committee on Irrigation of Arid Lands. *Reservoir Near San
Carlos, Arizona*. 56th Congress, 2d Session, 1901. H. R. Report
No. 2934.
United States Congress, Senate. Committee on Irrigation. *Investiga-
tion of the Reclamation Service Projects*. 61st Congress, 3d Session,
1909. S. Report No. 1281.
———. Committee of Special Advisers on Reclamation. *Federal
Reclamation by Irrigation*. 68th Congress, 1st Session, 1924.
S. Doc. No. 92.
———. *Report on the Irrigation Investigation for the Benefit of the Pima
and Other Indians on the Gila River Indian Reservation, Arizona*,
by Arthur Powell Davis. 54th Congress, 2d Session, 1897.
S. Doc. No. 27.
———. Special Committee on Irrigation. *Report of the Special Commit-
tee of the U.S. Senate on the Irrigation and Reclamation of Arid Lands*.
51st Congress, 1st Session, 1890. S. Report No. 928.
United States Congress, Joint Committee for the Investigation of the
Department of Interior and the Forest Service. *Investigation of the
Department of the Interior and the Forest Service*. 61st Congress,
3d Session, 1911. S. Doc. No. 719, pt. 5.

United States Department of Agriculture. *Irrigation in the Salt River Valley*, by W. H. Code. Bulletin No. 104. Washington, D.C.: Government Printing Office, 1902.

————. Arizona Agricultural Experiment Station. *Irrigation and Agricultural Practice in Arizona*, by R. H. Forbes. Bulletin No. 63. Washington, D.C.: Government Printing Office, 1911.

United States Department of Interior, Geological Survey. *Irrigation near Phoenix, Arizona*, by Arthur P. Davis. Water Supply and Irrigation Paper No. 2. Washington, D.C.: Government Printing Office, 1897.

————. *Proceedings of First Conference of Engineers of the U.S. Reclamation Service*. Water Supply and Irrigation Paper No. 93. Washington, D.C.: Government Printing Office, 1904.

————. *Twenty-First Annual Report of the U.S. Geological Survey, 1899–1900: Pt. 4: Hydrography*. Washington, D.C.: Government Printing Office, 1901.

————. *Underground Waters of Salt River Valley, Arizona*, by Willis T. Lee. Water Supply and Irrigation Paper No. 136. Washington, D.C.: Government Printing Office, 1905.

————. *Water Storage on Salt River, Arizona*, by Arthur P. Davis. Water Supply and Irrigation Paper No. 73. Washington, D.C.: Government Printing Office, 1903.

United States Department of Interior, Reclamation Service. *Annual Reports of the U.S. Reclamation Service*, 1902–1918.

————. *History of the Irrigation Movement*, by F. H. Newell. Washington, D.C.: Government Printing Office, 1903.

THESES AND DISSERTATIONS

Brown, Leahmae. "The Development of a National Policy With Respect to Water Resources." Ph.D. dissertation: University of Illinois, Urbana, 1937.

Davison, Stanley R. "The Leadership of the Reclamation Movement, 1875–1902." Ph.D. dissertation: University of California, Berkeley, 1951.

Heim, Peggy. "Financing the Federal Reclamation Program, 1902–1919: The Development of Repayment Policy." Ph.D. dissertation: Columbia University, 1953.

Henderson, Patrick. "The Public Domain in Arizona, 1863–1891." Ph.D. dissertation: University of New Mexico, 1965.

Hogan, Harry Joseph. "The 160-Acre Limitation: Conflict in Value Systems in the Federal Reclamation Program." Ph.D. dissertation: George Washington University, 1972.

Horning, E. C. "Reclamation of Arizona's Arid Lands." M. A. thesis: University of Oklahoma, 1942.

Mawn, Geoffrey P. "Phoenix, Arizona: Central City of the Southwest, 1870–1920." Ph.D. dissertation: Arizona State University, 1979.

Smith, Karen L. "From Town to City: A History of Phoenix, Arizona, 1870–1912." M. A. thesis: University of California, Santa Barbara, 1978.

Strebel, George Lofstrom. "Irrigation as a Factor in Western History, 1847–1890." Ph.D. dissertation: University of California, Berkeley, 1965.

Thomas, Robert Daniel. "Policy-Making in the American Federal System: Intergovernmental Responses to Water Problems in Arizona." Ph.D. dissertation: University of Arizona, 1970.

NEWSPAPERS AND PERIODICALS

The Arizona Democrat
The Arizona Gazette
The Arizona Republic
The Arizona Republican
Engineering News
The Engineering Record
The Phoenix Enterprise
The Reclamation Record

ARTICLES

Bates, J. Leonard. "Fulfilling American Democracy: The Conservation Movement, 1907–1921." *Mississippi Valley Historical Review* 44 (June 1957): 29–57.

Becker, Howard S. and Carper, James W. "The Development of Identification With an Occupation." *American Journal of Sociology* 61 (January 1956): 289–298.

Bien, Morris. "The Legal Problem of Reclamation of Lands by Means of Reclamation." *Annals of the American Academy of Political and Social Sciences* 33 (1909): 180–194.

Blanchard, C. J. "Great Work of Irrigation in the West: Story of the Town of Roosevelt." *Travel* 12 (August 1907): 482–484.

———. "National Reclamation of Arid Lands." *Annual Report of the Smithsonian Institution 1906*. Washington, D.C.: Government Printing Office, 1907.

———. "Home-Making by the Government." *National Geographic* (April 1908): 250–287.

Bolton, Herbert E. "The Epic of Greater America." *American Historical Review* 38 (April 1933): 448–474.

"Builders of State: Joseph H. Kibbey." *Arizona Magazine* (September 1906): 72–74.

Byrkit, James W. "A Log of the Verde: The 'Taming' of an Arizona

River." *The Journal of Arizona History* 19 (Spring 1978): 31–54.

Carter, O. C. S. "The Government Irrigation Project at Roosevelt Dam, Salt River, Arizona." *Journal of the Franklin Institute* 163 (January 1907): 277–301.

Caughey, John. "The Insignificance of Frontier in American History." *Western Historical Quarterly* 5 (1974): 5–16.

Clarke, E. P. "The Roosevelt Dam and the Salt River Project." *The Pacific Monthly* (September 1910): 301–310.

Coman, Katherine. "Some Unsettled Problems of Irrigation." *American Economic Review* I (March 1911): 1–19.

Conkin, Paul K. "The Vision of Elwood Mead." *Agricultural History* 34 (April 1960): 88–97.

Dana, Marshall N. "Reclamation, Its Influence and Impact on the History of the West." *Utah Historical Quarterly* 27 (1959): 39–49.

Davis, A. P. "Reclamation of the Arid West by the Federal Government." *Annals of the American Academy of Political and Social Science* 31 (January 1908): 203–218.

———. "The Salt River Project." *Engineering Record* 57 (June 20, 1908): 768–769.

Dean, W. H. "The Drama of the Desert." *Illustrated World* 23 (April 1915): 169–172.

Dobyns, Henry F. "Who Killed the Gila?" *The Journal of Arizona History* 19 (Spring 1978): 17–30.

Douglas, Ernest. "A Dream That Has Come True." *Arizona* 1 (March 1911): 3–10.

Englebert, Ernest A. "Federalism and Water Resources Development." *Law and Contemporary Problems* 22 (1957): 325–350.

Forbes, Robert H. "History of Irrigation Development in Arizona." *Reclamation Era* 26 (October 1936): 226–227.

Ganoe, John T. "The Beginnings of Irrigation in the United States." *Mississippi Valley Historical Review* 25 (1938): 59–78.

———. "The Origin of a National Reclamation Policy." *Mississippi Valley Historical Review* 18 (June 1931): 34–52.

"Genesis of the Salt River Project." *Arizona, the New State Magazine* 1 (March 1911): 7–9.

Gillette, Edward. "Reclamation Service From the Viewpoint of the Settler." *Irrigation Age* 31 (June 1916): 119–121.

Glass, Mary Ellen. "The First Nationally Sponsored Arid Land Reclamation Project: The Newlands Act in Churchill County, Nevada." *Nevada Historical Society Quarterly* (Spring 1971): 2–12.

———. "The Newlands Reclamation Project: Years of Innocence, 1903–1907." *Journal of the West* 7 (January 1978): 55–63.

Goodrich, Carter. "American Development Policy: The Case of Internal Improvements." *Journal of Economic History* 16 (December 1956): 449–460.

———. "The Revulsion Against Internal Improvements." *Journal of Economic History* 10 (November 1950): 145–169.

Hayden, T. A. "Cooperation Builds an Empire." *Nation's Business* 17 (March 1929): 66–70.

Hudanick, Andrew, Jr. "George Hebard Maxwell: Reclamation's Militant Evangelist." *Journal of the West* 14 (1975): 108–121.

Kinyon, Edmund G. "The Roosevelt Dam." *Scientific American Supplement* 69 (May 21, 1910): 321–323.

Lamar, Howard. "Persistent Frontier: The West in the Twentieth Century." *Western Historical Quarterly* 4 (1973): 5–25.

Lee, Lawrence B. "William Ellsworth Smythe and the Irrigation Movement: A Reconsideration." *Pacific Historical Review* 41 (August 1972): 289–311.

Lilley, William and Gould, Lewis L. "The Western Irrigation Movement, 1878–1902: A Reappraisal." In *The American West: A Reorientation*, edited by Gene M. Gressley, pp. 57–74. Laramie: University of Wyoming Press, 1966.

Lovin, Hugh. "A 'New West' Reclamation Tragedy: The Twin-Falls–Oakley Project in Idaho, 1908–1931." *Arizona and the West* 20 (Spring 1978): 5–24.

Luckingham, Bradford. "The City in the Westward Movement: A Bibliographical Note." *Western Historical Quarterly* 5 (July 974): 295–306.

McClintock, James H. "History and Development of the Salt River Valley." *Progressive Arizona* 1 (November 1925): 29.

McDaniel, Allen B. "Frederick Haynes Newell." *Transactions of the American Society of Civil Engineers* 98 (1933): 1597–1600.

Mead, Elwood. "Irrigation in the U.S." *Transactions of the American Society of Civil Engineers* 54 (1905): 83–110.

Mead, Elwood; Ripley, T. M.; Newell, F. H.; Maxwell, George H.; Croes, J. James R.; Haupt, L. M.; and Darrach, Charles G. "Irrigation Works. An Informal Discussion." *Transactions of the American Society of Civil Engineers* 49 (December 1902): 24–44.

Meier, E. D. "The Engineer and the Future." *Journal of the American Society of Mechanical Engineers* 34 (January 1912): 5.

Meredith, H. L. "Reclamation in the Salt River Valley, 1902–1917." *Journal of the West* 7 (January 1968): 76–83.

Newell, F. H. "The Arid Regions of the United States." *National Geographic Magazine* 5 (January 31, 1894): 167–172.

———. "Awakening of the Engineer." *Engineering News* 74 (September 16, 1915): 568.

———. Comments on "Present Policy of the U.S. Bureau of Reclamation Regarding Land Settlement," by Elwood Mead. *Transactions of the American Society of Civil Engineers* 90 (1927): 762–769.

———. Comments on "Some Phases of Irrigation Finance," by D. C. Henny. *Transactions of the American Society of Civil Engineers* 90 (1928): 563–568.

———. "The Engineer in Public Service." *Engineering News* 68 (July 25, 1912): 153–155.

———. "The Human Side of Engineering." *Engineering Record* 70 (August 29, 1914): 236.

———. "Irrigation: An Informal Discussion." *Transactions of the American Society of Civil Engineers* 62 (1909): 1–66.

———. "National Efforts at Home Making." *Annual Report of the Smithsonian Institution* (1922): 517–553.

———. "The National Problem of Land Reclamation." *The Scientific Monthly* 16 (April 1923): 337–343.

———. "Progress in Reclamation of Arid Lands in the Western U.S." *Annual Report of the Smithsonian Institution* (1910): 517–533.

———. "The Reclamation of the West." *Annual Report of the Smithsonian Institution* (1903): 827–841.

———. "Reclamation of the West." *National Geographic* 15 (January 1904): 15–30.

———. "The U.S. Reclamation Service in the Arid West." *Engineering News* 50 (November 26, 1903): 485–486.

———. "What I Am Trying To Do." *World's Work* 25 (February 1913): 396–399.

———. "Work of the U.S.R.S." *Journal of the Franklin Institute* 164 (July 1907): 29–42.

Peterson, Otis. "The Story of a Bureau." *Journal of the West* 7 (January 1968): 84–95.

Pinchot, Gifford. "How Conservation Began." *Agricultural History* 11 (October 1937): 255–265.

Pisani, Donald J. "Conflict Over Conservation: The Reclamation Service and the Tahoe Contract." *Western Historical Quarterly* 10 (April 1979): 167–190.

———. "Federal Reclamation and Water Rights in Nevada." *Agricultural History* 51:3 (1977): 540–558.

Pomeroy, Earl. "Toward a Reorientation of Western History: Continuity and Environment," *Mississippi Valley Historical Review* 41 (March 1955): 579–600.

"Pumping Water for Irrigation in Arizona." *Engineering News* 31 (May 31, 1894): 456.

Reed, Howard S. "The Salt River Project—Its Possibilities." *Arizona, the New State Magazine* 1 (April 1910): 3–4.

"The Roosevelt Irrigation Dam in Arizona." *Scientific American* 93 (December 16, 1905): 476–477.

"The Roosevelt Masonry Dam on Salt River, Arizona." *Engineering News* 53 (January 12, 1905): 34–37.

"Salt River Project." *Arizona, the New State Magazine* 3 (November 1912): 17.

"The Salt River Project, U.S. Reclamation Service." *Engineering Record* 52 (October 14, 1905): 422–423.

"Secretary Ballinger and the United States Reclamation Service." *Engineering News* 63 (January 13, 1910): 46–48.

Smith, Chester. "The Construction of Roosevelt Dam: An Account of the Difficulties Encountered in Constructing a High Masonry Dam in Arizona." *Engineering Record* 62 (December 31, 1910): 756–762.

———. "Progress on the Roosevelt Dam, Salt River Project, United States Reclamation Service." *Engineering News* 60 (September 10, 1908): 265–268.

———. "Reinforced Concrete Pipe for Carrying Water Under Pressure." *Transactions of the American Society of Civil Engineers*, 60 (1908): 124–141.

Smith, F. Dumont. "Phoenix, Arizona, and the Salt River Valley." *Kansas Magazine* VI (November 1911): 3–11.

Smith, Karen L. "The Campaign for Water in Central Arizona, 1890–1903." *Arizona and the West* 23 (Summer 1981): 127–148.

Tomlinson, F. L. "The Reclamation and Settlement of Land in the United States." *International Review of Agricultural Economics* (April–June 1926): 225–272.

Van der Veer, Charles A. "Brains and Water." *Arizona* 3 (January 1913): 7.

Widtsoe, John A. "History and Problems of Irrigation Development in the West." *Transactions of the American Society of Civil Engineers* 90 (1927): 680–709.

BOOKS

Bates, J. Leonard. *The United States 1898–1928: Progressivism and a Society in Transition.* New York: McGraw-Hill Book Co., 1976.

Bogue, Allan G.; Phillips, Thomas D.; and Wright, James E., eds. *The West of the American People.* Itasca, Illinois: F. E. Peacock, 1970.

Conners, Jo. *Who's Who in Arizona*, vol. 1. Tucson, Arizona: by the author, 1913.

Coyle, D. M. *Conservation: An American Story of Conflict and Accomplishment.* New Brunswick, N.J.: Rutgers University Press, 1957.

Davis, Arthur Powell. *Irrigation Works Constructed by the U.S. Government.* NY: John Wiley & Sons, Inc., 1917.

Gable, John A. *The Bull Moose Years: Theodore Roosevelt and the Progressive Party.* Port Washington, NY: Kennikat Press, 1978.

Graham, Otis L., Jr. *The Great Campaigns: Reform and War in America, 1900–1928.* Englewood Cliffs, N.J.: Prentice-Hall, Inc., 1971.

Hays, Samuel P. *American Political History as Social Analysis.* Knoxville: University of Tennessee Press, 1980.

———. *Conservation and the Gospel of Efficiency: The Progressive Conservation Movement, 1890–1920.* Cambridge: Harvard University Press, 1959; reprint ed., New York: Atheneum, 1975.

Hibbard, Benjamin Horace. *A History of the Public Land Policies.* New York: MacMillan Co., 1924; reprint ed., Madison: University of Wisconsin Press, 1965.

Hill, R. T. *The Public Domain and Democracy: A Study of Social, Economic and Political Problems in the United States in Relation to Western Development.* New York: Columbia University Press, 1910; reprint ed., New York: AMS Press, 1968.

Hodge, Carle, ed. *Aridity and Man: The Challenge of the Arid Lands in the United States.* Washington, D.C.: American Association for the Advancement of Science, Publication No. 74, 1963.

Hollon, W. Eugene. *The Great American Desert, Then and Now.* New York: Oxford University Press, 1966.

Huffman, Roy E. *Irrigation Development and Public Water Policy.* New York: Ronald Press Co., 1953.

Hundley, Norris, Jr. *Water and the West.* Berkeley: University of California Press, 1975.

Institute for Government Research. *The U.S. Reclamation Service: Its History, Activities, and Organization.* New York: D. Appleton & Co., 1919.

James, George W. *Reclaiming the Arid West.* New York: Dodd, Mead & Co., 1917.

Lampen, Dorothy. *Economic and Social Aspects of Federal Reclamation.* Baltimore: Johns Hopkins University Studies in Historical and Political Science, No. 48, 1930.

Lane, Anne Wintermute, and Wall, Louise Herrick, eds. *The Letters of Franklin K. Lane, Personal and Political.* Boston: Houghton Mifflin Co., 1922.

Layton, Edwin T., Jr. *The Revolt of the Engineers: Social Responsibility and the American Engineering Profession.* Cleveland: Case Western Reserve University, 1971.

Lee, Lawrence B. *Reclaiming the American West: An Historiography and Guide.* Santa Barbara, California: ABC-CLIO, 1980.

Link, Arthur S. *Woodrow Wilson and the Progressive Era, 1910–1917.* New York: Harper & Row, 1954.

McDonald, Angus. *One Hundred and Sixty Acres of Water: The Story of the Antimonopoly Law.* Washington, D.C.: Public Affairs Institute, 1958.

Mann, Dean E. *The Politics of Water in Arizona.* Tucson: University of Arizona Press, 1963.

Nash, Gerald D. *The American West in the Twentieth Century: A Short History of an Urban Oasis.* Englewood Cliffs, N.J.: Prentice-Hall, Inc., 1973.

Newell, Frederick Haynes. *Irrigation Management.* New York: D. Appleton & Co., 1916.

———. *Water Resources: Present and Future Uses.* New Haven: Yale University Press, 1920.

Newell, Frederick H., and Murphey, Daniel W. *Principles of Irrigation Engineering.* New York: McGraw-Hill, 1913.

Olson, Keith W. *Biography of a Progressive: Franklin K. Lane, 1864–1921.* Westport, CT: Greenwood Press, 1979.

Peffer, Louise. *The Closing of the Public Domain: Disposal and Reservation Policies, 1900 – 1950.* Stanford: Stanford University Press, 1951.

Pinchot, Gifford. *Breaking New Ground.* NY: Harcourt, Brace & Co., 1947.

Richardson, Elmo. *The Politics of Conservation: Crusades and Controversies.* Berkeley: University of California Press, 1962.

Robinson, Michael C. *Water for the West: A History of the U.S. Reclamation Service.* Chicago: Public Works Historical Society, 1979.

Schiff, Ashley L. *Fire and Water: Scientific Heresy in the Forest Service.* Cambridge: Harvard University Press, 1962.

Smith, Henry Nash. *Virgin Land: The American West as Symbol and Myth.* Cambridge: Harvard University Press, 1950.

Smith, Norman. *A History of Dams.* Secaucus, N.J.: Citadel Press, 1972.

Teele, Ray P. *The Economics of Land Reclamation in the United States.* Chicago: A. W. Shaw & Co., 1927.

———. *Irrigation in the United States.* New York: D. Appleton & Co., 1915.

Townley, John M. *Turn This Water Into Gold: The Story of the Newlands Project.* Reno, Nevada: Nevada Historical Society, 1977.

Vogt, Evon Z. *Modern Homesteaders: The Life of a Twentieth-Century Frontier Community.* Cambridge: Belknap Press of Harvard University, 1955.

Wagoner, Jay J. *Arizona Territory 1863 – 1912: A Political History.* Tucson: University of Arizona Press, 1970.

Warne, William E. *The Bureau of Reclamation.* New York: Praeger Publishers, 1973.

Widtsoe, John A. *Success on Irrigation Projects.* New York: John Wiley & Sons, Inc., 1928.

Wiebe, Robert H. *The Search for Order, 1877 – 1920.* New York: Hill and Wang, 1967.

Index

Throughout this index the term *Project* refers specifically to the Salt River Valley Project; other federal reclamation projects are identified in full.